POWER IN COLONIAL AFRICA

AFRICA AND THE DIASPORA
History, Politics, Culture

SERIES EDITORS

Thomas Spear
David Henige
Michael Schatzberg

A Hill among a Thousand: Transformations and Ruptures in Rural Rwanda
Danielle de Lame

Power in Colonial Africa: Conflict and Discourse in Lesotho, 1870–1960
Elizabeth A. Eldredge

Nachituti's Gift: Economy, Society, and Environment in Central Africa
David M. Gordon

*Intermediaries, Interpreters, and Clerks: African Employees
in the Making of Colonial Africa*
Edited by Benjamin N. Lawrance, Emily Lynn Osborn, and
Richard L. Roberts

Antecedents to Modern Rwanda: The Nyiginya Kingdom
Jan Vansina

POWER IN COLONIAL AFRICA

CONFLICT AND DISCOURSE IN LESOTHO, 1870-1960

Elizabeth A. Eldredge

THE UNIVERSITY OF WISCONSIN PRESS

The University of Wisconsin Press
1930 Monroe Street, 3rd Floor
Madison, Wisconsin 53711-2059

www.wisc.edu/wisconsinpress/

3 Henrietta Street
London WC2E 8LU, England

1   3   5   4   2

Printed in the United States of America

Library of Congress Cataloging-in-Publication Data
Eldredge, Elizabeth A.
Power in colonial Africa: conflict and
discourse in Lesotho, 1870–1960 / Elizabeth A. Eldredge.
p.   cm.—(Africa and the diaspora. History, politics, culture)
Includes bibliographical references and index.
ISBN 0-299-22370-1 (cloth: alk. paper)
1. Power (Social sciences)—Lesotho.
2. Lesotho—Politics and government—To 1966.
3. Lesotho—History—To 1966.
4. Sotho (African people)—Lesotho—History.
I. Title.   II. Series: Africa and the diaspora.
DT2638.E43   2007
968.85′02—dc22   2007012905

CONTENTS

PREFACE

Historians by definition are "time travelers," traversing the presumed boundaries of differences in culture created by the passage of time. The project of writing history requires the ability to identify and take into account cultural difference in our interpretations of the past, whether that project involves a translation across time or across space and differences of language and culture. The ability to generate the trust necessary to gain access to information as well as the sensitivity to nuances of representation in the information gathered shapes the interpretations of scholars and intellectuals who seek to represent the past of a people. Even if the conceptualization of them and the expressions of understanding about them are mediated by culture, nevertheless the experiences of birth, hunger, pain, love, and death are irrefutable as truths that all humans experience in every cultural context. At the same time that we identify differences in how we understand and represent these common experiences, we also find and explore those elements of experience that know no linguistic or cultural barriers.

I first saw Lesotho from the window of a twin engine propeller plane flying in from Johannesburg in 1981. I spent the next eighteen months living and traveling among villages and small towns in every district of the country, interviewing more than eighty old people about their memories of their childhood. My oldest interviewee had been born in 1873 and had lived his long life as a chief in the highest mountains of the Mokhotlong District; we were only able to reach his village by horseback after a long, four-hour ride. Over the years I have returned many times and trudged along the packed-dirt paths of villages and of the university campus at Roma, where I was always welcomed by the friendly library staff on my way in and out of the archives. I have watched the children of my friends and colleagues be born and come of age, and they in turn helped care for my children, who chased chickens and rode donkeys in villages as I carried out my research. I don't have to tell the people of Lesotho that they have long since won my heart as well as my respect.

When I first went to southern Africa I changed planes in Johannesburg in the international section of Jan Smuts Airport, where passengers without visas or welcomes into then-apartheid South Africa could still travel in and out of the landlocked country of Lesotho. Years later, in the early months of 1994, my family watched South Africans struggle to attain a peaceful transition to a postapartheid era in which democracy was extended to every person across the country. I was there as a senior Fulbright scholar, and my children were enrolled in school in Durban. On election day we drove downtown to look at the long line of voters winding around city hall and then found other lines at other voting places, the ones seen on the news around the world. On inauguration day the following month we drove to Lesotho, our home away from home, celebrating the feeling of democracy arrived. But in Lesotho, which had enjoyed democratic elections the previous year, we found the moment had been used to foment turmoil there, and my children went to sleep to the sound of mortar fire a mile or two from where we slept. Guns and democracy do not mix well, and democracy is sustained only by the constant vigilance of everyone. Over twelve months in 1994 I traveled and conducted research and gave seminars and lectures in Lesotho, Swaziland, South Africa, and Mozambique, and it is to all the people of these countries that I dedicate my work.

The research for this book was supported by grants from York University in Toronto, the University of North Carolina at Greensboro, Michigan State University, and the Social Science and Humanities Research Council of Canada. This work would not have been possible without the support of my many colleagues and friends at the National University of Lesotho and the communities of Roma and Mafefoane. Special thanks go to the staff of the library and archives and of the Institute of Southern African Studies and to the faculty of the Department of History. I am especially grateful for the years of help and encouragement I have received from Burns Machobane and his family, Lois and Molapi Sebatane and their family, Roshan Fitter and the staff at the Roma Primary School, and David Ambrose and his family. Thanks to every archivist who has ever assisted me, especially Albert Brutsch and Steve Gill at the archives of the Lesotho Evangelical Church in Morija. I received invaluable assistance from the keepers of history who shared with me the historical traditions, including James J. Machobane, Mo-sebi Damane, Patrick Lehloenya II, A. C. Manyeli, Charles Dube Mo-lapo, and Gerard Tlalinyane Ramoreboli, and from their families who assisted in arranging interviews. Many thanks to Patrick Malefetsane Marabe, who assisted me in conducting most of these and other inter-views in 1988 and 1989, and thanks to the people who spoke with us about their personal histories and memories, which enriched my under-standing of Lesotho in the twentieth century. I am grateful to David Plank, who accompanied me on so many research trips and interviews in 1981–82 and 1988 and valued with me the work and the people. Thanks to my many friends far and wide who rescued me in times of trouble, especially Steve Goldblatt in recent years. Finally, thanks to my family and especially Mike and Jim, who spent so much of their early lives in southern Africa as I pursued my work in the hope of helping to bring peace, justice, and freedom to the world.

NAMES AND TERMS

BaSotho	people of the country of Lesotho or of SeSotho culture
Basutoland	British colonial name for Lesotho
Bereng Griffith	son of Paramount Chief Griffith, brother of Paramount Chief Seeiso
Griffith, Charles D.	Governor's Agent in Basutoland under Cape Colony rule, 1871–81
Lagden, Godfrey	Assistant Resident Commissioner and Resident Commissioner in Lesotho, 1884–1901
LNA	Lesotho National Archives
Lesotho	southern African country formed by SeSotho-speaking chiefdoms and other immigrants under Moshoeshoe in 1824, known as Basutoland under British colonial rule from 1868 to 1966; a modern kingdom since its independence in 1966
liretlo	term for so-called medicine murders, committed to obtain human flesh for use in medicine horns
MoSotho	a person of the country of Lesotho or of SeSotho culture
Paramount Chief	*Morena e Moholo,* or highest central authority in Lesotho, designated "king" since independence in 1966. The country's Paramount Chiefs and each man's years as Paramount Chief, beginning with the founding *morena e moholo,* Moshoeshoe I, to independence, are the following:

Moshoeshoe (Moshesh, Moshweshwe) (b. 1876), 1824–70

Letsie (I), son of Moshoeshoe, 1870–91

Lerotholi (Lerothodi), son of Letsie, 1891–1905

Letsie II, or Letsienyana, son of Lerotholi, 1905–13

Griffith, son of Lerotholi and brother of Letsie II (Letsienyana), 1913–39

Seeiso, son of Griffith, 1939–40

'Mantsebo, senior wife of Paramount Chief Seeiso Griffith, who served as Regent Paramount Chief during the minority of the heir, Constantine Bereng Seeiso, from 1940 to 1960

Constantine Bereng Seeiso, son of Seeiso, named heir in 1940, installed in 1960, designated as King Moshoeshoe II

pitso   public meeting called by a chief and his counselors to consult with the adult men in the country or district about major policy decisions and used by colonial officials to make official announcements

SeSotho   proper term for the southern Bantu language and culture, associated with the root term *Sotho;* also used as a modifier, as in the designation of "SeSotho-speaking people" living in culturally related chiefdoms prior to the emergence of the centralized country of Lesotho after 1824

Sotho   linguistic root, also used alone in European language texts, to designate SeSotho-speaking peoples or their language or culture; alternatively, used to designate the larger linguistic grouping that includes peoples who speak SeTswana and northern Sotho or SePedi as well as SeSotho.

POWER IN COLONIAL AFRICA

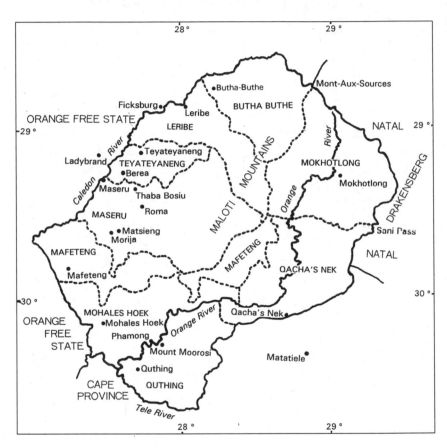

Colonial Lesotho, District Boundaries after 1945

1

Power in Theory and Practice

Actions speak louder than words.[1]

This is a study of power and how it operates. Studying the operation of power in a colonial setting is particularly appropriate because colonial rule has been so often misunderstood in terms of unremitting and successful domination through both coercion and persuasion. Virtually the entire world has been shaped by the colonial experience through the historical actions of people, individually and collectively, as colonizers or as colonized. The widespread influence of Western modernity across the globe has inspired various theories about power, domination, discourse, and hegemony among contemporary scholars.[1]

The study of power is hardly new. Issues of domination and resistance, economy and ideology were so much a preoccupation of nineteenth-century scholars and intellectuals that as we theorize about them there is a danger of reinventing the wheel. Scholars studying society and history from what has been defined as a postmodern perspective have focused on the examination of discourses as a source of power exerting control over society and politics, although the definition of terms used by self-defined postmodernists, including the term *discourse,* has varied, as have their assumptions and conclusions.[2] Postmodernism draws its influence from the field that claims the study of culture as its own, anthropology. It has been the goal of Western anthropology to discover and reveal the internal logic of a non-Western culture in order to bring into question the apparent naturalness of Western culture, to have a benchmark from which to measure Western culture, and to question our Western selves and our humanity and way of life by putting them next to a non-Western culture and society. Hence the colonial setting is a suitable arena for examining questions of power, political rule, knowledge, and discourse because of the blatant initial preexisting distance, contestation, and countervalence between two nodes or foci of power and discourse representing two distinct, intersecting cultures.

Like ethnographers and anthropologists of the late nineteenth and early twentieth centuries, postmodern scholars laudably assert the value and difference of non-Western cultures. Just like their predecessors of one hundred years ago, postmodernists decry the assumption that what is taken for granted in Western culture is universal, natural, and better. For generations Western anthropologists have sought to understand and critique Western society by achieving an understanding of alternative cultural worldviews in terms of both explicit beliefs and unstated habits and practices, the world of the "taken-for-granted." The validation of non-Western cultural beliefs and practices by postmodernists who are insistent that there are no universals in the human experience borders on the repetition and glorification of "othering," which today, as in the past, tends to exoticize the expression of non-Western cultural experiences, set in contrast to Western culture, rather than actually decentering the Western mindset. Intellectuals hailing from the realms of the colonial empire who experience most thoroughly the fuzzy cultural borders between the Western and non-Western worlds that were once the realms of the colonizers and the colonized have brought eloquence to the expression of postcolonial ideas in their attempts to speak for their kith and kin in former colonial outposts. These intellectuals, still cognizant of the imbalance of political and cultural power in the modern world, cannot afford to adopt a postmodernist view that romanticizes difference and seems to refute the possibility for liberation from oppression.[3] For the postcolonial world themes of domination, ideology, and discourse are not merely academic.

Definitions of power that equate power with domination and assume implicitly that power flows downward from those who hold political authority ignore the play of power outside the realm of officially recognized channels of authority. We are able to perceive power when it produces results, whether it appears as the ability to cause action or the ability to prevent action. The ability of individuals and groups to exercise power as political and cultural domination has been demonstrated throughout history, but less evident has been the ability of people and groups to resist successfully their domination by others, culturally as well as politically. The potential for the abuse of power through domination in the name of politically recognized authority has historically been kept in check by a universal drive for political and cultural self-determination and autonomy from control by others. The preservation of freedom, as much as the extension of political domination, is the product of the exercise of power. Where political domination occurs it is a reflection of an imbalance of power rather than the monopoly of power by one group over another. Domination is achieved through the mobilization of various tools of power, which in turn operate through processes of both coercion and persuasion. The tools of power range from the obvious deployment of military strength in manpower and technology to the subtle exercise of individual influence. Wealth and authority are often used to mobilize tools of power, but they do not constitute power in and of themselves. Force, ideology, knowledge, and discourse are tools of power, but they are not merely tools of domination; all are also employed by the dominated as means of resistance to domination.

Violence, terror, and the threat of violence are tools of coercion that operate to achieve domination through force. Ideology, or the diffusion of ideologies, is sometimes deployed in an attempt to achieve domination through consent, albeit consent offered by those who have been convinced through ideological forces that the domination is either beneficial or, at least, inevitable and natural. Discourses, the collective body of statements about given subjects, reflect, convey, and support the diffusion of ideologies, whether in the service of domination or in that of resistance. The fact that ideology, diffused through public discourses, can achieve the apparent consent of the ruled to domination indicates the importance of understanding how ideologies are deployed and how discourses emerge and achieve influence. The apparent acceptance of domination by the dominated can be deceptive, however, as the mere threat of violence or terror can elicit cooperation, acquiescence, and silence and can suppress all discernible signs of nonconsent and resistance to domination. The use of violence, what has been termed *violence douce* as well as *violence directe*, has supported domination generally throughout history, and not only in colonial settings.[4] Conversely, resistance does not always reflect rejection of the dominant sociopolitical and cultural order and may emerge from the desire of the resisters to become part of the established political order.[5]

Written statements have been the focus of discursive analysis because of Western favoring of literacy and written representations in the legitimation of knowledge. But alternative forms of expression contain statements that constitute evidence of alternative discourses. Such alternative

forms of expression include oral testimony, visual arts, music, clothing and adornment, and public actions carrying intended meanings.
The privileging of written forms of discursive expression in the analysis
of power relations and attributions of power falsely portrays illiterate
people, or people whose voices are not permitted access to the printed
record, as powerless. The recovery of oral traditions and oral history
has deeply enriched our ability to discern historical agency among
people whose perspectives remain, for a variety of reasons, unrepre-
sented in the written historical record. Gaining access to unwritten and
nonverbal expressions can be difficult, but historians have come to recognize the importance of reading all forms of cultural expressions as
"texts," albeit with the caution necessary in the use of all sources, such
as in the attribution of intention where necessity or constraint rather
than choice might have prevailed. The adoption of forms of expression
can reflect conscious choice, bearing a strong message, or unconscious
acceptance of cultural norms, indicating cultural "hegemony" in operation or sociopolitical pressures necessitating involuntary conformity.
Nonverbal indicators of culture must be read with caution, then, since
forces of repression may inhibit or prevent any indication of resistance
and create an illusion of unchallenged dominance or "hegemony." Both
public and private statements and actions may contain secret or coded
messages, whether they are generated by the dominators or the dominated. Private messages meant to be kept secret might subsequently be
revealed, deliberately or unintentionally. Therefore, in the recovery and
interpretation of sources it is important to recognize that the boundaries between public and private are sometimes ambiguous.

Michel Foucault has made one of the most original contributions to
the study of power in recent Western intellectual history. His own intellectual growth is evident in the progressive change of his ideas over the
course of his career; thus there is slippage in Foucault's definitions and
uses of terms such as *discourse* and *power*. He asserts that the structure and
functioning of power in any society determine what is given legitimacy
as knowledge and what is excluded from such legitimation and recognition. Foucault rejects the validity of Western universalistic theories,
which is the characteristic feature of postmodern thought, but in alternative non-Western perspectives he identifies alternative sources of
power. Foucault seeks to unmask the power structures that dictate what is
seen as truth and reality by pointing to alternative sites of knowledge that
contest the dominant regime and perspective, what he refers to as "subjugated knowledges." Foucault argues, to use his own words in reverse,

that an historical struggle of knowledges arises because of the historical knowledge of struggles: "In the case of the erudite as in that of the disqualified knowledges—with what in fact were these buried, subjugated knowledges really concerned? They were concerned with a *historical knowledge of struggles*. In the specialised areas of erudition as in the disqualified, popular knowledge there lay the memory of hostile encounters which even up to this day have been confined to the margins of knowledge."

Foucault's work reflects not a nihilism, then, as is often assumed about his thought and that of other postmodernists, but, rather, a profound hope that with the elimination of "the tyranny of globalising discourses" the potential had been created for the success of the heretofore hidden struggles for power as well as knowledge. Indicating his goal of liberation, he wrote, "Our task . . . will be to expose and specify the issue at stake in this opposition, this struggle, this insurrection of knowledges against the institutions and against effects of the knowledge and power that invests scientific discourse."

Foucault questioned the Marxist conception of power and the conceptualization of power as "essentially that which represses," to which he had himself previously subscribed.[6] Foucault abandoned the conceptualization of power as intrinsically flowing downward as part of domination, in particular as associated with the state: "I don't want to say that the State isn't important; what I want to say is that relations of power, and hence the analysis that must be made of them, necessarily extend beyond the limits of the State. In two senses: first of all because the State, for all the omnipotence of its apparatuses, is far from being able to occupy the whole field of actual power relations, and further because the State can only operate on the basis of other, already existing power relations."[7] Instead of focusing on the apparent centers of power such as the state, Foucault adopted a view of power operating through countless channels in every direction. These interconnected channels of power constitute power relations through which power operates but only sometimes through evident dominating structures such as the state.

Since the association of power with domination has given it negative connotations, that is, as primarily a tool of or means for domination and repression, Foucault was forced to explain why his reconceptualization of power as an inescapable web did not imply the inevitability of domination: "It seems to me that power *is* 'always already there,' that one is never 'outside' it, that there are no 'margins' for those who break with the system to gambol in. But this does not entail the necessity of accepting an inescapable form of domination or an absolute privilege on the side of the law. To say that one can never be 'outside' power does not mean that one is trapped and condemned to defeat no matter what."[8]

Never a nihilist, on the contrary, Foucault perceived power as an ability to produce effects that are positive as well as negative. For Foucault, power "traverses and produces things, it induces pleasure, forms knowledge, produces discourse. It needs to be considered as a productive network which runs through the whole social body, much more than as a negative instance whose function is repression."[9] Because "power is exercised from innumerable points, in the interplay of nonegalitarian and mobile relations," it is widely accessible and not monopolized by those who hold political domination: "Power comes from below; that is, there is no binary and all-encompassing opposition between rulers and ruled at the root of power relations."[10]

Arguing that "power exists only when it is put into action," Foucault also rejects a simplistic reduction of power to the use of force or violence.[11] Force and violence, like ideology and discourse, are instruments employed in the exercise of power but are not intrinsic to power itself. Foucault is not blind to the problem of domination; rather, he perceives that domination, not inevitable, is a temporary "strategic situation" in the relations of power that may shift at any time.

If discourse is the means through which power produces truth, it is clear that discourse is one key element in Foucault's propositions about power. Specifically, Foucault writes that, "indeed, it is in discourse that power and knowledge are joined together." Foucault concedes that ideology or, more specifically, "ideological productions" accompany the "major mechanisms of power," but he considers the term limited by its use and connotations, for example, as standing in opposition to "truth."[12] Discourse includes all statements about a given subject, whether they are considered true or false; it is within the context of the discourse that statements come to be legitimated and validated or fail to be, as "truth" and "knowledge," but all statements become part of the discourse, including "the things said and those concealed, the enunciations required and those forbidden." He writes: "We must not imagine a world of discourse divided between accepted discourse and excluded discourse, or between the dominant discourse and excluded discourse; but as a multiplicity of discursive elements that can come into play in various strategies. It is this distribution that we must reconstruct, with the things said and those concealed, the enunciations required and those forbidden, that it comprises."[13] As a comprehensive collection of statements about a subject, discourse cannot be merely equivalent to or a tool of ideology that excludes countervailing perspectives and opinions. Discourse is not merely a tool of domination; rather, it is an instrument of power. Those who make statements in any venue, publicly or privately, openly or secretly, participate in the creation of a discourse and may wield power accordingly. Discourse does not serve merely the goal of domination, it can also serve the goal of liberation. As Foucault puts it,

> Discourses are not once and for all subservient to power or raised up against it, any more than silences are. We must make allowance for the complex and unstable process whereby discourse can be both an instrument and an effect of power, but also a hindrance, a stumbling-block, a point of resistance and a starting point for an opposing strategy.
>
> Discourse transmits and produces power; it reinforces it, but also undermines and exposes it, renders it fragile and makes it possible to thwart it. In like manner, silence and secrecy are a shelter for power, anchoring its prohibitions; but they also loosen its holds and provide for relatively obscure areas of tolerance. . . . There is not, on the one side, a discourse of power, and opposite it, another discourse that runs counter to it. Discourses are tactical elements or blocks operating in the field of force relations; there can exist different and even contradictory discourses within the same strategy; they can, on the contrary, circulate without changing their form from one strategy to another, opposing strategy.[14]

Once again, it is clear that Foucault's conceptualization of power allows for explicit and effective opposition to domination. Ideology may be a tool of domination through which the dominant attempt to control belief and the popular understanding of what is right and natural, but discourse stands outside of such control.

In an incisive analysis of discourse Richard Terdiman examines the contradictory position of intellectuals as producers of knowledge. His work explores how nineteenth-century French intellectuals sought to counter the dominance of the middle-class bourgeois culture, which they abhorred, through both subversive texts and subversive means, such as in the invention of a new form, the prose poem. Terdiman argues that the dilemma for these intellectuals was how to be a critic observing from outside a dominant discourse, culture, and language within which they themselves worked—how to use the language of the dominant to critique it without becoming part of it and absorbed by it and thus reinforcing it. Analyzing the ways in which they demonstrated their ability to transcend the dominant discourse and escape its constraints, Terdiman developed the concept of "counter-discourses," although he observes that "from within dominant discourse, 'difference' nearly eludes us."[15]

Terdiman argues that those seeking to dominate through the dissemination of an ideology, posed through a dominant discourse, cannot afford even to acknowledge the existence of alternative discourses and ideologies because insofar as they must protest against and suppress alternatives with violence, they create a perceptible contradiction, a cognitive dissonance, that enhances the visibility and reinforces the viability of the very alternatives they seek to suppress. The suppression of alternatives normalizes the dominators' language, ideology, and practices such that alternatives become almost inconceivable. Terdiman writes, "A certain discourse is always normalized within speech communities and social formations. Certain linguistic and conceptual elements, from pronunciation and vocabulary to the large and methodologically diffuse question of 'world view,' are valorized by and infused with the implicit acceptance by and of the norm. This is what gives theoretical substance to the widely articulated notion 'domination by the code.'"[16] Linking linguistic codes and language to ideology and power, Terdiman asserts, "The overarching regulation of the cultural field by codes, specifically linguistic and languagelike, transcends the generative and critical capacities of any individual speaker or speech act. And when it is adequately historicized, this systematicity turns into the structure of ideological *power* which organizes a social formation."[17] Such codes are not insurmountable, however: "Essentially the problem is to achieve the necessary distance, to project the metalanguage on the basis of which a hegemonic discourse can be reconfigured as relative, as contingent, and thus as potentially transcendable." Nevertheless, explaining the notion of dominant discourse in everyday terms, Terdiman acknowledges how powerful it is:

> The dominant discourses thus came to appear as the naturalized expression of the social formation itself, as the self-evident form of utterance, the system of sense-making which, precisely, "went without saying."
>
> In modern societies it is by this transparency that the "ruling ideas" rule. . . . The dominant becomes the discourse within which the consecrated phrase "and so forth" represents a usable discursive move. For we know the next line of the social script, even without knowing *that* we know it or how we learned it. The dominant is

the discourse whose content is always already performable by the general member of the population.

The apparent or near "hegemony" of dominant discourses may be overcome, however, because the "dominant" is internally fragmented, and all languages, "even the discourse of dominant power" are "heteroglot." The heterogeneity of dominant languages and discourses implicitly opens the door to a countervailing language, perception, and discourse and even the eventual normalization of this counterdiscourse into a newly dominant discourse. Thus Terdiman acknowledges that "discourses of resistance ceaselessly interrupt what would otherwise be the seamless serenity of the dominant, its obliviousness to any contestation," and, further, that "counterdominant strains challenge and subvert the appearance of inevitability which is ideology's primary mechanism for sustaining its own self-reproduction." As a result, the "structural limitation of social control" opens space for counterdiscourse(s), "so no dominant discourse is ever fully protected from contestation."[18]

In the colonial setting self-evident difference preexisted in language itself, and the dominant order of the intruding Europeans was marked clearly by a European language, even when individual colonial officials or missionaries learned the local language. Therefore, if we turn Terdiman's proposition on its head, we have a better idea of the situation at the onset of colonial rule and the imposition of a colonial "order": it was the West, that which was European, that represented that which was different and outside of the prevailing local dominant discourse. If we see that which was Western as being the "different" and "other," then we realize that what Westerners, including the missionaries, were up against in trying to undermine, disrupt, overturn, and replace the precolonial "order" with its own "discourse" and unchallenged dominance. The preexisting order was much more resilient and resistant than Europeans anticipated or allowed themselves to believe. Much of the mindset, the local understanding of what was natural and right, both explicitly in beliefs and implicitly in practices, was sustained throughout the colonial era and survived into the postcolonial period throughout Africa. It was the precolonial "order" or "discursive system" that subverted and absorbed new elements of the Western world to keep the new, intrusive "other" from subverting it.

Scholars have commonly adopted, if unconsciously, a Eurocentric perspective that assumes the prevailing dominant discourse in a colonial setting is the discourse of the colonizer. This ignores the reality of most colonial settings, in which the colonizers are few numerically and interact only in limited settings with the colonized, leaving the precolonial order with its own dominant discourse about the natural order of things fundamentally intact. Even in settler colonies, marked by extensive interaction between local and colonial populations, the preexisting prevailing dominant discourses of the colonized have been remarkably resilient, putting Western colonial culture and discourse at a disadvantage.

Part of the project of colonizers was to destabilize African cultural systems, to undermine them, and to replace them. Often the colonized have historically tried to proscribe imported beliefs, practices, objects, and styles in the effort to protect indigenous forms and customs and preserve the cultural supports to power. At other times they have taken elements of the imported culture and turned them to their own advantage, adopting, for example, Islam and literacy in Arabic or Christianity and literacy in a European language, as tools and sets of beliefs and practices to be absorbed and subverted into a new cultural underpinning for the existing indigenous power system. It is a mistake to assume that the presence of imported cultural elements implies subversion from the outside, operating in the service and control of outsiders, when historically these cultural elements have often been converted and subverted in service of the local sociopolitical order and stability. It is the association of culture with politics that imbues cultural elements with power, so that power-laden beliefs and practices must be seen as the proverbial "two-edged sword," to be wielded by either side in a contest of power.

European colonizers carried their dominant Western discourse and covalent ideologies with them intentionally as well as unconsciously because they were products as well as producers of those discourses and ideologies. Many Europeans believed or pretended that there was no countervailing discourse on the other side of the cultural divide, and many assumed that the colonized had no culture of value and had no desire to resist the imposition of what the colonized assumed was a superior cultural system. Colonizers sought to exclude the old as abnormal and unacceptable and to replace the old worldview, but this required a blindness over time to evidence of the persistence of the old order, which in language and in everyday habits and practices was counterdiscursive, perpetuating a rupture in consensus over what was normal and possible.

In colonial situations the imported Western discourse competed with the prevailing discourses of the colonized, and two competing discursive systems coexisted, sometimes overlapping and sometimes oblivious to each other. The theoretical problem created by the definition of either discourse or hegemony as supposedly reflecting the "taken-for-granted" and as defining the boundaries and limits of possibility, truth, and knowledge is that it leaves no room for explaining how a discourse or "hegemonic" order can ever be contestable. The colonial setting, as a cultural intersection laden with the competition for power, provides an opportunity to explore the possibility or impossibility of the achievement of unquestioned and unquestionable authority or "hegemony." We ask the wrong question if we look for, politically and culturally, "hegemonic" colonial rule; rather, we must examine a local culturally defined political order in which colonial discourse is the marginal outsider and not necessarily successful in becoming the natural, accepted, everyday order of things for the vast majority of the colonized.

James C. Scott makes a compelling case that studies of power relations that only focus on the public transcript are bound to fail in their objective because the public transcript masks hidden transcripts and hidden struggles. He urges the uncovering of hidden transcripts and argues that a "coded version of the hidden transcript is always present in the public discourse of subordinate groups."[19] Evidence from meetings and official correspondence in colonial settings can reveal much about how a "public transcript" concerning power and authority was constructed and maintained and how public meetings served as "symbolic displays" of power for a local audience. Colonial rulers could stage public performances to undergird their public authority, but on the same stage representatives of the colonized community could display defiant insolence. Unable to voice openly their dissent and disapproval of spoken or written agreements into which they were compelled, by force or the threat of force, to enter, they were able to use insolent gestures to contradict their constrained spoken words. The result was an overt acquiescence to colonial rule that conformed with a colonial need to maintain an appearance of hegemony in order to maintain order. Any gestures of defiance, however, were well understood by an audience of the colonized, who understood the compulsion behind a formal public transcript of loyalty and obedience.

Power and Colonial Rule in Africa

The study of power in colonial Africa has focused on colonial rule and the role of the state as an agent of imperialist and capitalist expansionism, resulting in a tendency to attribute to the colonial state greater powers of coercion and influence in the political, economic, social, and cultural spheres of activity among the colonized than is justified, as empirical studies have borne out. The centrality of African initiatives and agency in the era of colonial rule stands out in the historiography of Africa, which has addressed issues of power in various contexts, if sometimes only implicitly.[20] Thomas Spear has challenged the exaggerated role attributed to colonial rulers in what has been termed the "invention of tradition." His article highlights the need to delve into the precolonial context if we are to be able to assess the presence or absence of change in the colonial era and identify and analyze the character and origins of those changes.[21] In a central contribution to the study of colonial Africa Fred Cooper has argued that overemphasis on "the binaries of colonizer\colonized, Western\non-Western, and domination\resistance . . . end up constraining the search for precise ways in which power is deployed and the ways in which power is engaged, contested, deflected, and appropriated."[22] He identifies factors that constrained the power of colonial rulers even as they were dominant and dominating. A multitude of initiatives in various political, social, cultural, and religious forms have demonstrated African agency, which limited the coercive and convincing powers of colonial rule.

Perhaps because the concern of Africanist historians has been focused on the perspectives of the colonized since the inception of the field of African history as a discipline, a more sophisticated and nuanced understanding of the complexity and multiplicity of African voices has helped scholars to overcome overly simplified categorizations. Since the 1960s the field of African history, guided by the groundbreaking work of Jan Vansina, has pursued the agenda of retrieving oral traditions and oral histories in order to preserve them in a world that had so come to value the printed word that oral sources and the indigenous voices they conveyed were at risk of being lost forever to future generations.[23] Persistent scholars have also uncovered evidence of African perspectives on colonial rule from local written sources, both published and private. Theoretical approaches to history, dominated by Marxist and neo-Marxist agendas, have been confronted with strong evidence from indigenous sources, written and oral, that contradict Marxist assumptions about historical stages of development, dubbed "modes of production," and about the "consciousness" of the colonized and the inevitability of class conflict as the primary motive force in history. The unexpected result, whether acknowledged or not, has been an overturning of the Marxist paradigm even in the work of Marxist scholars. Thus in his close critique of Kikuyu political thought in 1950s Kenya, which exposed wide scope and variation in the conscious experience and response of a colonized people in a settler colony, John Lonsdale shattered many Marxist theoretical assumptions. Lonsdale identified culture as being as important as social and economic status in influencing the consciousness and actions of the participants in the "Mau Mau" Rebellion of 1950s Kenya, and the privileging of African perspectives by Lonsdale in his work marked an important break from the tunnel vision of many earlier Marxist studies.[24] Similarly, Steven Feierman's groundbreaking work on those to whom he refers as "peasant intellectuals" in Tanzania forced scholars to acknowledge the independent vitality of indigenous perspectives evident in local discourses, which explained the world in local terms. The "peasant intellectuals" who conveyed these worldviews continuously renewed old terms of discourse but often adapted old terminology and invested the tropes of local discourse with new meanings.[25]

Power and colonialism in southern Africa has also been addressed from a Marxist perspective by John and Jean Comaroff, anthropologists who based their rich theoretical propositions on a thin historical study of a small BaTswana group, from which they projected their results hypothetically to colonialism in southern Africa more generally. Exploring the colonization of "the" consciousness of "the" southern Tswana, the Comaroffs assert that "among the Southern Tswana this process began with the entry of mission Christianity onto the historical landscape" and that the missionaries of their study, the Nonconformist evangelists, were the vanguard of the British presence in this part of South Africa who achieved this goal. They have adopted Gramscian Marxist theory, which attempts to explain why people fail to rebel in terms of ruling-class "hegemony" based on ideological values imbued across a society and culture, preventing people from recognizing their conflict of interest with the state and ruling class and producing "consent" to domination. The Comaroffs adhere to a definition of "hegemony" as "non-negotiable and therefore beyond direct argument" as well as distinct from "ideology," which is open to contestation. The Comaroffs maintain that "the making of hegemony involves the assertion of control over various modes of symbolic production: over such things as educational and ritual processes, patterns of socialization, political and legal procedures, canons of style and self-representation, public communication, health and bodily discipline, and so on."[26] They purport to demonstrate that colonialism in southern Africa resulted in "the colonization of consciousness" through the means of Western cultural values inscribed upon Africans through the Christian missionary project.

In their effort to contest postcolonial depictions of the agency of the colonized the Comaroffs appear patronizingly to underestimate the conscious self-awareness of the colonized about their own cultures and their predicament. They depict southern Africans as being "drawn unwittingly into the dominion of European 'civilization'" and implicitly suggest their diminished capacity to achieve anything more than "partial recognition" or "inchoate awareness" of "ambiguous perception," so that they "cannot or do not order them into narrative descriptions or even into articulate conceptions of the world."[27]

The Comaroffs' focus on the "battle" for "signs and symbols" has underestimated the extent to which the agenda of the European missionaries, if it was the "colonization of consciousness," was undermined and indeed precluded by regional violence that discredited their imported culture. The precolonial order, modes of thought, ways of understanding reality, parameters of reality and acceptability of thought, practice, and habit were resilient and did not easily succumb to the project and agenda of the colonizers, even on the subliminal level examined by the Comaroffs. As they selected evidence to support their case the Comaroffs ignored significant countervailing evidence. For example, the conscious resistance of BaTswana to the cultural influence, both material and religious, of Christian missionaries was well documented by one of the Comaroffs' main sources, Robert Moffat of the London Missionary Society. He and his colleagues were perpetually frustrated in their attempts to proselytize BaTswana and change their material as well as spiritual cultural habits. Describing his missionary work among BaTswana in the 1820s, Moffat wrote that the missionaries had hoped to introduce European dress, "however much the natives might condemn our doctrines, as being in direct opposition to their customs," but were unable to make progress in this regard because

> any thing like an infringement on the ancient garb of the nation, was looked on as a caricature of ours, and therefore it appeared in their eyes, what a man in this country would be with a lady's bonnet or cap on his head—a merry Andrew. Various articles of clothing were sent from England for the queen and noblesse of Lithako; but none of these made their appearance.

Moreover, the thoughts and "consciousness" of the BaTswana could not be discerned from their behavior, and these nineteenth-century missionaries were deliberately deceived, as Moffat came to discover:

> Replies to questions as to what they thought of the Word of God, were very cheap; and if they supposed that by such means they had obtained favour and respect, their success would be the subject of merriment in their own circles. Some individuals, to my knowledge, who had carried on this deception in the early period of the mission, many years afterwards boasted how expert they had been in thus gulling the missionary.[28]

Moffat was also aware that missionary efforts were undermined by other negative, and violent, European influences in the area at least a generation prior to their arrival. Hence for SeTswana speakers European "culture" and "civilization" were associated first not with missionaries but with a small and specific number of people, Europeans and the Europeanized Bastaards and Griqua, some of whom raided for cattle, children, and women and brutally murdered their victims during raids.[29]

Nor were the everyday practices of the BaTswana changed in ways that subverted or "colonized" their "consciousness." Some European practices were adopted, self-consciously, and then subverted to the old ways, as when traditional medicines were used to doctor square houses. The form and function changed, but the consciousness, the way of conceiving of the house, whether round or square, did not. The church bell announced the time when missionaries wanted things done, but women had long been rising far earlier, long before dawn, to do their work, and the missionary work ethic must have seemed a slovenly one to African women. The first missionaries were met with caution, and their efforts were controlled by southern Africans, generally chiefs, who were aware of their connection and sometimes conscious collusion with violent and expansive imperial European forces. The evidence does not support the Comaroffs' contention that elements of this foreign, invasive culture, carried by a violent frontier population as well as missionaries, were unconsciously absorbed in a process that involved the "colonization of consciousness." When southern Africans discovered their affinity with elements of Western culture, especially Christianity, they incorporated them into their own culture without abandoning the latter, much to the chagrin of the missionaries, who saw evidence of continued participation in indigenous rituals and practices by members of their congregations as backsliding. Perhaps because the Comaroffs limited the scope of their study to the missionary effort, their choice of words, depicting colonialism as a "long conversation," underplays the violence and implicit force underlying the colonial encounter and conveys a false image of balanced power. However, they make the important argument that the advent of Europeans in Africa set in motion "a process in which signifiers were set afloat, fought over, and recaptured on both sides of the colonial encounter."[30]

Far more insightful for understanding the power-laden role of religion in a colonial setting is the approach and analysis of Pier M. Larson in his study of unexpected spontaneous, locally controlled religious responses in the Malagasy culture of Madagascar to the missionary message and practices brought in the 1820s.[31] Scholars must not assume that the early interaction between missions and Africans yielded the results desired by the missionaries, and Larson shows us how complex cultural and conceptual frameworks of local discourses could determine the outcome of religious encounters. Larson's study is in the tradition of that of Gabriel M. Setiloane, whose work demonstrates the complexity of religious and intellectual exchanges originating out of the Christian missionary enterprise in southern Africa because of the centrality and resilience of indigenous religious beliefs.[32] Paul Landau similarly privileges indigenous African perspectives and initiatives in his important study of the emergence of a southern African kingdom in Botswana. He demonstrates how Christianity intersected with society and politics but in ways that were shaped and controlled by the Ngwato king in his extension of geopolitical control and in ways compatible with local discourses and meanings beyond the control of missionaries.[33]

A variety of other scholars have produced important works on various aspects of colonial rule in southern Africa that also shed light on aspects of domination and on the local, internal resilience of the politics and culture of colonized African communities, even in the face of severe oppression. Jeanne Marie Penvenne recorded the oral histories of workers in Lourenço Marques who had endured extreme brutality during the colonial era; in spite of or perhaps because of their close encounter with a white settler colonial system they retained their local discourses and messages.[34] African coal shovelers on the waterfront sang as they worked, "The Portuguese live by stealing our wages, Heave that shovel, heave."[35] The incisive essays of Leroy Vail and Landeg White demonstrate that the voices and perspectives of Africans subjected to a variety of suppressive constraints can be recovered from cultural traditions sustained in songs, poetry, and praises that were beyond the reach of colonial controls.[36]

It is not surprising, considering the extremes of racial domination that emerged in colonial southern Africa, that scholars have continued to be interested in factors related to the emergence of the state. The influence of culture and local indigenous discourses in the shaping of the emerging state in South Africa and neighboring countries is the focus of a series of essays edited by Clifton Crais on the culture of power in southern Africa. Although the embedded language of Marxist scholarship with a postmodern gloss, marked by terms like "hegemony," "conversation," and the reduction of Africans to being "subaltern," reflects a reluctance to jettison dated and discredited assumptions and theories, these essays provide important empirical evidence about the processes of the expansion of state controls as constrained and shaped by local understandings of politics, authority, and power.[37] Timothy Keegan has provided an important overview and analysis of how colonial rule and expansion were driven by various interests. Privileging the centrality of economic factors and Western commercial expansion as the driving force in the expansion of European settlement and domination in the Cape Colony and beyond its borders during the first half of the nineteenth century, Keegan identifies the disparate interests and actions of British officials and colonial settlers that shaped the legal and economic context in which emerged a structured and repressive racial order.[38] More narrow in focus is the study by Crais on the advent of colonial rule in the eastern Cape Colony between 1770 and 1865.[39] In a work that tries to balance a variety of theoretical approaches Crais has made an important contribution to our understanding of the colonial experience in South Africa from the perspective of Africans and Europeans with reference to cultural as well as economic, political, and legal influences. The experience of the southern Tswana with the expansion of colonial rule and colonial policy following the discovery of diamonds in Griqualand West is traced by Kevin Shillington in a model study of how geopolitical, demographic, economic, and social forces interacted on the northern borders of the Cape Colony between 1870 and 1900.[40] Thomas McClendon brings the insights from work elsewhere to his study of the influence of specific Africans over the shaping of colonial policies as they were formulated under Sir Theophilus Shepstone in early Natal.[41] McClendon identifies deliberate African influences at work as the judicial system and codification of laws emerged and underscores the authenticity of local indigenous cultural roots in what came to be understood as customary law. Keletso E. Atkins opened up new perspectives on the colonial encounter in South Africa when she explored the cultural clash between European and African perspectives that underlay labor relations in Natal between 1843 and 1900.[42]

This study of colonial Lesotho breaks new ground in the study of power because of my focus on the roles of individual colonial officials and BaSotho chiefs and their use of diplomacy, rhetoric, and moral suasion as well as violence and the threat of violence in their attempts to wield power. In my earlier work on the BaSotho I explored the intersection between economic, political, and social change to demonstrate the self-conscious initiative of the BaSotho in creating and sustaining their nation from its foundations in 1824 as an emergent kingdom through the early decades of colonial rule. Tracing geopolitical factors, agricultural production, the rise and decline of craft specialization, the shifting allocation of labor, and socioeconomic considerations, I explained the amalgamation of diverse peoples into a kingdom and their conscious decision to retain their assimilated identity as the BaSotho ruled by their own chiefs, even after seeking colonial protection from Great Britain in order to sustain their independence from intrusive Dutch-speaking Boer farmers in the neighboring Orange Free State. In my earlier book I contested prevailing Marxist assumptions that exaggerated the control and dominance of chiefs over their people in decisions related to production, migration, labor, and politics, and I highlighted the self-conscious roles of women in contributing to the economic, social, and political welfare of their households, community, and nation. The evidence from Lesotho in the precolonial and early colonial periods demonstrates that the BaSotho, although conscious of differentiation and stratification based on wealth and status, willingly supported their chiefs who were not excessively exploitative and who engaged in precolonial practices of social welfare, ensuring the survival of even the most indigent in society. As the BaSotho encountered the Christian missionary enterprise they self-consciously engaged in open dialogue with individual missionaries, distinguished them readily from other European settlers and colonial officials, and only selectively adopted aspects of Western culture, preserving the symbolic elements of their own culture, which they valued more highly.[43]

This is a more focused study of hidden aspects of diplomacy in which I have uncovered evidence of the operation of power at multiple levels of authority and by use of various tools, strategies, and mechanisms. Here I examine the case of colonial Lesotho to explore the alternative uses of coercion and force, rhetoric, and diplomacy as colonial rulers and their subjects engaged in a struggle to control the political fate of the country and the people.

Colonial Lesotho, also known as Basutoland, provides an appropriate case study for understanding these broader issues of power. Southern Africa experienced the influx of European settlers from as early as 1652, when the Dutch East India Company established its first refreshment station at the Cape of Good Hope for the benefit of merchants carrying trade to the Indian Ocean and Asia. By the late eighteenth century Dutch-speaking herders, or Boers, as well as communities of mixed-race descendants of renegade Europeans, Khoi, and slaves had expanded their settlements, encountering AmaXhosa chiefdoms eastward and BaTswana chiefdoms to the north. The expansion of Boer communities into the interior was hastened by the advent of the British during the Napoleonic Wars, first from 1795 to 1803 and then permanently from 1806, changing the character of society and politics in the Colony of the Cape of Good Hope. From the late 1820s the SeSotho-speaking peoples, who, joined by others, had created the emerging kingdom of Lesotho under their first *Morena e Moholo* (Great Chief), Moshoeshoe, began to feel the repercussions of violence to their west. Moshoeshoe invited French missionaries who had come to the region to establish a mission in Lesotho, but successive wars with first Boers and later British settlers induced Moshoeshoe in 1868 to seek formal protection from the British Queen, which was granted. Although a brief period of rule by the Cape Colony itself distinguished the BaSotho experience from that of Africans elsewhere in the region and from colonial subjects in other British colonies, the reestablishment of direct British rule in 1884 initiated colonial rule that was fairly typical of British colonial Africa.

The extensive colonial records for Lesotho provide an unusual opportunity for a close scrutiny of the dynamics of power in a colonial setting. They reveal hidden diplomatic tactics, including threats and conciliation, shedding light on the nuances of the African response to colonial rule individually and collectively. This has allowed me to develop a deeper understanding of mechanisms through which colonial officers exercised domination, tried to exercise domination, and were subject to constraints in the exercise of power because of the strategies employed by the colonized, which are not readily apparent without a close examination of dialogue and discourse. By looking at episodes of conflict, some of which culminated in violence and war, I examine closely the moments at which power was employed by the British in colonial

Basutoland to maintain domination. I explore hidden discourse and dissent among the BaSotho as well as open conflicts that revealed the cracks in the colonial order and the failure of the colonial ideology to take root and establish "hegemonic" control through channels of consent. Instances of overt conflict forced the colonizers to show their hand and revealed the constant threat of force that undergirded colonial rule.

This project is complicated by two factors: no single voice represented all BaSotho and there were struggles over power within the indigenous sociopolitical system that were also supported by force and discourse. The "colonial discourse" of the colonized, like that of the colonizers, was not homogeneous and harmonious. A wide range of voices reflected social differences, gender divisions, and differences of rank, status, power, influence, authority, wealth, occupation, residence, and so on. A Western-educated elite, presumably inculcated with Western values and perceptions, has often been taken as the legitimate representative of the indigenous population, whereas their location on the borders of two cultures has left the shaping of their perspectives and interests an open question in each individual case. The written records of the colonized often originated from people who did not necessarily reflect or portray prevailing, commonly held perceptions, attitudes, and beliefs, although they might. Sometimes the educated were the sons or daughters of chiefs, and, conversely, sometimes they were the children of the indigent who were dependent on missionary support, so that the indigenous forces and influences shaping their consciousnesses could vary greatly. In short, there is no one voice of the colonized to be retrieved and put forward as representing "the African perspective," and each individual African voice must be given due weight and consideration in any analysis of a parallel indigenous discourse or set of communications concerning colonial rule and the colonial order.

Oral sources present problems in their use because they reflect both past and present attitudes and interpretations of the past, which must be disentangled as far as possible. Oral traditions purporting to be the collective history of a people often contain the myths, praise poetry, and genealogies that legitimize those in power. If oral traditions are often the record of the powerful, then the voices of the subordinate are often only retrievable through the collection of oral history, that is, the recollections of direct participants providing information about their firsthand experiences in the past.

Colonial sources, whether published or private, reveal an official position that may deliberately obscure the deeper knowledge of the colonial official who originally created a given record, for example, if he were unwilling to reveal vulnerabilities in the system or evidence of his own incapacity to govern. Alternately, an official might not credit certain reports and therefore might exclude them, or he might remain totally oblivious to the actions and intentions of the Africans around him. Dissembling was a favorite strategy of African chiefs and commoners alike in dealing with colonial officials. Whether or not the official creating a colonial record was aware of counterhegemonic discourses and strategies among the colonized, part of a parallel African discourse, these rarely appear in the record unless they resulted in open conflict.

In colonial Basutoland public meetings, or *pitsos*, which had been consultative forums between chiefs and their followers during the precolonial era, were the forums for the public announcement of British policies and actions and for the BaSotho to respond to these colonial initiatives; thus the negotiation of power through hidden and overt forms of communication and discourse often took place on this public stage. The British were adept at signaling British power through words and rituals designed to bolster their authority in such public arenas, but the BaSotho also used these meetings to convey counterdiscursive messages of disapproval and discontent, even when couched in terms of loyalty. When signs of resistance became public, officials could not afford to ignore them. British colonial officials in Basutoland found it necessary to respond to public displays of insolence even when the chiefs were verbally conceding to the ideology of loyalty to the British Crown. Undisguised challenges required a response from the rulers, because "when a practical failure to comply is joined with a pointed, public refusal it constitutes a throwing down of the gauntlet, a symbolic declaration of war."[44]

This study of the dynamics of power in colonial Lesotho is possible because of the strength of the existing historiography on Lesotho. The historical study of Lesotho emerged with two groundbreaking and complementary works by Leonard Thompson and by Peter Sanders, each of whom studied precolonial nineteenth-century history to 1870 through the lens of biographies of Moshoeshoe, founder of the BaSotho nation.[45] Sanders's work is notable for its analysis of political dynamics in the precolonial era, while Thompson provides important insight into cultural responses of the BaSotho under Moshoeshoe's rule, including early responses to the efforts of Christian missionaries. Covering both the precolonial and colonial eras, L. B. B. J. Machobane produced a penetrating analysis of the historical development of political institutions of

Lesotho during the nineteenth and twentieth centuries, demonstrating the indigenous sources of legal and democratic impulses leading to independence in 1966. Sandra S. Burman has carefully studied the politics of Lesotho in the era of direct rule by the Cape Colony from 1871 to 1884, including the period of the Gun War. Economic and political developments and organizations have been studied by Judith M. Kimble and by Robert Edgar, who have explored the experiences of ordinary BaSotho during the colonial era. The end of the colonial era is traced by Richard F. Weisfelder in his study of political movements and constitutional developments from 1952 to 1965.[46] My work reflects the influences of this previous scholarship and builds upon it as I construct what might alternatively be considered a social history of politics or a cultural interpretation of diplomatic and political history that unmasks the underlying dynamics in the struggles for power in colonial Lesotho.

My goal, consistent throughout my earlier work and in this new study, is to demonstrate the self-conscious initiatives of BaSotho, from all levels of society, in directing their own affairs and determining, as far as possible, their own fates and their own history. This is consistent with my personal experience of the country and of the many people of the nineteenth and twentieth centuries who left evidence to that effect. Presumptions of hegemonic colonial rule disable and disempower the people whose voices have been submerged and suppressed in public discourse and in the historical record. By contrast, hidden transcripts such as those appearing in oral traditions and oral histories reflect conscious knowledge and understanding on the part of the not quite "silenced" oppressed of the means of oppression, including both overt force and control over the elements of daily life. Hidden transcripts reveal the consciousness of involuntary compromise in the face of domination and the conscious deception by the politically colonized who rejected not only political colonization but also the colonization of consciousness, of culture, and of daily life.

2

Transcripts of the Past

The BaSotho under Colonial Rule

A snake in the house.

After a series of wars against their aggressive Boer neighbors, to whom the BaSotho had gradually lost most of their arable land, Paramount Chief Moshoeshoe requested and received British colonial protection. In 1868 Lesotho was annexed to the British Crown, and in 1871 it was turned over to the Cape Colony, which had just received the status of Responsible Government from Great Britain. Moshoeshoe had hoped for protection rather than a loss of sovereignty under colonial rule, and he never anticipated that after his death in 1870 his son and heir, Letsie, would be faced with colonial overrule from the white Cape Colony settler government. Because of this unanticipated twist of affairs, the fate of the country was to hinge on Letsie's ability to negotiate power through every means at his disposal, from diplomacy to warfare. The colonial presence in Lesotho constituted, in the BaSotho discourse on colonialism, "a snake in the house," while the collective Western interpretation of the BaSotho experience of colonial rule defined this experience as one of "benign neglect" through a system of indirect rule.

The myth of Basutoland is this myth of benign neglect, but a close reconstruction of the colonial period from both colonial sources and African sources, written and oral, reveals continual struggles over power at various levels and rule by force and the threat of force. The BaSotho have always faced dilemmas of accommodation and resistance to agents of white rule. When Moshoeshoe first requested British protection

25

against the Boers, he was trying to choose the lesser of two evils: indirect British colonial rule in preference to total dispossession by the Boers of the Orange Free State. From that time forward the BaSotho were constrained in their ability to resist colonial oppression by the British because they feared a worse fate at the hands of the Boers. For over a hundred years, then, the BaSotho accommodated themselves to one form of political oppression at home in preference to what was perceived to be the potential for worse oppression, which would come with direct South African rule.

The constant negotiation of power at any given level of politics in colonial Lesotho was contingent on the dispensation of power at other levels, creating a complex interplay of power relations between the British and successive Paramount Chiefs, between Paramount Chiefs and their subordinate chiefs, and between the chiefs and their people. The dynamics of struggle over power in these various relationships was revealed historically during moments of overt conflict and turmoil, so it is these moments that provide the focal points for this study. Toward this end three specific periods of conflict in the nineteenth century are examined: 1879–1880, which encompassed Moorosi's rebellion; 1880–84, or the Gun War and its immediate aftermath; and the so-called civil war between chiefs Masopha and Lerotholi in 1898. These wars involved conflict between opposing BaSotho parties and might therefore be mistakenly characterized as civil wars. In fact, however, all of these conflicts arose out of the direct interference of the colonial rulers, who used direct threats to coerce certain portions of the BaSotho population to support the colonial order in opposition to a group of rebels. In each case BaSotho initially resisted colonial interference but in the end chose to retain the British colonial connection out of fear of the strength of the Boers across the border.

The historical narrative continues in a chapter on political and administrative developments of the early twentieth century that reveal BaSotho perceptions and discourses on international dimensions of power and the internal dispensation of power and authority. Colonialism became more oppressive as the British succeeded in introducing measures that centralized power in the hands of the Paramount Chief and fewer subordinate chiefs, allowing for growing exploitation and abuse of office. Struggles for power at multiple levels became evident in the disputes over succession to the paramountcy in 1939 and 1940, which brought about the long reign of the Queen Regent, 'Mantsebo, during the minority of the young male heir to the Paramount Chieftaincy. The remainder of the book explores political dynamics and power struggles that manifested themselves in the turmoil that subsequently erupted in the form of the widespread incidence of "medicine murders" in the 1940s and 1950s, revealing cracks in the British ideology of indirect rule in colonial Basutoland.

Stories of the precolonial history of the people who came to be known as the BaSotho of Moshoeshoe have been transmitted through oral tradition and written narratives many times since the founding of the Lesotho kingdom, or nation, in about 1824. The precolonial history of the BaSotho has received considerable attention from historians, including myself, and indicates the strong self-awareness, initiative, and political savvy of BaSotho leadership, including Moshoeshoe, founder and first Paramount Chief of the BaSotho. The case of Lesotho is particularly appropriate for a study of power and discourse in the era of the transition from precolonial politics to colonial rule precisely because there is a rich body of primary sources and a developed historiography on which to build a close analysis of the BaSotho experience and BaSotho perspectives on their own history.

Perhaps most indispensable are the BaSotho oral traditions that have been edited and analyzed by Mosebi Damane and Peter B. Sanders. Not only have Damane and Sanders translated a collection of *lithoko*, or praise poems, as faithfully as possible, conveying the idioms of SeSotho without distorting the meaning in English, but they have also provided extensive explanatory notes about the people and places involved, and they interpret the poetic qualities of the poems with reference to their structure and elements of their composition. The authors explain that the poems are not often useful to establish historical accounts, as they are convoluted in presentation because of the aesthetic requirements of the poetry, and the original composers naturally took poetic license with their subjects. Damane and Sanders write that the praise poets "may often convey an account of what has happened by combining straightforward statements with hypotheses, questions, and most commonly, exhortations and commands." And they discourage scholars from attempting to use the poems as historical sources because "such information as they do provide is often incoherent and distorted. Nor is this surprising, for their primary aim is not to give a lucid factual account of what the chief has done, but to extol and praise him. They are not historical narratives, but poetry with historical allusions. In general, accuracy and clarity have been sacrificed for the sake of eulogy and aesthetic excellence."[1]

Nevertheless, Sanders and Damane concede the usefulness of the poems in conveying BaSotho perspectives of the people and events to which they refer. The praise poems convey a critical piece of the BaSotho discourse on the past because "the *lithoko* . . . have been composed for a Sotho audience alone, and this gives them a certain spontaneity and freedom. . . . Nothing has been altered to satisfy the requirements of outsiders."[2] The hidden transcripts of the BaSotho are thus present in these oral traditions, and their undisguised rejection of European domination resounds throughout. The rejection of the value of things European was perpetuated across generations through transmission of these attitudes in the oral traditions. The glorification of most BaSotho warriors came through praises of their roles in wars fought against Europeans, both Boers and British; hence the oral traditions kept the popular sentiment against and understanding of Europeans and colonialism alive throughout the colonial period.

Power in BaSotho History: A Culture of Diplomacy

The BaSotho nation was born of the astute strategies and diplomatic maneuvers of its founder, Moshoeshoe I, during a period of regional turmoil in the 1820s. Moshoeshoe is best known for his diplomacy, as recorded in BaSotho oral traditions and European accounts of his leadership and negotiating skills and evident in early stories about his consolidation of power. An oral tradition, perhaps true and perhaps apocryphal, reflects the myths that have been passed down for generations to illustrate Moshoeshoe's astute leadership skills, which explained why he gained followers and became so powerful. The founding of Moshoeshoe's nation may be dated to 1824, when he gathered his followers and led them from his parental home in Butha Buthe south to the Mountain of Night, Thaba Bosiu, a mountain fortress discovered by his scouts seeking a permanent place of refuge for his cattle and people. On that arduous march Moshoeshoe's grandfather was captured and killed, allegedly by people who had in their desperate hunger turned to cannibalism. According to traditions, Moshoeshoe later made peace with these captors not by killing them but by purifying them and incorporating them into his nation with the explanation that they were the tomb of his ancestor.[3] The nation survived because Moshoeshoe continued to exercise diplomacy in the face of danger, sending tribute in the form of cattle and ostrich feathers to the Zulu king, Shaka, and subsequently his heirs, Dingane and Mpande, and giving cattle to the AmaNgwane leader, Matiwane, in the wake of an attack in order to ward off further conflict. When Moshoeshoe found his territorial possessions and sovereignty similarly threatened by Europeans in the decades that followed, he used the same skills in ways that won him scorn as a duplicitous negotiator as well as praise as a peacemaker. Sir Godfrey Lagden, a colonial official with longstanding experience of the BaSotho through years of turmoil, provided a lengthy historical interpretation of the BaSotho past based on some of the hidden transcripts of both British officials and BaSotho to which he had gained access.[4] We can "read through" the colonial text of Lagden, that is, see through its biases, with its derogatory comments and opinions, in order to glean much of the hidden history of the BaSotho.

From Lagden we discover a pattern of diplomatic behavior on the part of the BaSotho that predated the advent of formal colonial rule. It was evidently Moshoeshoe himself who taught his children the techniques of disguise and dissembling by providing precedents for diplomatic maneuvers that were to stand them in good stead as they struggled to employ hidden strategies of resistance against colonial rule. Surprisingly, Lagden displays overt sympathy for Moshoeshoe, even serving as an apologist on his behalf:

> Stirred by intense patriotism, a virtue possessed in no small degree, he burned with a desire to make his people into a nation. That desire absorbed all his energies and if the means he employed to satisfy it were not invariably approved he may be acquitted of guilt for any wanton bloodshed or needless violence. Were apology necessary for his methods of statecraft, be it remembered that during the greater part of his career the tribe was plunged in struggles so keen as to threaten its extinction; in extricating it he was compelled at times to adopt daring expedients, diplomatic and otherwise.

These passages are significant because they are written by a colonial official who was not inclined to sympathize with the "wanton bloodshed or needless violence" that was attributed to Moshoeshoe. Lagden credited Moshoeshoe with conscious, astute strategies designed to protect his nation even if it meant using "deceit and perfidy," what we can recognize as forms of dissembling, to gain his ends:

> The instinct of self-preservation accounted for many of the faults, vices they were called, of which he was held culpable, such as deceit and perfidy; but his detractors could never fairly charge him with seeking personal gain or committing misdeeds not hallowed by other nations in the name of patriotism. Though his policy was

in the main fortunate it frequently appeared to miscarry and was then described as foolish and perverse by those who were either unwilling or unable to realize the far-reaching consequences of heroic measures they advocated.

Lagden was almost effusive when he noted that Moshoeshoe had a "gift of foresight" and that he used it with intelligence, to the chagrin of British colonial officials who had preceded Lagden in dealings with the BaSotho. Lagden implies that Moshoeshoe was justified both by the legitimacy of his goal and by the similar behavior of those with whom he was dealing, an implicit reference to Europeans:

> The gift of foresight was peculiarly his; it was because he exercised it intelligently that British Governors one after another challenged his bad faith and ingratitude for not following advice or orders which he knew for a certainty would prove fatal to national interests. If his besetting sin was crookedness, the times were crooked. Broken pledges were not his alone.[5]

Many anecdotes and observations in Lagden's work indicate that he was often privy to information gathered informally, evidently through oral channels, making him a rather astute observer about events to which he was witness. Other Europeans were not as generous, and one called Moshoeshoe "a great humbug, an old liar and deceiver, without one particle of truth, faith, honesty, or sincerity."[6] Moshoeshoe engaged in strategic dissembling:

> Doubtless he was a very capable chameleon, always presenting himself in the colour most likely to appeal to the eye of the man with whom he was treating at the moment; equally, with every appearance of complete submission, he would industriously elaborate plans for future emergencies; every change in the political atmosphere he carefully meditated upon and he generally turned every opportunity to account; and he was a master of evasion. Nevertheless, his leanings were always towards peace, and he clearly saw that it was only through peace that his people could thrive.[7]

Moshoeshoe appears to have been well able to take on whatever demeanor best suited him in a given situation. Lagden described him both as intelligent and gifted with foresight and as handicapped by a lack of understanding. He concludes that Moshoeshoe was "staggering under the weight of intrigues domestic and foreign, and worried perpetually

both by envoys from all parts and correspondence hard for his untu-
tored mind to grasp the meaning of."[8]

Moshoeshoe's strategy of dissembling was employed by his heir,
Letsie, and by Letsie's heir, Lerotholi, who deliberately presented themselves as weak or confused or ignorant (or intoxicated) in order to explain why they were unable to comply with the demands of a given colonial official. This, then, was the character of power and diplomacy at
the time of the imposition of colonial rule in Lesotho. Moshoeshoe had
left his heirs with a culture of diplomatic maneuvering and a legacy of
diplomatic strategies, but Moshoeshoe had also left British colonialism,
"a snake in the house." My story here is the story of how Letsie and his
people and his heirs dealt with the snake in the house.

British Rule in Basutoland: A Narrative

Moshoeshoe had presided over a country that saw a succession of wars
resulting in land dispossession but also sociopolitical consolidation, an
economic boom in production and trade, and the advent of Protestant
and Catholic missions with concomitant access to Western literacy and
technology. He left a truncated country in the hands of Letsie, but one
with tremendous potential based on past performance. This potential
was to be but briefly realized in large part because of the rapacious ap-
petite of the Cape Colony settler government for more and more land.
Administratively, the policy of the Cape Colony was to undermine the
power of the BaSotho chiefs, but it could not afford to send in more
than a handful of magistrates, so in practice it relied on indirect rule
through the chiefs. This meant that all orders from above and appeals
from below were supposed to go through the *Morena e Moholo*, now given
the English label of Paramount Chief, but Lagden's observations suggest that even from the beginning Letsie did not trust colonial officials,
and their trust in him was, as a result, misplaced. Although Lagden was
writing in retrospect, his knowledge of "hidden transcripts" and his intuition served him well as he observed:

> One of his [Letsie's] first acts was to relinquish the fortress seat of
> government at Thaba Bosigo, which had never succumbed to as-
> sault, in favour of his brother Masupha. That arrangement had a
> hidden meaning. It meant that the new Paramount Chief pur-
> posed to disguise his intention of resisting if needs be in future any
> unpopular form of government by avoiding residence in a fortified
> position that looked menacing to authority; to that authority he

would diplomatically bow under pressure whilst the "will of the people" under Masupha revolted if desirable and showed its teeth from the summit of Thaba Bosigo. It was a clever subterfuge which made it difficult for the authorities to discern whether they had to deal with the passive voice of Letsie or the resolute bearing of his brother—a puzzling problem for many years to come.[9]

Letsie served as Paramount Chief from the year of his father's death in 1870 until his own death in 1891. One brother, Molapo, had settled in the northeast district of Leribe, and another, Masopha, was settled in the central district of Thaba Bosiu, while Letsie remained in Matsieng, the village he had established a few miles from the French mission station of Morija. The territory of Moorosi, the old chief of the BaPhuthi who had long before offered his allegiance to Moshoeshoe, was annexed to Basutoland in the south before its final borders were fixed in 1871. Nehemiah Sekhonyana, yet another son of Moshoeshoe from a junior house, tried to establish himself with a following in the mountain area along the southern border of Basutoland, which had been ceded to Moshoeshoe by the AmaMpondo years before, but his claims were contested by the Griqua, who had migrated there in the 1860s to establish a new home, Griqualand East, after losing most of their land in their old Cape Colony homes of Griqualand West.

During Letsie's reign the people of colonial Basutoland, as it was now called, experienced a dramatic period of confrontation with their colonial rulers. As the Cape Colony made its rule felt through the imposition of magistrates who usurped the powers of the chiefs through new laws and control over courts and law enforcement, the new dispensation of power immediately revealed itself as far more interventionist than is suggested by the myth of benign neglect. The first chief to rebel openly was Moorosi, who had placed his people under Moshoeshoe in the earliest years of the nation's history. Having maintained a subordinate chieftaincy owing allegiance to Moshoeshoe, Moorosi rejected the imposition of courts, laws, and taxes that came with the person of a new District Magistrate in 1877. After more than a year of wrangling, open rebellion in the southernmost district of the country finally broke out in 1879. Paramount Chief Letsie was pressed to remain loyal and supply troops to suppress Moorosi's rebellion, and colonial troops eventually defeated the old chief, who died on his mountain during the final assault. But his rebellion was only the preface to stronger defiance across Basutoland. Within less than a decade it had become clear that the Cape Colony did not feel bound by the 1868 promises of the Imperial government to ensure and protect the sovereignty of the country and by 1880 had so threatened the security of the BaSotho that open rebellion, in what has been called the Gun War, broke out. While Letsie proclaimed his loyalty to the British, his brother Masopha and sons, including Lerotholi, led the rebel troops in order to protect BaSotho territorial possessions and their right to bear arms. When Cape Colony forces were unable to defeat the BaSotho, the two sides reached a standoff, and the Cape Colony decided to cut its losses and withdraw, an action formalized in the Disannexation Act of 1884. Letsie remained Paramount Chief, and his brother and sons remained patriotic heroes in the eyes of the population at large. The BaSotho then had to decide whether to remain under direct British Imperial rule or choose complete independence. There was dissension among the people, but the majority felt threatened by the potential aggression of the nearby Boers in the Orange Free State, and the decision was made to remain a colony under the British Crown.

The colonial administration changed, then, in 1884, and the Governor's Agents of the Cape Colony were replaced by Resident Commissioners, who reported to the British High Commissioner for the Cape Colony and Natal and subsequently for the Union of South Africa. The war had destroyed any pretense of rule by consent or the "hegemony" to which colonial rulers aspired, but pragmatism dictated that the British continue to employ a policy of indirect rule through chiefs. This policy called for not undermining the paramountcy but rather strengthening the central chieftainship, a strategic goal that the British pursued throughout the reigns of Letsie and his heir, Lerotholi, who reigned from 1891 to 1905, so that these chiefs naturally became strongly associated with the British colonial administration. BaSotho chiefs had always expropriated surpluses in the form of tribute labor and taxation, and under colonial rule their powers for exploitation increased. Nevertheless, the chieftainship, or institution of chiefs, remained popular in Lesotho, and both Letsie and Lerotholi enjoyed popular support, indicating that there has always been a hidden transcript concealing the popular understanding of the activities and roles of these two leaders.

Letsie had reigned during the final years of his country's economic prosperity, before overpopulation and land degradation limited the potential for sustained economic growth. Political pressures across the border sent waves of immigrants into Lesotho in the 1870s and 1880s, including the BaTlokoa under their chief, Lelingoana; the BaRolong from Thaba Nchu; thousands of AmaXhosa from the Transkei; immigrants from Natal; and BaSotho families who had been working as migrants outside of the country and who now returned with the livestock they had earned.[10] These population pressures intensified processes of land overuse and degradation that were already under way, and by the 1890s the formerly uninhabited mountains, previously used only seasonally for grazing herds, had become filled with permanent residents who scraped out their fields on the sides of mountain slopes.

Overcrowding reduced the land resources available to families and made those lacking reserves in food or capital resources (i.e., cattle) especially vulnerable to famine and disease in times of scarcity. The Ba-Sotho were always subject to periodic droughts, which brought food scarcity and sometimes famine, and the 1880s were no exception. But the 1890s were devastating in every way: crop production was adversely affected almost every year of the decade either by locusts, which appeared in 1892, 1893, 1895, and 1898, or by drought, which lasted from 1894 through 1898. Eighty percent of the cattle population died from the rinderpest epizootic that swept across the continent, hitting southern Africa in 1896, and famine conditions ensued.[11] The challenges that faced the country following Letsie's death in 1891 were formidable.

Lerotholi's succession to the paramountcy in 1891 was insecure because he was the issue of Letsie's second house, his first wife having produced a daughter, Senate, but no son. Letsie himself had favored his son from his third house, Maama, over Lerotholi, so that the British confirmation of Lerotholi as the new Paramount Chief after Letsie's death was decisive and created a precedent for direct British intervention in all future succession decisions.[12] Lerotholi's uncle Masopha and brother Maama were both strong, popular chiefs, and both were resistant to colonial interference, intensifying the need for the British to consolidate and centralize power in the hands of Lerotholi in order to meet their own goals of ensuring the stability of colonial rule through the Paramount Chieftaincy.

Lerotholi faced formidable political and economic challenges during his reign from 1891 to 1905. The economic disasters of the 1890s exacerbated festering competition for land and the cattle herds that had survived, creating tensions among a number of subordinate chiefs. The arrest of Masopha's son Moeketsi across the border in the Orange Free State created the pretext that the British needed to insist that Lerotholi subdue this recalcitrant chief, his uncle Masopha, and consolidate his power. Several dozen people died in the short battle that ensued in 1898, and Masopha was finally driven from his stronghold at Thaba Bosiu. This "civil war" was the last war of colonial intervention and achieved the British objective of the centralization of power under the Paramount Chief. Pressing their advantage and insensitive to the misery affecting the country from drought, famine, and disease, the British doubled the hut tax in 1898, although they deferred implementation until the following year. The South African War of 1899–1902 provided the opportunity for some BaSotho to recoup their losses of the 1890s by selling their horses at high prices to the British troops and by earning relatively high wages in service to the British war effort along their borders. Much of this newly earned wealth was used to purchase cattle, and crops were successfully harvested from 1900 to 1902. A renewal of drought in 1903 finally ended BaSotho self-sufficiency in food production, however, and created a permanent dependence on food imports to support the population. This, then, also marked the time from which the BaSotho became dependent upon the wages of migrant laborers working across the border on the farms of the Orange Free State, in the Kimberley diamond mines, and in the gold mines of the Transvaal.[13]

Social and economic disruptions brought on by droughts, diseases, famine, and war thus constituted the context for the political and administrative changes that marked Lerotholi's reign. A council of one hundred BaSotho men, the Basutoland National Council, which had been originally proposed by the Cape Colony government as a "Council of Advice" in 1883, was finally created in 1903 to assist the Paramount Chief in his administrative duties and to serve in an advisory capacity to the British Resident Commissioner.[14] The members of the council, along with Paramount Chief Lerotholi, regarded the council as a legitimate body for legislation and in their first session appointed a committee that met for an intense three-day session to draft in writing the laws that were believed to be those observed under Moshoeshoe and that, by virtue of the fact that they were still in force in the chiefs' courts, were deemed legitimate on the basis of their observance. Considered by the British to represent "traditional" law and thus the appropriate basis for legal action in the chiefs' courts, these laws became known as the "Laws of Lerotholi" and underwent periodic revisions by the council in the following decades. These laws continued to serve as the basis for court decisions in the BaSotho chiefs' courts, but these courts existed side by side with the courts of the European magistrates who took cases on appeal; eventually, in 1942, the laws were ruled by the British High Court to be advisory only.

Women were affected in various ways by the social, economic, political, and administrative changes introduced during the colonial era.

Their labor in the fields and in manufacturing goods for household use and exchange undergirded the economy and brought economic security to their families.[15] In times of economic stress, however, women and children tended to suffer more because their options for mobility and alternative forms of employment were more limited than were those of men, and men were given priority in the allocation of food. Women shouldered the burden of additional labor as men left to work in the mines, even as the economic returns to women's labor in the fields declined because of shrinking landholdings and declining soil fertility. Men nevertheless depended on their wives to stay home and retain the family claim to the land, intensifying male incentives to dominate and control women. Over time, however, the long absences of men working in the mines and the decline in the power, prestige, and wealth accruing to the positions of chiefs opened up new opportunities for women to serve in the role of chiefs during the twentieth century.

By the beginning of the twentieth century a mission-educated elite had also emerged to make its mark in BaSotho politics. Missionaries from the Paris Evangelical Missionary Society, whose predecessors had first arrived in Lesotho in 1833, were operating schools and a hospital. Catholic missionaries had established a mission in the 1860s and by the early twentieth century had gained a following especially among the chiefs and the wealthy. Not until after the advent of colonialism did missionaries from the Anglican Church venture across the border from the Orange Free State to establish missions in Basutoland, where they too opened schools and hospitals. The BaSotho teachers and clerks produced by these schools envisioned the world both from the perspective of their parents and from a Western perspective and created the first modern political association, the Basutoland Progressive Association (BPA), in 1907. As the name implies, their primary goal was to serve as leaders in helping their people achieve "progress," with implied connotations of Westernization, opening them up to criticism from those who strongly defended BaSotho culture and past indigenous practices. Thus the political world that Letsie II inherited upon the death of his father in 1905 was entering a new era.

Letsie II, commonly referred to as Letsienyana ("Little Letsie"), was faced with the same threat that had challenged each of his predecessors: the threat of incorporation into a country ruled by their old Boer enemies. After the conclusion of the South African War in 1902 the British oversaw a transition period leading up to the amalgamation of their two possessions, the Cape Colony and Natal, with the formerly independent

Boer republics, that is, the Orange Free State and the South African Republic, or Transvaal. No longer concerned about the Boer threat in the region, the British had no incentive to continue administering their other three possessions, the Bechuanaland Protectorate, Swaziland, and Basutoland, independently. Not surprisingly, Africans from all three of these colonial possessions objected vociferously to incorporation into the Union of South Africa, and in 1908 Letsienyana and his subordinate chiefs, in the name of all the people of the country, successfully petitioned His Majesty King Edward VII to retain their status under the Crown and independent of the proposed union, which came into being as the Union of South Africa in 1910. After a relatively short and uneventful reign Letsie II died in 1913, failing to leave behind an obvious successor to the paramountcy.

Griffith Lerotholi, Letsienyana's younger brother, was eventually installed as Paramount Chief after some controversy. The only son born to one of Letsienyana's wives was reputed not to be his biological son, although the original payment of bridewealth by Letsienyana to this wife's family legitimized all of her children as his.[16] Chief Griffith was asked to serve as regent on behalf of this child, who was still a toddler, but Griffith declared that he was only willing to serve as Paramount Chief in his own right, and the infant heir died a somewhat mysterious death, reportedly poisoned by an uncle. Griffith could have taken one of his brother's wives through the levirate system, thereby siring a son who would be considered the legitimate heir of the late Lerotholi rather than his own son, but Griffith prevailed in his demand to be made Paramount Chief himself and was so recognized by the British High Commissioner in April 1913.

Paramount Chief Griffith came to power on the eve of World War I and ensured the continuation of official BaSotho loyalty to the Crown in spite of growing political agitation against British colonial rule. The BPA had supported the concept of the Basutoland National Council and also supported the new council's efforts to resist Basutoland's incorporation into the Union of South Africa in 1908–9. However, the BPA also perceived the council as it was configured to be merely an assembly of chiefs serving the interests of the chiefs, and BPA members devoted their efforts toward the constant reform of the council to make it genuinely representative of the population at large. The delegation of responsibilities only to chiefs and to the exclusion of commoners came under more stringent attack by Josiel Lefela. Lefela started his political career serving as secretary to his local chief, Peete, who delegated Lefela as his representative to the Basutoland National Council in 1916. Eventually disillusioned by the chiefs in the council, Lefela sought to establish a second council chamber for representatives of "commoners." His proposal for a "Council of Commons" was not well received by the chiefs in the National Council, who rejected the proposal, prompting him to form a separate political association, the Lekhotla la Bafo, or Council of Commoners, in 1919. Expelled from the National Council the following year, he became a thorn in the side of Griffith but eventually became outspoken in support of the institution of the chieftaincy as a statement of his strong anticolonial views.[17]

Many of the political and administrative changes that came about during Griffith's reign were the product of regional and international economic and geopolitical forces beyond his control. BaSotho supported the war effort of Great Britain in World War I with men and donations, while closer to home more and more men were drawn into the migrant labor system, staying for longer and longer periods across the border in the new Union of South Africa. Christian missionaries expanded their efforts in the country, and Paramount Chief Griffith's conversion to Catholicism in 1913 was responsible for advancing the influence of the Catholic mission in particular. All of the Christian missions grew during this era, but the Catholic mission grew the fastest, and conversion to various denominations tended to reflect socioeconomic status, with the Catholic Church attracting chiefs and their supporters, largely the royal line and the wealthy, and the Protestant denominations appealing to educated commoners whose forebears had been the first recruits to these churches the previous century. These missions provided virtually the only Western-style education available through their schools, relieving the British of the burden of this social service, although the government did provide state aid to the schools. Still concerned primarily with achieving efficient administration at the lowest possible cost, the British pursued their goal of centralization of authority by pressing for administrative reforms. First mooted in draft proposals during the late 1920s but resisted by the chiefs, these received new attention after a British report commissioned in 1935 recommended streamlining administration by drastically cutting back the numbers of officially recognized chiefs and courts.

The death of Griffith ushered in a succession dispute between his sons Bereng and Seeiso in 1939. Griffith had supported the former, but most of the country was in favor of the latter, who was approved as Paramount Chief with a dramatic and spontaneous national display of genuine support. Seeiso lived only a year after his accession to the throne, however, and after his suspicious death a new succession dispute arose between his brother Bereng and his son, who was only two years old at the time. Eventually, the government passed over Bereng a second time and recognized as heir to the paramountcy Seeiso's infant son by his second wife, with his first wife, 'Mantsebo, to serve as regent and Acting Paramount Chief. Bereng took his challenge all the way to the High Court, and when he failed in the courts he turned to illicit methods of influence to expand his power. The rising incidence of a new form of terror and control, *liretlo*, commonly referred to as "medicine murder," was clearly connected to the struggles for power between Queen Regent 'Mantsebo and her deceased husband's brother Bereng in the 1940s. Bereng and a coconspirator named Gabashane Masopha, fourth in line to the paramountcy, were hanged after being convicted of medicine murder, but the rash of murders continued throughout the reign of 'Mantsebo, who was eventually forced to step aside for the new young king, Moshoeshoe II, in 1960. The supposed colonial regime of "benign neglect" had turned into a regime of terror, exposing the corruption of the British pretense of enlightened colonial rule. As the British achieved their longstanding goal of the centralization of power to serve their own needs they had strengthened the hands of corrupt leadership. In the end it was the pressure of the BaSotho who expanded the presence of commoners in the Basutoland National Council, circumscribed the power of the paramountcy, and forced the process of democraticization, which eventually yielded independence in 1966. After a century of domination Lesotho finally emerged from the shadow of colonialism.

3

Prelude to Rebellion

Pitsos, *Magistrates, and the Imposition of Colonial Rule*

The transfer of Lesotho, now called Basutoland, from British imperial hands into the care of the government of the Cape Colony signaled only minor changes in the new colonial administration in 1872. The Governor's Agent, responsible to the governor of the Cape Colony, consolidated colonial authority with the creation of administrative districts placed under the authority of District Magistrates, who in turn oversaw the collection of colonial taxes and the preservation of law and order through the chiefs, police, and a layered court system. But there had been sporadic wars between the BaSotho and their European neighbors for three decades, and it is not surprising that an attitude of defiance toward European rulers persisted in spite of the voluntary act of requesting British protection that had initiated that rule. From the outset, even as BaSotho chiefs, now charged with maintaining order and collecting taxes in cash and kind, complied with practices of indirect rule, subcurrents of discontent persisted. The colonial records show a varied awareness on the part of colonial officials to the signs and signals of BaSotho resistance to their authority, which were couched in careful and polite discourse and rhetoric accompanied by silent discursive acts of insolence.

The mountain areas between Lesotho, the Transkei, and Natal remained distant from colonial oversight and provided the opportunity for BaSotho to cultivate plans of resistance with their African neighbors to the south and east. When war broke out in the eastern Cape Colony in August 1877, Col. Charles D. Griffith, Governor's Agent in Basutoland, left to lead the colonial troops in the struggle involving the AmaXhosa. Émile Rolland, son of one of the first French missionaries to Lesotho and who was fluent in SeSotho and well acquainted with BaSotho politics, became Acting Governor's Agent. In September 1878 he reported to the Secretary for Native Affairs on a "riotous meeting" during which Nehemiah Sekhonyana Moshoeshoe and two others were said to have used "treasonable or seditious expressions," Rolland noting that "the meeting was a very noisy and tumultuous one and the general tone of it was disloyal."[1] The headman contested the authority of the Governor's Agent to allocate land, insisting, "I recognize no one but Letsie" and "the country belongs to Letsie and not to Mr. Griffith." The tone was contemptuous: "You hear, Basutos, that Lemousi says he has not been located [assigned the land] by Letsie but by the *Makhoa*." After pointing out that the term *makhooa* was "a contemptuous term meaning the white man" or, more literally, "white people," Rolland ended his report with a broader interpretation of political dynamics at the time: "I felt morally certain that a treasonable agitation was on foot, in which a number of the younger chiefs were taking part, presumably to cooperate with the Pondas and Zulus in case of a rising," but he believed that "Letsie was too deficient in courage to promote any open acts of hostility."[2] The incident became a part of the historical record only because of the sensitivity of this observer and suggests that rebellion was always brewing beneath a surface of complacency.

Rolland was not complacent; he held a public inquiry into the incident at Lemousi's village and reported that the young chiefs, Nehemiah and his compatriots, expressed strong denials of disloyalty. These were couched in vague and ambiguous language, however, and Rolland wrote that "the language used, though purposely made vague, was intended to arouse a feeling against the Government." Rolland believed that the BaSotho chiefs retained "sentimental regrets for the loss of their independence" and were influenced by the anticolonial resistance efforts of their neighbors.[3] The British were testing their authority by usurping the rights of chiefs to allocate land, adjudicate disputes, and collect punitive fines in court cases.

Nearby and at the same time it was the attempt of a British official to extend British authority over judicial procedures that eventually sparked trouble in the BaPhuthi chiefdom of Moorosi, in the southernmost district of the country. Moorosi had offered his allegiance to Moshoeshoe in the 1820s, and, with his approval, his territory had been incorporated into the boundaries of the country in 1872. Eventually, a controversy concerning Moorosi's son Lehana, referred to as "Doda" in the colonial documentation, triggered rebellion.

The story began in 1877, when the southern Basutoland district of Cornet Spruit was deemed too large and difficult to administer and was subdivided in two. The newly created district, Quthing, was Moorosi's territory, and suddenly for the first time Moorosi found himself with a new colonial official intent on imposing colonial control over both the chief and his people. The new Resident Magistrate of Quthing, Hamilton Hope, reported difficulties with Chief Moorosi from July 1877, just after his arrival. Their first encounter was at a district *pitso*, or public assembly, and set an ominous tone for events to follow. Moorosi's men were required to stack their arms before the meeting began, and when they sought to retrieve them after an angered Hope withdrew peremptorily one person was accidentally killed by a rifle shot. This gave Hope the reason he needed to ban weapons from future *pitso*s, and this ban on weapons became a bone of contention itself.

Chief Moorosi sent a statement to the Governor's Agent, then Colonel Griffith, explaining his perspective on complaints that Hope had raised against him following the abortive *pitso*. By his own account Moorosi had called a meeting of his people in order to introduce the new Resident Magistrate to them and to afford Mr. Hope the opportunity of explaining to the public any instructions to the chief or the people. This formal introduction was in accord with previous British colonial practices in the area and was proper according to BaSotho expectations of the right and responsibility of their chiefs to keep them informed and to control, if only nominally, the right of newcomers to establish themselves. Such official recognition should have been welcomed by Hope, and it suited the colonial administration's policy of working with and through the chiefs whenever possible. Moorosi was upset, however, because Hope had already taken action in several cases even before he had been officially welcomed and recognized by Moorosi. Moreover, the cases in which he had acted were not ones in which other magistrates would have intervened, and Moorosi had good reason to suppose that he was being subjected to greater interference by his magistrate than was the case elsewhere. While Moorosi denied that he had intended to insult the government, he had chastised his people for going to Hope's court before he had been officially recognized by the chief. Dissembling, Moorosi wrote later that "I had all unconsciously committed a fault, and stabbed the magistrate with my words. For thereupon Mr. Hope immediately rose and went away into the house."[4]

Hope's account of the same meeting is in basic agreement with Moorosi's, and it is clear he understood Moorosi's intentions. He reported that after the initial greetings and speeches of introduction, followed by the reading of the colonial laws by Maitin, Moorosi said to his people:

> Are you my people, or are you the Government people? If you are Government people you are fools. Do you obey this man (pointing to me) or do you obey me? They all with one voice cried out, we obey Morosi. I at once got up and left the meeting with Mr. Maitin, and the police and constables.

Hope left the meeting as a sign of disagreement and protest, showing his awareness that acts as well as words were important signifiers in the discourse of colonial rule and the discourse of the colonized. His report shows he believed that Moorosi was astute and deliberate in his words and actions, and he referred to signs of disrespect, which he considered a significant indicator of the attitude of Moorosi and his people. Hope understood Moorosi's message, which he referred to as a "text":

> Believing it to be expedient to overlook many other marks of the want of respect for the Government, I listened patiently to all that Morosi had to say, which occupied the time until sunset, when I answered him, and explained everything with the utmost care; but he still keeps to his text, that you and Mr. Austen said, that I was in all cases subordinate to him, and upon my asking him plainly what he wanted, adding that my most earnest wish was to govern this district well and to deal kindly and justly to everybody, he said he would never give in until I consented, in all cases, whether Civil or Criminal, first to report to him, and, upon receiving his permission, commence proceedings, but if I adjudicated in any cases before doing this he would complain, and justly too, that I was killing him.

Hope confirmed that he had told Moorosi that "they were liable to be treated as rebels" and that "it was too late to talk of his independence, that he should have said this to Moshesh before Basutoland was given over to the Government, but he only replied that he had never given *his* country to the Government." The tension rose:

> Even at this point I preserved my composure, and warned him that his language was rebellious. He said, you may kill me but I will not submit or resign any of my privileges.

Hope did not deny that his practices deviated from those of his prede-cessor, John Austen, as Moorosi had stated, but according to Moorosi he retorted, "Do you want me also to act like him, and stumble over the same stone over which he stumbled?" Prophetically, however, Hope added, "I will stumble over my own stone."[5]

Hope stumbled not only because he interfered with cases that had not yet been seen by Moorosi but also because his judgments were not in accord with established SeSotho legal precepts and practices, and he imposed extraordinarily onerous punishments such as exorbitant fines for infringements. Hope contested the customary authority of Moorosi to levy fines, telling him, "No, Morosi, all that kind of payments no longer belongs to you."[6] The colonial government expected chiefs to meet their customary responsibility to supply food and clothing to the poor and indigent but was simultaneously whittling away at the source of revenue from which chiefs made charitable disbursements as a mat-ter of course.

The day after the contentious meeting, at the urging of his son Le-tuka Moorosi returned to see Hope. He made clear his concerns about Hope's usurpation of his own authority but told Hope, "I give in about the beer, and the gardens, and the gun, but I give in grudgingly," com-plaining, "I can see that I am no longer anybody in this land." Moorosi told the Governor's Agent, "Then we shook hands, and cried, 'Hurrah! Hurrah! Hurrah! May God save the Queen!'"[7]

Hope's report of the second meeting was one of victory in the battle of words, as he stated that "after a final struggle to-day, he [Moorosi] had come to a complete understanding."

> I asked him plainly whether he would submit to my authority
> or not; that if he did I would shake his hands as a faithful Brit-
> ish subject, but that if not, he was a rebel, and I must treat him
> accordingly.[8]

Moorosi shook Hope's hand and in doing so signaled acquiescence, if only for the moment. Secretary for Native Affairs Charles Brownlee told Griffith that "Government is not able to accept Morosi's statement, as being true and correct, yet it does not now desire to enter into any fur-ther question with him upon this subject."[9] Griffith in turn instructed Hope to "substitute diplomacy and moral persuasion for physical force or high-handed proceedings."[10]

Not surprisingly, trouble reappeared within months. The new magistrate's seat at Quthing was only ten miles from Palmietfontein, which was in the Herschel District in the Cape Colony across the Tele River, a stream that marked the southern colonial boundary of Basutoland. By November Hope was expecting serious trouble. Moorosi was expected to arrive on 3 December at the magistracy, where "the whole tribe [was] to assemble armed."[11] He apparently believed that a military showdown was only a matter of time but did not want troops sent across the border yet because he hoped to buy some time.[12]

Hope and Moorosi then exchanged letters debating whether Moorosi and his people had the right to bear arms to a *pitso*. Moorosi insisted that it was "our custom; I have not invented it, it is so from ancient times," but the message, carried by the messenger Segata, was mixed. Moorosi insisted that he was willing to meet and implied that his loyalty was evident in his payment of taxes, yet he continued:

> When a bull goes out to pasture, he does not leave his horns in the kraal, he goes out with them, that he may defend himself by them from his assailant, and gore it also. I will not leave my weapons. I used to go and visit even Moshesh with my weapons. O, Segata, intercede for me with the magistrate; I should be weak if I were unarmed. If the magistrate says I must leave my arms, then it is that he refuses to see me; we shall then not meet, and the magistrate will prove that he does not wish to speak with me. See you, I do not want to walk stark naked, this is my nature. Even to pay hut-tax I go with these arms; they do not prevent me from paying tax, I pay it all right.
>
> These arms I bear with a glad heart; I do not carry them with my heart crooked; these arms are harmless to produce a wound unless a man's heart is crooked.[13]

This was the moment when the diplomatic game really began, and both sides employed colonial jargon, part and parcel of the discourse of the colonizers, to justify themselves in the struggle that ensued. The colonial officials, including District Magistrates Hope and Austen and Governor's Agents Rolland and Griffith, had to contend with conflicting reports and rumors that they knew might be unreliable. After Hope reported rumors that Moorosi was planning either to expel him by force or extract a concession of Moorosi's superior authority, Rolland sent a written response to Moorosi in which he insisted Moorosi show respect and obey the ban on weapons at public meetings:

> The great thing is that it is not you, Morosi, who must dictate your customs to the Queen's Government; it is the Queen's Government

which must teach you its custom, and that is, that people do not attend a pitso armed. We are not like God who can see into men's hearts whilst they are afar off; we are only men, and when we see armed men coming to us, we suppose they want war. Although your words may deny it, your actions call out in a loud clear voice.

No, Morosi, your duty is to obey and to humble yourself. If you go about with bands of armed men after you have received an order to the contrary, it will be impossible for the Government to recognize you as a subject. "A bull that carries its horns with it in order to gore its assailant" (to use your own words) is very like an enemy.

Rolland went on to order that the *pitso* not be held and told Moorosi directly, "You have done wrong," ending with the usual incongruous discourse of friendship: "Fare-you-well in peace! My words to you are the advice of a true friend."[14] Both men, the Governor's Agent and the principal chief of the BaPhuthi, were playing a game of veiled threats and counterfeit claims of friendship, and each recognized the intent and strategy of the other.

It is not difficult to read Rolland's intentions, since he made them explicit in the accompanying letter he sent to Hope at Quthing. The terminology, including reference to "ignorant barbarians," is, not surprisingly, racist and again suggestive of the colonizer's fear of the "other":

> No advantage can possibly accrue from a "pitso" held at the suggestion of this unruly chief, and which will give him the opportunity of being insolent to his magistrate, and of contrasting his large physical resources, in the shape of a body of armed men, with the (to native eye) defenceless and weak position of the magistrate.
>
> The chief Morosi is evidently trying to make use of these armed demonstrations in order to convince his people of his power and supremacy, being unaffected by the presence of the magistrate, and to a tribe of ignorant barbarians no argument could be more conclusive, especially if the demonstration be accompanied by a defiant bearing.

Perhaps most revealing of Rolland's understanding of the hidden discourse of the colonized was his reference to the public display of insolence that he feared from Moorosi. He advised Hope not to attend the *pitso* if Moorosi should arrive in spite of his orders not to come or, alternatively, to receive him privately in his office or private residence to "avoid giving him any opportunity of making a display before his people of his power and eloquence, a display which must necessarily be at your expense."

> [Y]our wisest policy will be to keep quiet, avoid trials of strength, gain time, and allow the moral influence of the Government to gain ground insensibly as it has in the more advanced districts. . . . [B]ear in mind that your highest and most lasting triumphs will be those which are the most gradually and noiselessly obtained, and that profound tranquillity is the most successful result of good government.[15]

Rolland also tried to resolve the problem through Letsie, but Hope, in order to demonstrate the seriousness of the situation, sent Rolland two sworn depositions indicating that Letsie supported Moorosi's defiance. The depositions are remarkable. Monaheng, a private in the Basutoland Police, had reported to Charles Maitin, Justice of the Peace in Quthing, that another man, Makhoa, had returned from a *pitso* at Maseru and spread a report that Letsie had publicly used defiant language to Austen. According to Monaheng, Makhoa told him and others that at a *pitso* Letsie said:

> "I hear that Mr. Hope is very hard on the people and torments them, that he (Mr. Hope) is simply running a stick in Morosi's rectum. Who has established Mr. Hope in the Quthing District, that he might be so hard upon Morosi and run a stick in the rectum of that chief. I do not understand you, Austen, how I am ruled by the Government? If the Government rules me in this way, I have only to say: The Maaoas [BaPedi] have perished, the Kafirs [amaXhosa] are also dead." Then Letsie stood up, and throwing his hat on the ground stamped upon it, saying: "This country is also dying."[16]

The second deposition was from Makhoa himself. At first he denied that he had reported this but then signed a statement after being confronted with that of Monaheng. According to Makhoa, the confrontation was unmistakable: "Then Letsie took the cap off his head and threw it on the ground, and said: 'I swear that if we are treated in this way there will be a war!'" Makhoa's desire to cover up the story, evident in his initial denial, suggests that he never intended it to reach colonial ears and that it was not fabricated for such purposes. On the contrary, he had to be intimidated in order to get the deposition out of him. Then he became defiant, adhering to the story: "If Letsie or Mr. Austen were to deny what I have said I should still insist upon it, and tell them it was the truth."[17] But Rolland's world would have been turned upside down if he had believed Letsie could be disloyal, so he rejected these stories even before he checked with Austen. He told Hope, "I consider

Mokhoa's statements, both as related by Monaheng, and as made before
Mr. Martin [*sic*], to be either gross exaggerations or perversions, or else
direct falsehoods in regard to what actually took place at Letsie['s]."[18]
To Austen Rolland wrote:

> I have informed Mr. Hope that I place no confidence in these state-
> ments, and that had Letsie so emphatically threatened the Govern-
> ment with war as is alleged, you would not have allowed such a
> threat to pass unreproved, nor would you have failed to report the
> matter to this office.[19]

Although the truth of whether or not Letsie made these statements
cannot be established, Makhoa's listeners were obviously willing to believe that he had. The Cape Colonial Native Affairs Office instructed
Rolland specifically to "take steps for the punishment of Makhoa, informing him that while he could be protected and confidence kept with
him in any statement made *bona fide,* though in error, that he cannot be
permitted to make a false statement knowing it to be false." Rolland accordingly gave orders for the punishment of Makhoa "for making false
and mischievous statements to his magistrate."[20] Punishing those who
transmitted unwelcome reports of resistance was a sure way of suppressing such reporting when actual resistance was brewing, but it preserved
the semblance of colonial order.

Rolland then requested Letsie to send a messenger to Moorosi to
bring him into line, informing Hope that "Letsie has responded most
heartily to my appeal, and has sent down his messenger, Mothlepu, to
bring Morosi to reason."[21] Later Rolland reported that Letsie's mission
had been a success: "The messenger spoke very strongly to Morosi on
the part of Letsie, in the presence of official witnesses, and administered
a very sensible and severe reprimand that was suitably responded to by
Morosi." Rolland had no choice in the matter, however, as he noted to
Hope that "we are not at present in a position to meet force with force . . .
and our only wise policy is to keep quiet as much as possible to avoid
giving the chiefs opportunities of displaying their physical superiority."
He told Hope that he did not want Hope's "moral influence" with Moorosi to be undermined, in spite of irrefutable evidence that Hope had no
moral influence over Moorosi whatsoever.[22]

Rolland reported the public transcript, produced self-consciously
by the BaSotho participants, and he ignored the possibility of a private
hidden transcript in unofficial conversations that might have transpired
between Letsie, via his messenger, and Moorosi. That other matters

were on the minds of the BaSotho is made evident by the fact, reported by Rolland in the same message, that Moorosi had also asked Hope for news of the war and for permission to hold a meeting of his people to warn them "to be careful to preserve order and quietness." Under the guise of loyalty Moorosi was seeking an opportunity to tell his people collectively about a war of colonial resistance just beyond their own borders. Surely the message was not lost on his listeners.

The Cape Colonial Native Affairs Office was not taking any chance with Moorosi, however. William Ayliff, the Secretary for Native Affairs, sent a letter insisting that a strong warning be issued to Moorosi, embodying implied threats of war if he did not submit to the colonial order. Rolland was "to intimate to Morosi" that the government was glad that he had seen and acknowledged his "error before he had gone too far" and remind him, in an implicit threat, that he had "narrowly escaped what many are suffering here for their rebellion and disobedience." Ayliff told Rolland that Moorosi "must not be led by this to believe that when he does wrong he has only to apologise in order to escape punishment." Ayliff also instructed Rolland to

> express to Letsie the approval of Government of his action in using his influence with Morosi to save him and his people from great trouble.
>
> It is better that a chief should use his influence in giving good advice to his neighbours than that he should, like chiefs in this neighbourhood, lead them to destruction.[23]

Ayliff was thus issuing implied threats to Letsie as well, trying to ensure that if Letsie had any inclinations toward disloyalty he would think twice about them. But the troubles brewing gained momentum when Hope took a provocative action by imposing a hut tax on four widows who had never previously paid this tax. As Hope reported:

> [T]his morning one of my policemen told me that for a week past all Doda's men have been assembled, armed with guns and assegais, with instructions that if I attempted to arrest any one or to attach any stock, they were to shoot the constables, and that Doda himself had been to his father Morosi to tell him of the case, and that Morosi had said, "You talk like a child. What have you done? If you had done any manly deed you might have something to report, but as yet you seem to have done nothing."[24]

Hope was certain Moorosi was provoking his son into resistance. After Hope had issued a writ against a village chief subordinate to Doda because of his failure to pay these hut taxes, seventy or eighty men, reported by Rolland to be following Doda's orders, "mobbed the constables" who were trying to take two head of cattle as payment, resulting subsequently in criminal summons against Doda and the others. The discourse of resistance was summarized in Doda's reported words, stating that no appeal was made in the case because "I have nothing to do with Makhoa [*makhooa;* i.e., white people, colonial officials]; I only know Morosi."[25] Doda was openly and explicitly contesting the legitimacy of colonial jurisdiction, which was the heart of the matter. Following the confrontation, all but sixteen of Doda's men fled with their livestock, and Moorosi declined the order to arrest them on the basis that he did not know where they were. Hope dismissed the usefulness of calling upon Letsie's help in the matter and worried about "a very cleverly planned scheme being hatched between those two chiefs."[26] Rolland immediately planned for a war in which he assumed Letsie would fight against Moorosi.[27]

As obnoxious as Hope was to the BaSotho, he read them more astutely than did his more sympathetic supervisors. The Secretary for Native Affairs regretted Hope's imprudence in the matter, wondering why partial payment of the taxes might not have been accepted, and he informed Rolland that "the Government would not wish to resort to the extreme measure you propose for coercing sixty or seventy men, that is of calling out an addition to the forces of Basutoland, the European forces from New England and Aliwal North."[28] Ayliff's mistake was to assume that the forces of resistance would in the end amount to only those sixty or seventy men now hiding in the hills with Doda.

Hope believed that Moorosi would never act alone, because resistance without Letsie's support would be futile. In light of the future rebel role of Letsie's son Lerotholi in the Gun War, it is also significant that at this moment Hope reported Lerotholi to be at Moorosi's. Finally, unaware that he was predicting the future, Hope noted that it was difficult to punish Doda because "if I sentence Doda to pay a fine he will hardly suffer at all personally, and if I sentence him to imprisonment I cannot keep him here, for he would either escape or be rescued."[29]

J. H. Bowker arrived on 13 March 1878 to take up the duties of Governor's Agent, and Austen replaced Hope in April. Bowker was an old hand, having been in Lesotho at the time of the British extension of protection to Moshoeshoe and his country in 1868. Upon his arrival Bowker adopted contingency plans for military action and then proceeded with a risky strategy. He took seven hundred men, mustered by

Letsie, to Mohale's Hoek and there learned from Austen that "the true state of the case was that the war spirit had spread up to the Orange River, and that there was a connecting link from thence to the Tembu chiefs on the sources of the Kei." Bowker was able to mobilize Letsie's support because of an old basis of trust, but Letsie made him aware of his own misgivings. Lerotholi himself served as one of Bowker's advisers and apparently told him what he needed to know to defuse the situation. Bowker certainly discovered more than less trusted officials might have and played a deep game of strategy to bring in Doda and Moorosi:

> The scheme of Doda and the cave was a plan to induce me to bring on a fight by sending a party to capture him, it being the plan to let us fire the first shot, and then if Doda had been captured, or not, the retreating or retiring [colonial] party would have been met in the rear by Tyali's Tembus. Finding this to be the case, I set aside all thoughts of giving them the opportunity wished for. Message after message was sent merely to gain time, and give me the chance of tiring them out, and it had its good effect, as at last Morosi agreed to meet me and hand over Doda.[30]

Even more remarkable was the subsequent strategy Bowker adopted, which entailed great risks. Since Doda was afraid to come in unarmed and, according to Lerotholi, would rather declare open defiance against the government, Bowker allowed an armed *pitso* of two thousand men to assemble, precisely the scenario Hope had so feared the previous year. Yet Bowker did not believe he was taking any chances:

> Morosi and his sons and family advanced in front of the mass of the people, and seated themselves in a position where not one of them could have escaped our bullets, and the living wall behind prevented their escape, so that in the event of a death struggle on our part, though lasting only a minute or two, every shot fired by my little compact party of well-armed men would have told with fatal effect upon the chief. This was sufficient to assure me that there was no danger to be apprehended; one accidental shot, however, might have brought on a mêlée of some sort.

Bowker, then, was mighty cool under pressure, and this was not lost on his BaSotho audience, a volatile group of two thousand armed men who had been expecting war for months. The outcome was a remarkable success for the colonial government, and even Bowker sounded surprised:

> The ring of a shilling might have been heard from any point during the time the case was being "talked"; but from the time the

sentence was pronounced there was a general murmur of congrat-
ulations, and the serious faces of the chiefs and people relapsed
into good humour. I never saw such a change in my life.[31]

Bowker's experience had served him well. He explained later that he
expected to have to fight, saying, "I was told I could not pull through
without." The situation required careful diplomacy:

> I kept up a correspondence through Letsea's messengers every day;
> we had our messengers going and coming, and after this had been
> going on for several days I informed Lerothodi that the thing was
> played out, and I must have a decided answer from Morosi by the
> next Saturday. After some conversation, Lerothodi went himself
> and returned with the reply, that Morosi was quite willing to come
> out and talk the case over, but he was afraid he would be caught
> like Langalabelele. If I would allow him to come armed, he would
> come most willingly.
>
> As soon as this was agreed to, I consulted the Chief Lerothodi
> and others. Lerothodi was almost crying at the time for fear I
> would not agree; he said it was the only way of saving the country
> from a war by allowing it.

The colonial ideology of indirect rule through the chiefs had been employed to good effect, but Bowker was only being realistic:

> I am not aware what view Government will take of my plan of
> bringing the matter to a close through the chiefs; but it must be
> borne in mind that I was without other means of meeting the diffi-
> culty, with only about seventy untrained native police and a few
> thousand rounds of ammunition, one-half of which would not
> ignite—there was no help for us.[32]

Cape Colony officials were unsympathetic with his tolerance of the
chiefs' influence and power, as the Secretary for Native Affairs let him
know. Already the colonial government was interested in the centralization of power, which would allow for tighter control from above:

> While justifying this course of action in extraordinary circum-
> stances, in ordinary times it would be best to rely upon your own
> sources of strength, than to lean too much on the support of the
> chiefs for the maintenance of order.[33]

As was common when colonial officials first arrived on the scene,
Bowker wrote a broader analysis of the situation in Lesotho and

concluded about the BaSotho that "their attachment to the chiefs is quite as strong as when I took over the country from Moshesh in 1868." Bowker underestimated Letsie but was not deceived with regard to the other principal BaSotho chiefs:

> Much will be said relative to the Basuto chiefs Letsie, Molappo, and Masupha. The latter is the least to be depended upon; easily led away by evil counsellors, no reliance can be placed in him; it is, however, different with Letsie. A coward by nature, old, and feeble as well, he is not likely to make any attempt to throw off his allegiance; add to this a bitter hatred of his brother Molappo; and I think, with ordinary care on the part of his magistrate, we will have nothing to fear. Molappo, from the position of his country, is more in contact with the Natal Zulus, and even the Transvaal, and he must be looked after in that direction. It is only known to a few that some years ago Molappo had strong hopes of being elected chief of the Zulus residing within the Natal boundary. This was the very cause of his wishing to be annexed to Natal instead of the Cape Colony. His chief warriors and guards are also composed of Zulus, and in the Langalabelele affair there is but little doubt that the old chief came over on an invitation from him.[34]

Affairs in Lesotho remained quiet until the end of 1878, when John Austen, now Resident Magistrate at Quthing, tried to take decisive action against Doda once again. His actions were presumably approved by Colonel Griffith, who was back at his post as Governor's Agent by October 1878. Several of the men who had hidden out with Doda the previous April had subsequently been jailed for stock thefts and then in September had broken out of the Aliwal North jail. Austen, referring to "detectives" who kept him informed, explained that he had adopted a strategy of group punishment to recapture the escapees, seizing the livestock of their relatives in retaliation for having assisted them. Further investigation caused him to arrest two of Moorosi's other sons, a brother and a half-brother of Doda, for having planned and assisted in these earlier thefts. By November Austen had also arrested and convicted Doda himself of these April thefts and sentenced him to four years of imprisonment and hard labor.[35] Although the conviction was for theft, Doda was actually being punished for rebellion, as the official correspondence demonstrates, and Austen conceded that there was "no direct evidence" against Doda.[36] It is not surprising that Doda's subsequent escape from jail was to mark the beginning of overt resistance to colonialism in Basutoland.

So Moorosi's rebellion was not unforeseen by the British. The timing was not coincidental: in the late 1800s the British were making a concerted effort to establish their dominance across the region over both their Dutch-speaking rivals and the centralized chiefdoms that had not yet been broken. Throughout the region Africans were keenly aware of their joint interest in resisting British encroachment. When Moorosi finally rebelled, he expected and received widespread sympathy and support from other Africans, including those BaSotho who were recruited to suppress his rebellion.

Colonial activities along the border between Basutoland and the Cape Colony to the south were the catalyst for the ultimate rebellion. The Yeomen stationed at Palmietfontein were among the troops being sent to take up defensive positions on the frontiers of the colony in the wake of the disastrous defeat of the British by AmaZulu troops at Isandlwana, but they were naturally seen by the BaSotho across the border in Basutoland as a potential invasion force. Closer to home, the poor relationships between the BaPhuthi and the colonial officials with whom they had to deal did not bode well. The BaPhuthi did not respect Hope and disliked Austen because he was identified with the so-called Fingo people whose land claims against the BaSotho he had supported in the Cape Colony, where he had previously served as a colonial magistrate.[37]

The trigger for rebellion finally came on New Year's Eve, 1878. A handful of Moorosi's men rode to the rickety jail at the side of the district magistracy where Doda and his companions had been held since their conviction. While the guards drank liquor, celebrated, and slept some distance from the jail, the night horsemen opened the jailhouse door and released the imprisoned men, who escaped into the night and into the mountains. Over the next few days Austen panicked and soon fled across the border, the people in the area made preparations for war, and the telegraph lines hummed between Basutoland and Cape Town. Moorosi denied involvement in the jailbreak and called upon his people to assist the government, thus delaying the British response to the impending crisis, but by March 1879 the Cape government had concurred with the Governor's Agent that troop intervention was necessary, and "Moorosi's Rebellion" began.

4

The White Horse and the Jailhouse Key

Moorosi's Rebellion

Colonial and BaSotho reactions to the jailhouse escape exposed the dynamics of colonial rule at various levels. The Cape Colony had hoped to wield power and administer the colony without the use of military force by means of the authority of the District Magistrates with the support of the chiefs. The District Magistrates, however, were aware that their authority was fragile because it lacked moral legitimacy among the chiefs and the population at large. The chiefs, in turn, were aware that colonial officials had the ability to call up military force from the Cape Colony in order to enforce administrative decisions, and their memory of sustaining military losses against colonial troops, resulting in the loss of land and independence, deterred them from resorting to violent rebellion. The exchange of communications between colonial officials and BaSotho chiefs at this time indicates a careful use of rhetoric by both sides in an effort to deploy moral suasion instead of armed forces to accomplish their conflicting goals.

The stakes were high for everyone in Moorosi's rebellion. The events were rather dramatic and have never been in dispute.[1] Rebellions across the region had prompted the Cape Colony to pass the notorious Peace Preservation Act, which was enabling legislation for preemptive disarmament of any group where rebellion had occurred or was feared. On 3 January 1879 Charles Griffith reported to the Secretary for Native Affairs in Cape Town that he had received information from Major Bell, Resident Magistrate in the Leribe District, who had in turn received it from his Chief Constable, Jan Magadlani, that made "reference to a message said to have been sent by Letsie to Molapo to the effect that the

people must not give up their arms." Yet Griffith also noted that the informants were unknown, so he could not judge the reliability of the information, and he downplayed the legitimacy of the report with the
comment that "Jan Mogadlani himself although a *loyal trustworthy* man
is yet an alarmist and inclined to exaggerate any information which he
may gather from other Basutos." The desire of the British to believe
their own rhetoric, their own discourses about loyal Africans, allowed
them to be blindsided as confrontations approached. Thus Griffith,
with no apparent awareness of the contradictions imbedded in his statements, concluded:

> The question of disarming the Basutos has caused & is still causing
> a good deal of discontent & many of the Chiefs think that we have
> an ulterior object in view and it was only yesterday that I was told
> that one of Letsie's sons had been heard to say that after the Basu-
> tos were disarmed that then they would be made slaves of and op-
> pressed in every way.[2]

The association of colonial rule with slavery was part of the BaSotho discourse of colonialism, and this was not the only time this charac-
terization appeared in BaSotho statements, but its significance was lost
on the British. Griffith was no wiser by the end of January, still insisting
on BaSotho loyalty even as he presented evidence to the contrary:

> There are no symptoms of disaffection amongst the people—At
> the same time I am well aware that all eyes & ears are directed to
> Zululand and the operations going on there, and I have no doubt
> that the pulse of the people will be regulated by the reports which
> will be circulated in this country as to the success or otherwise of
> our troops.[3]

By the following week Griffith was worried that the "partial disaster"
of the British, that is, their disastrous loss at the battle of Isandlwana in
their invasion of Zululand, would give confidence to the BaSotho or
perhaps frighten them into "Rebellion."[4] Griffith and Austen did not
believe that Paramount Chief Letsie and his vassal Moorosi could agree
and therefore disbelieved a report that Letsie's own messenger was
preaching disloyalty to the British "Government."[5] Griffith also began
to see the possibility of his worst fears being played out, those of unified
African resistance to the British, because of messengers traveling between the chiefs in Basutoland, Zululand, East Griqualand, Pondoland,
and Herschel.[6]

The British colonial officials in Basutoland were in a position to calculate the rebellious sentiments of the BaSotho in concert with their neighbors. In February 1879 Charles Maitin, a missionary's son who had become a Justice of the Peace in the colonial government, wrote to Griffith, who was back in his position as Governor's Agent in Maseru, that the "natives are trying to play a deep game with us, and without being alarmists we must be on our guard."[7] After Doda escaped from jail Griffith strongly suspected that Doda's father, Moorosi, had played a significant role in planning the escape. He wrote to Austen that he should keep in custody two people he had captured because they were important witnesses whose "evidence will go far to show the complicity of Morosi"; at the same time he ordered Austen to treat Moorosi as innocent until he had "been found guilty or given an opportunity of answering for himself."[8] Austen reported to Griffith that "Moorosi had sent a messenger to Pondoland to ask shelter for Doda and his companions" and was told to collect evidence against Moorosi. At the same time Griffith wanted desperately to believe in the loyalty of the Paramount Chief to the British colonial government.

The Colonial Discourse of Loyalty and Rebellion

A presumption of loyalty was embedded in the discourse of colonialism, as was immediately evident in the government's response to Doda's escape from jail. Austen sent a message to Moorosi informing him of the jailbreak and calling upon his loyalty to assist in returning the prisoners. On the one hand, Austen's message clearly indicates that he was reading the signs of the alternative discourse of BaPhuthi resistance, since he immediately inquired, "The magistrate asks why have the cattle been removed from the out-posts, thereby causing alarm in the country without a cause." This reference to the telltale signs of preparation for war shows that Austen knew there was more to the jailbreak than the individual actions of the escaped prisoners, and he was letting Moorosi know this. He therefore did not mince words and stated emphatically that the prisoners had been freed by some men "who are no true friends to the Basutos or the Government; that this is a very serious matter, and is tantamount to an open act of rebellion." Having thus informed Moorosi that the government was prepared to take the jailbreak as a sign that the BaPhuthi had rebelled, he underscored the collective responsibility for the action, stating that "in this case the chief Morosi and his principal sons will be held responsible for the act of breaking open the gaol door from outside."[9] To prove their loyalty, Moorosi and his people were to apprehend the fugitives.

At the same time Griffith was furious with Austen for having allowed Doda to escape:

> The idea of a prison guard sleeping in a hut sixty yards away from the "Lock-up" is so absurd that for all practical purposes they might as well have been sixty miles away. Under these circumstances I cannot help feeling that you have been guilty of great carelessness in the matter and that had ordinary precautions been taken the prisoners could not have effected their escape.[10]

The frustration Griffith felt with his subordinate blinded him to the wisdom of some of Austen's advice. Austen himself was prone to misjudging the BaSotho with whom he dealt, but at this point in time he appears to have been more cautious than Griffith with regard to Letsie's position in the dispute. Griffith thus found himself reassuring Austen that although Letsie should not be seen as speaking for the government, "Chief Letsie is for his own sake as well as for the welfare of the whole territory anxious to bring about a peaceful solution of the difficulty with Morosi."[11] But Austen fled across the border to Palmietfontein for help.

Although he would have approved of Austen's actions in the face of real danger, Griffith chastised him because he doubted Austen's information and thought all was safe. Griffith went so far as to accuse Austen of "thus precipitating matters and causing alarm & excitement throughout the whole country," and he told him to take two months' leave while he sent someone to take his place.[12] Within days Griffith was forced to eat his words and acknowledge that Austen "had good grounds for leaving."[13] He wrote to the magistrates in each of the country's districts:

> I have the honour to inform you that the Chief Morosi and his people are in open revolt. On Sunday last Mr. Austen had to abandon his seat of Magistracy in consequence of information which he had received as to Morosi's intention to send down an armed party to attack him—Since then on Monday and Tuesday Morosi carried out his intention by sacking the Magistracy plundering a trader & taking property & stock from all loyal people in the neighborhood.[14]

Griffith's calls for help to the BaSotho chiefs of the various districts are models of colonial discourse about loyalty and duty. Each chief was told he now had "an opportunity of showing his loyalty to the Queen" by sending troops to put down "this rebellion."[15] Of course, the call to display loyalty was accompanied by the pledge to reward the troops with the booty of cattle, suggesting Griffith's doubt that loyalty alone was enough to bring out the BaSotho and that he was also able to exploit elements of the BaSotho discourse of power that from precolonial days had conferred approval on those who captured booty in cattle raids and war. In his direct messages to Letsie, Griffith also deployed typical colonial rhetoric. Describing the initial acts of destruction in Quthing, he wrote, "By these acts you will see that Morosi has thrown off the cloak under which he had been hiding for so long and has openly rebelled against the Government of the Queen," and he signed off with the phrase "I am your friend."[16]

The need to maintain prestige was at the forefront of colonial discourse and always played a role in decision making when it came to colonial rule. In August 1879 Rolland told the Committee on Basutoland Hostilities, appointed by order of the Cape Colony House of Assembly, that the Cape government should reject Moorosi's offer of conditional surrender and properly invest the mountain to cut off supplies, because "I do not think it would be consistent with our prestige to accept anything but an unconditional surrender." Rolland also believed that Moorosi would not surrender even if promised that his life would be spared, because "his great fear is of being exiled to Robben Island," which had already entered into the discourse of colonialism and resistance.[17]

William Ayliff, the Secretary for Native Affairs, used the discourse of colonialism in communications with Griffith. Ayliff wrote that "if we are to maintain our position as masters in Basutoland we shall need to be prepared for such accidents as they come about."[18] Reference to the carefully planned and executed jailbreak as an "accident" reflected the colonial denial of the possibility of planned and deliberate resistance indicating dissatisfaction with colonial rule. Juxtaposed against this is the common colonial jargon referring to the colonizers as "masters," reflecting some awareness of the inequalities that could foment resistance. The divergence between discourse and the need to address reality could lead to convoluted and contradictory statements in official colonial statements.

Even before he heard of the rebellion Griffith was aware of the delicate balance between persuasion and force that was necessary. After Austen's flight Griffith was immediately ready to resort to the use of armed force to maintain control and to send a clear message of colonial domination:

> This matter cannot be allowed to pass over without our punishing Morosi severely; if this is not done we shall be the laughing-stock of the whole country.
>
> Last year he was let off with a mere nominal punishment, and hence his arrogance and disobedience now.[19]

This was the position adopted by the colonial government. Ayliff ordered Colonel C. Y. Brabant, in charge of the colonial military camp at Moorosi's mountain, "You do not withdraw one inch from the position taken up," and wrote him that if the rebels asked for terms of surrender, "those only admissible by the Government will be an unconditional surrender."[20]

The BaSotho Discourse of Resistance and War

The BaSotho conveyed and read a discourse through actions as well as words. The removal of cattle, women, and children from an area portended the beginning of hostilities. Similarly, the doctoring of troops indicated that war was expected. The signs of war were discursive acts that were understood, as intended, by the BaSotho and by some Europeans. Miscellaneous BaSotho testified later to this. One MoSotho witness considered it significant in late January 1879 that "all the men of this village sleep with their guns at the Sigotla [court]" and that a number of men went "daily with their arms to the gardens [fields]."[21] Mapara testified that he only believed the war was coming when he heard that Moorosi had ordered Lesala "to put the little children out of danger."[22] He was told by Mosueu that he did not need to fear participating in the jailbreak because "it is to be war." The sending of the cattle into the mountains was further confirmation to Mapara and all the BaSotho that war was expected, while others testified that they considered Austen's flight and the capturing of the cattle of loyal people as sure signs of war.[23]

Various white farmers across the border also became aware of impending war because their employees asked to be released from service. Two of these farmers testified in June 1879 that in the previous December and January they had been explicitly told that "Moorosi intended making war," and in early February one had learned from "the natives [who] were passing in numbers (armed) over my farms towards Moorosi's country" that they "were going to assist Moorosi in an outbreak."[24] Maso, a witness, related that "the war-cry had been sounded" and that on the day the trader's shop was looted just before open rebellion on arrival at the chief Mahlonzo's place, at the Buffalo River, [he had] found all the men assembled, and the doctor at work, doctoring the army to make it strong and invincible, "ukukufula."[25]

This witness also noted that the BaSotho were driving their stock away and fleeing and that "it was customary at the time for all the men to go about armed," which he took as signs of impending war. The issue of disarmament was central to the discussion of rebellion, but Maso stated definitively:

The cause of this rebellion is not the disarmament question, it is the old war spirit of the previous year; we did not want to be ruled by the Government, and pay hut-tax; we wanted our independence and to govern ourselves.[26]

The hegemonic discourse among Moorosi's people was a durable and persisting discourse of African rule. This African discourse could take colonial discourse and turn it on its head, with mockery a sign that it had never held sway. Hence on the Tuesday after Austen fled his magistracy, the magistracy was "looted," but it was not merely an act of theft. Rather, the premises were systematically destroyed as a symbolic act. According to the missionary D. F. Ellenberger, who stayed throughout the rebellion and had continuous contact with both sides, Moorosi's sons Ratsuanyane, Nk'a, and Lemena traveled through Quthing and sent other messengers "to call up the people." They found that a Thembu chief who resided in the Quthing District under Moorosi had already begun raiding. Lemena found the magistracy "tenantless, lonely and deserted," and "after holding a mock trial, Matushela and his men tore down the Magistrate's Bench, smashed the furniture, tore the office books to pieces and scattered the papers around."[27]

Although these men then went on to loot the items in the magistrate's residence, more significant is the fact that they took the time to hold a mock trial before proceeding to destroy the colonial seat of "justice."[28] The importance of this act of defiance in the prevailing discourse was made further evident the next day:

When Mathlokolo and his companions arrived at the camp of Ratsuanyane they found him and his brother Nk'a engaged in the performance of a light comedy piece. Ratsuanyane sat in front of a rock representing the Magisterial desk, personating Mr. Austen. Nk'a sat below with a book before him, a short stump of wood in his hand, writing down the evidence,—or rather simulating to

write as they do on the stage. At the end of the mock trial Ratsuanyane solemnly sentenced the sham prisoner to receive 24 [lashes]
with the cat-o-nine-tails. At the conclusion of the farce Ratsuanyane interviewed the messengers.[29]

The prevailing discourse was a resilient discourse of independence and self-governance; a colonial discourse had never taken hold or
achieved hegemonic status among the colonized peoples. The disarmament question would be the rallying point for coordinated resistance,
but it was the colonial order that was under attack. The old order of
African rulers remained the legitimate authority of African discourse,
which rejected the perceived evils of the European world. Austen reported that when he sent those who had remained loyal or surrendered
into the Cape Colony to serve as laborers, he learned that the BaSotho
told the men who had surrendered that "they were being sent to Aliwal
North to be killed, and their wives to be sold as slaves."[30]

"Moral Castration": Disarmament as *Causus Belli*

The issue of disarmament was present from the very beginning of Moorosi's rebellion. Mhlowoa, one of the six prisoners who escaped with
Doda, later testified that he heard from other prisoners that they would
be rescued before being transferred to Aliwal and before the war they
had heard would break out if Mr. Austen imposed disarmament.[31] Mapara's testimony reveals that the disarmament issue was at the heart of
BaSotho discourse of the moment. In a lengthy "voluntary" statement
to the Resident Magistrate at Quthing he reported that the day after
Christmas he had had the following conversation:

> Somatube said to me, "have you heard that the arms would be
> taken away from us and in all Basutoland, and that war would
> break out directly; that Letlatsa had been sent to the chief Letsie's
> when he returns, if it is true, Mtsapi says it is better that the gaol be
> broken open, the prisoners liberated, and we all die together."
> I asked if it is really true that war would break out? He said
> "Yes."[32]

As they investigated the causes of Moorosi's rebellion, colonial officials at the Cape asked all the witnesses whether they expected the Ba-
Sotho to resist disarmament. Joseph M. Orpen, a Member of Parliament in the Cape Colony who had first visited Lesotho in 1854 as an

elected member of the first Orange Free State Volksraad, noted that disarmament was "a cause of general irritation" among the Basotho. He stated that although disarmament was advisable, the timing was wrong.[33] Similarly, Bowker was outspoken in opposing the disarmament of the BaSotho because he considered them "friendly" but that disarmament would be seen as provocative, and during an inquiry he foretold the coming of the Gun War, telling the committee:

> I believe if the Peace Preservation Act was put into operation in Basutoland, you would at once have 20,000 men against you.

Questioned again about imposing disarmament on the BaSotho, Bowker was even more unequivocal, saying, "I think it would be insanity." Bowker pressed the point home once more later in the questioning with his statement: "I think it would unite every black face in South Africa against us." Removing all doubt about this warning, Bowker concluded, "I think if there is anything calculated to unite the natives, it is this disarmament act; it is moral castration."[34]

Rolland asserted that disarmament had been the cause of Moorosi's rebellion and that "it lay at the bottom of everything." According to Rolland, Moorosi believed the movement of colonial troops up to Palmietfontein, across the border but a mere ten miles from the magistracy in his district, which had been part of a general defensive move on the colonial borders because of the Zulu War, was in fact a preparation to attack him. Hence,

> the moment Mr. Austin left his magistracy, it was taken as a declaration of war; it was looked upon that the magistrate had fallen back on the army, and that war was practically declared.[35]

Loyals or Rebels? The Role of BaSotho Troops

From the beginning colonial officials realized that they needed to mobilize BaSotho troops under Letsie's command and debated whether this would be feasible and effective.[36] According to a later report of Secretary for Native Affairs Ayliff, about two thousand BaSotho troops took "part in suppressing the rebellion," supplied with equipment and horses "entirely at their own expense" under their chief, with the approval of the government. Moreover, he emphasized that they "rendered their services throughout this campaign without pay." When asked if the BaSotho were "long in raising that force" Ayliff replied:

> No, at first there seemed some difficulty in getting them out; Mr. Griffith attributed it to slowness of action on their part rather than any unwillingness.[37]

While it is not clear to what extent the military officials or their colonial counterparts trusted the BaSotho to fight their own BaPhuthi people, Griffith was encouraged after Lerotholi captured rebel cattle and reported in the first week that no more troops would be needed, misled because the rebels had put up no resistance.[38] Griffith was wrong, however, and more troops were needed as the war dragged on. Less than a week after his first report the Colonial Secretary's Office wired that one hundred more Cape Mounted Rifles should be sent as reinforcements, stipulating that "this rebellion must be decisively crushed."[39] Griffith reported BaSotho troop movements, but his optimism had waned somewhat, as he noted, "I suppose if Morosi is on his mountain we shall have to besiege it until the two guns come up, or we shall have to storm it."[40]

It did not take long for the colonial officers in the field to recognize that the BaSotho troops were not necessarily reliable. One colonial official noticed that "there appeared to be a little hanging back on the part of some of the Basutos in turning out to guard the Drakensberg passes," and one chief

> absolutely refused to turn out, and prevented the men under him from doing so. I tried Leshuta in camp, found him guilty of disobedience, and sentenced him to six months imprisonment with hard labour, and a fine of fifty pounds.

While many men did not believe they would be punished for refusing to fight because they thought Letsie himself would refuse or "even render Morosi aid," open rebellion did not suit Letsie's goals because it would provoke the full suppression of the BaSotho by the Cape Colony, whereas by appearing to serve the colonial order he could maintain his authority, albeit restricted in scope.[41] Hence Lerotholi's troops captured the cattle of both rebels and "loyals" but did not play a significant role in suppressing Moorosi's rebellion.

Mr. Stevens, a long-term resident of the Herschel District, believed that Letsie and Moorosi had an "understanding." He observed that the timing of BaPhuthi attacks suggested prior coordination between Moorosi and Letsie's troops, and he wrote that when Lerotholi had visited Moorosi he took a message from his father Letsie saying he, Moorosi, should give up the prisoners, his sons who had broken gaol to be punished by Govt and that he, Letsie was not yet prepared for war so the big thing was yet coming.[42]

When pressed, Ayliff later conceded that the BaSotho had not taken part in the first attack on Moorosi's mountain, and eventually he made clear they had not really ever engaged in any attack.[43]

Mr. J. Wood, a member of the House, served as a captain of the Yeomanry who were sent to the conflict and provided a picture of operations on the ground. He testified that "with the exception of the Fingoes, all the friendly natives were a cowardly lot, and their sympathies were very much more with Morosi than with us." Without consciousness of irony he employed the colonial jargon of "friendly natives" but then indicated they were not so friendly after all: "I was informed by some of the Fingoes that the Basutos were plotting to shoot me and the other officers."[44]

So the loyalty of the BaSotho remained in question to the extent that their European commanders even believed there had been plots to shoot their European commanding officers, a highly problematic scenario for dealing with a rebellion. When the final assault was planned in November, this problem was again apparent. In the end the mountain was "successfully attacked and taken by a force of 1400 men of the Cape Mounted Rifles and Herschel Native Levies with a score of the Barkly Border Guard all under the Command of the Colonel Commanding the C.M.R., Col. Zachary Bayly." The force would have been larger but for the last-minute discovery of the intent of Thembu troops from Herschel to betray the colonial forces to Moorosi. An African assistant from the hospital who was assisting Dr. Hartley and Dr. Cummings on the front line overheard voices near a mountain road where they were passing, and "after attentively listening for a few minutes he said they are Tambookies who are saying 'that they don't want to "schit" (shoot) a Maphuti on the mountain but would get up into the schantzes and help "schit" the whiteman!'"[45]

The Contest of Indirect Rule: The Role of Paramount Chief Letsie

As early as February 1879 Maitin, the Justice of the Peace, reported from Quthing to Griffith, who had returned to his position as Governor's

Agent in Maseru, about serious reports of emerging rebellion. In the reports Maitin had heard locally Letsie was portrayed as the key player, with his influence said to be determining popular reaction in a manner that reflected the strong popular base of his leadership. Maitin, who as a missionary child grew up among the BaSotho, was well positioned to recognize that the BaSotho chiefs were playing what he referred to as a "deep game" with the colonial officials.

During the month of February colonial officials openly considered Letsie's position and role. They had to determine whether Letsie was loyal and trustworthy, as there was some evidence to the contrary. Moeletsi, who accompanied Letsie's messenger Makhube to Moorosi on Austen's orders, reported in a formal statement that Makhube seemed to be stirring up trouble, and it was not clear whether this was Letsie's intention. Contradictory evidence suggests that Letsie was sending two messages, one as public discourse for British consumption, the other as a hidden transcript to a BaSotho audience. According to Moeletsi, Makhube told Moorosi and his sons Motsapi and Letuka that they should assist Austen in apprehending Doda and those who had helped him to escape and that if they fought against the government they would have to "fight [their] own battle." However, Makhube went on to make some inflammatory statements that implied Letsie's support for rebellion against the colonial government. Moeletsi reported further that Chief Molapo had told his brother Letsie that "he was tired of the Government, and that the time had come to fight the Government," and that Letsie had informed Moorosi he planned to refuse to disarm.[46]

Letsie sent a messenger to the Governor's Agent and denied that Makhube had been sent by him to participate in Doda's rescue, noting, "I am at peace with the Queen. I am her servant in very truth." Letsie, using a metaphor of a leather blanket, then challenged Moorosi and his rebel sons:

> If he is afraid to bring them up to Austen, let him bring them here, and give them to me. What makes me (Letsie) say so is that Morosi has no country of his own, he wishes to dispute with me the ownership of Moshesh's kaross, and tear it up into little tatters.[47]

Letsie therefore went on record as having denounced the rescue of Doda and any further act of rebellion that might occur. At the same time, both he and Moorosi had, through their messages, taken refuge in the colonial dispensation that in theory continued to recognize Letsie's authority over Moorosi, thus providing a form of protection for Moorosi.

The colonial officials appear to have been conscious of the problems inherent in reinforcing Letsie's authority by allowing him to deal with Moorosi, and Ayliff wrote specifically to Griffith: "Don't think it well that Letsie should alone punish Morosi."[48] Playing it safe, Letsie adhered to colonial discourse when he wrote directly to Ayliff on the occasion of Ayliff's visit to Basutoland during the rebellion, insisting:

> I believe that our interests are safe in your hands; and that, as you get better acquainted with us, you will more and more be convinced of our loyalty and faithfulness to the Queen's Government. May we continually live in peace and security under it.[49]

Austen had a fairly realistic understanding of Letsie's position by the middle of June. He wrote Ayliff:

> In the case of Letsie I believe that every principal chief in Basutoland has no love for our rule—and would gladly shake off the yoke if they thought they could—but the time has not come yet. He doubtless had and still has his sympathies with Morosi, and urged him to hold out at the beginning, but I don't think that he intended him to carry matters so far.[50]

Bowker, the old hand who had first received the country under British protection, seemed to enjoy Letsie's trust and certainly would not hear anything of disloyalty on the part of Letsie.[51] Rolland believed that Moorosi only rebelled because of his certainty that the rest of the BaSotho, including Letsie, would support him and join him, concluding, "He did not think he was going to fight single-handed." The hidden transcript evidently provided compelling reason to Moorosi to expect widespread support from his BaSotho compatriots. One rebel later testified that "Moorosi said that he trusted to the assistance of all the black people . . . [and] his dependence was upon a general rising."[52]

"Letsie's Old General": Moorosi and the Rebellion

Moorosi's role was never really in doubt, although it took awhile for the colonial officials to prove his complicity in freeing Doda from jail. This was in part because Moorosi tried to manipulate the discourse of the colonizer to his own advantage while sending messages of a hidden discourse of resistance to his followers. When Moorosi was first approached by a government messenger carrying the order that he track and apprehend the fugitives and send them back to jail, the sergeant reported that Moorosi was "very sulky." It is notable that the colonial officers realized the importance of the deportment of Moorosi as he spoke, since this might convey additional information about hidden intentions.

Austen had been immediately aware that the audacity of the action—freeing the prisoners—suggested the complicity of Moorosi, something that would also have been obvious to Moorosi's people:

> The chief Mtsapi, Morosi's principal son, next in rank to Letsika, thinks that his father must be in the secret, that no common man would have committed such an outrage, and has promised to do his best to trace out the fugitives.

But the public discourse was different: Moorosi held two public meetings, and Austen reported that "Morosi's object was at each meeting to impress upon the minds of the people that the prisoners had broken out themselves, and were not rescued, and that he is held responsible unjustly for the act, and also the public."[53] The message was for the public record only.

Moorosi's complicity was confirmed, deliberately, to the BaPhuthi and the rest of the BaSotho when it became widely known that on the night of the escape Moorosi's own distinctive white horse was used. Mapara testified that Somatube "came with his horse (the white horse Morosi always rides)," and the implication of Moorosi's complicity was not lost on him.[54] Moorosi would only have allowed the use of his horse if he had wanted his role in the escape to be widely known. In his report of one of these meetings Sergeant Masin stated that he had received "private information to the effect that the rescue of the prisoners had been planned by Morosi, and that the gaol had been broken open by his orders, and that the prisoners were hidden on the top of the mountain."[55]

So Austen was never deceived, reporting as early as 18 January that "I have no longer any doubt in my mind but that the prisoners were released by the orders of Morosi by the men named, and that the prisoners are secreted at the present time on Morosi's Mountain."[56] But Griffith pointed out to the Secretary for Native Affairs that there was "no positive proof" and that "both Mr. Austen and Sergeant Isaak Masin are to a certain extent interested in endeavouring to throw the blame on Morosi, in order to avoid their own responsibility in not having taken proper precautions to keep the prisoners in safe custody."[57] Griffith was gradually convinced by a growing body of evidence implicating Moorosi, and subsequent events demonstrated beyond a doubt his complicity in the rebellion, which began with Doda's escape. By 17 February

Maitin had in hand testimony from two participants stating explicitly that Moorosi had personally given the jailhouse key to Somathube so that he could free Doda.[58] When Moorosi heard Letsie's message that he should give up the prisoners because Letsie was not yet prepared for a rebellion, Moorosi is reported to have replied,

> I have now gone too far as blood has already been spilt. I now find
> I am alone. My children and people can do as they like; for my own
> part I shall go back to my stronghold and die, if need be, in defence
> of my own home.[59]

Moorosi had indeed launched the rebellion that took his name, and, after successfully resisting two attacks (on 8 March and 5 June), he perished in the final assault on his mountain on 21 November 1879. The Cape Colony mounted a carefully planned surprise nighttime attack using specially built tall ladders held in place by some soldiers while others climbed to the summit. The colonial troops took the BaPhuthi rebels by surprise under a moonlit sky just before dawn. As the soldiers swarmed the mountain, meeting with little resistance, Private Whitehead directed their attention to a ledge below the peak, where Moorosi then met his end:

> It appeared that he had found Moirosi in a sort of cave or hollow
> ledge with Dodo the original cause of Moirosi's rebellion [who]
> had fired upon Whitehead. With some other men they attempted
> to capture Moirosi whom Whitehead shot. Moirosi's body had two
> fatal wounds in it one in the left side of the neck another in the
> ribs.[60]

Doda and some of his men had jumped from the ledge and survived, to surrender or be caught over the next two years. But Moorosi had met his end, and this European witness concluded that "Letsea's old general had a fine head full of crafty intelligence" and wrote that in death he had a "curious disdainful smiling expression."[61] In an act of brutality the white colonial troops dismembered Moorosi's body and sent his head to Kingwilliamstown, but the colonial office prevented the carrying out of plans to send it to London and ordered Moorosi's head to be returned and buried with the body.[62]

After the mountain was taken the troops explored it, and "one searcher picked up Moirosi's Bible a large quarto in brown leather binding."[63] The Bible and the Christian message it carried, although kept by Moorosi with his karosses, powderhorns, and "bags for medicine containing curious little bits of wood, beads, copper bracelets, bullet moulds and sulpher," had not succeeded in establishing the hegemonic discourse of the Christian European colonizers. The legacy of Moorosi's rebellion, a challenge to the legitimacy of the colonial order, was a terrain of resistance in both discourse and reality that set the stage for the coming Gun War, when all of the BaSotho fought to defend their own home.

5

Guns, Diplomacy, and Discourse

The Gun War

Even before the end of Moorosi's rebellion the BaSotho chiefs were preparing for their own fight against the Cape Colony in what became known as the Gun War of 1880–81. Ostensibly fought over the right of the BaSotho to bear arms, this was a war over issues of land, sovereignty, and the establishment of colonial rule by the Cape Colony. In April 1880 the Cape government extended the Peace Preservation Act, which had already been imposed in the Cape Colony, to Basutoland and ordered the surrender of all guns to local magistrates in exchange for monetary compensation. About half of the adult male population of Basutoland owned a gun, and the majority had paid ten pounds for their guns, with many guns valued at twenty-five pounds.[1] Guns had determined the outcomes of battles over land, cattle, and people in southern Africa for fifty years; the BaSotho insistence on the retention of their arms derived not from the hours of labor and the capital they had invested to obtain them but from the desire to protect their land, property, and freedom. From the beginning it was clear that those who would comply with the order to turn in their guns were in the minority, and by July 1880 those who refused were attacking these so-called loyals and confiscating their land and property. By August the rebel leader, Chief Masopha, was well ensconced in his refortified stronghold at Thaba Bosiu, and last-minute attempts by the Cape Colony to forestall the inevitable rebellion only highlighted its powerlessness. A colonial contingent of Cape Mounted Rifles rode into the country on 13 September 1880, and the first battle of the war was engaged.

The BaSotho were fighting for much more than the right to bear arms. In spite of the fact that they had maintained the appearance of loyalty and served the Cape Colony during Moorosi's rebellion, the Cape Colony subsequently planned to double the hut tax, appropriate £12,500 from Basutoland to pay for the expenses of the colony, and, most important, confiscate the fertile Quthing District so that the land could be sold to white farmers. While disarmament was an important grievance and precipitated the rebellion, the planned confiscation of the Quthing District for white settlement was perceived by the BaSotho as having much more serious ramifications because of the precedent it would set for future land expropriation. This was the intention of the Cape government, which explicitly stated that it did not accept that Basutoland would be maintained as a "reserve" for the use of BaSotho only. The stage was set for another colonial war, this time bigger and with a different outcome.

Griffith's dilemma was that the Cape government, driven by colonial politics and politicians, refused to recognize that its policies of disarmament and land dispossession were fated to have disastrous results. Griffith's letters of early 1880 are filled with his apprehensions of rebellion by the BaSotho and explanations and pleas about the folly of colonial policy. The colonial enterprise was driven by diverse factors, and colonial discourse encompassed dramatic disagreements over the wisdom of land expropriation for the benefit of white settlers, as is evident in Griffith's letters to the Secretary for Native Affairs in Cape Town. From the beginning Griffith was firmly opposed to any land expropriation from the BaSotho and was not afraid to say so, citing historic agreements and the possible ramifications: "They will naturally conclude that this is only the thin end of the wedge, and that, upon one pretext or another, they will eventually be deprived of all their country."[2]

Griffith's letters quickly moved away from historical rationales to realistic warnings. He carefully employed the jargon of a colonial subordinate, framing his advisory warning in terms of "honour" and "respect," prefatory to challenging the wisdom of his superiors. In the same vein he employed the colonial trope of "loyalty," that of the BaSotho, knowing that no colonial official could argue against the ideal and wisdom of winning and sustaining such loyalty. Referring to the punitive measures of land expropriation, the financial indemnity, and the doubling of the hut tax, Griffith told the Cape Colony officials:

> I cannot but feel that I have been placed in an equivocal position, one which must naturally create a wide gap in that good feeling

which has hitherto existed between the whole nation & myself as
their "Father" and the Government representative.

Griffith believed he had achieved a positive paternalistic working relationship with the BaSotho, and he clearly resented the fact that his entire credibility was endangered among the people he hoped saw him as
"Father." Griffith further worried about his reputation as a colonial official more broadly and wrote that he felt his "unsullied reputation" for
thirty-two years in service was now threatened.[3] He continued to press
for BaSotho interests and challenge the colonial policies that he was expected to implement.

Griffith's sense of the futility of his struggle against the colonial office for which he worked as well as his understanding of the politics
behind the colonial policy decision for disarmament were evident in a
letter he wrote to the prominent French Protestant missionary, Adolphe
Mabille, on 25 February 1880. Marking the letter "Private," he confided
to Mabille about the Cape Colony Prime Minister that "there is no
chance of Mr. [Gordon] Sprigg's Ministry falling upon this question,
because it is a popular measure in the colony."[4] Griffith also had to deal
with discontented BaSotho who faced the prospect of permanent land
dispossession. One of his own subordinates, Austen, was chairman of
the Land Commission, which was making the decisions he was expected
to enforce. Griffith was upset that the Land Commission was already
communicating with the missionary, Ellenberger, about land surrounding the mission's Industrial School without his knowledge or input, and
he insisted that all instructions from the Cape government to the Land
Commission be transmitted through him.[5]

By March 1880 Griffith was making preparations for conflict; he
sent the Secretary for Native Affairs a "Sketch of scheme of Basutoland
Militia."[6] Griffith also found himself in the unfortunate position of now
attacking the actions of Mabille, one of the few people who clearly
shared his perspective on the folly of disarmament. On 17 March 1880
Griffith sent a copy of the Peace Preservation Act to Mabille, requesting
that he translate it into SeSotho and use the Paris Evangelical Missionary Society's printing press, the only one in the country, to print two
thousand copies.[7] But Mabille took a principled position, refusing to
allow the missionary society's printing press to be used to print the Disarmament Proclamation for dissemination in Lesotho, thereby seriously
inconveniencing the colonial office, an act that had the support, as Griffith learned upon complaining to them, of Mabille's entire missionary
society.[8] It was Griffith's duty to rebuke him, which he did in a letter, but

Griffith knew that the missionaries, working as they did so closely with the BaSotho throughout the country, were likely to be able to predict accurately BaSotho popular reactions to colonial policies and actions. Griffith intensified the urgent tone of his messages to Cape Town and in the end pointed out that the underlying colonial policy of relying upon moral suasion rather than direct force was no longer possible because "the people now look with suspicion upon their magistrates and other Government officers."[9]

It was a colonial hope that people had become alienated from their chiefs as a result of oppression, but this illusion was possible only because of colonial ignorance of an indigenous discourse of political rule that allowed for political dominance in the context of what was perceived as the natural, legitimate rule of indigenous rulers. Griffith implied that to date the colonial magistrates had managed to rule by means of the confidence and respect they inspired, choosing to ignore the implicit force by which colonialism was maintained. But now, he wrote, "the policy which has been forced upon me, the circumstances over which I have had no control, of carrying on the Govt of a large tribe, like this, by what is known as 'moral force' or 'moral persuasion' has been played out."[10]

Griffith struggled to prevent the ensuing disorder. He responded to an inquiry from a trader by writing, disingenuously, that he did not foresee trouble and asked the European resident in Lesotho what he meant by his reference to "the critical state of the country?"[11] But only two weeks later he himself wrote to a missionary that "from reports which have been brought to me within the last 24 hours I regret to say that matters in this country are in a most critical state & I do not think the lives & property of Europeans are safe for any time longer."[12] At that point he realized he would need the help of all available Europeans in any fighting, and he sent a letter to three other traders that they should help defend the country, or their property would be confiscated.[13] He was evidently aware that he did not have the resources to defend against rebellion, for he wrote at this point in frustration to the Secretary for Native Affairs that "a law obnoxious to the people of this Territory has been forced upon them and no steps have been taken by the Govt to support the authority of its officers to enable them to protect the loyal & those who have obeyed the law in question."[14] As the reality of the precariousness of colonial defenses became evident, the irony of the disarmament was revealed: those loyal to the colonial government had obeyed the Disarmament Proclamation and were now disarmed, while the rebels had kept their guns. Griffith sent word immediately to his subordinate magistrates to correct this situation, notifying them: "You are authorized to return arms surrendered to any loyal people in whom you have confidence giving them to understand that the guns are only lent to them to defend themselves & property until quieter times."[15] He did not yet know that the distinction between "loyalists" and "rebels" would be in doubt throughout the war.

Of Tropes and Guns: Loyalty or Force of Arms?

The war of words that preceded the war of guns over the right of the BaSotho to carry guns reveals the public and hidden transcripts of British and BaSotho protagonists regarding the legitimacy of colonial rule. BaSotho transcripts of resistance reveal a concern not merely for the right to bear arms but rather for the right to protect their land, children, and property from colonial expropriation, a right ensured only by the retention of their guns. Colonial officials and those who subscribed to their discourse of colonial rule, including some missionaries, minimized or obscured the deeper concerns of the BaSotho and focused solely on the issue of guns, at least in part because they could not imagine a hidden transcript that questioned the legitimacy of colonial rule. The tone of Griffith's communications with Paramount Chief Letsie revealed his paternalistic belief that Letsie would take anything Griffith said about his intentions and the intentions of the colonial government at face value. On 22 December 1879 Griffith wrote to Chief Letsie and "the other Chiefs and People of Basutoland":

> As Governor's Agent in this country, and also as your friend and well-wisher, I think the time has arrived when I should draw your attention to, and remind you of the words spoken to you by the Honorable the Colonial Secretary at the Pitso, also at the meeting held on the following day in the school room.
>
> You were all told that the Government was of opinion that it would be a good thing for the Basutos to be disarmed in order that Peace & Prosperity might reign throughout the country.[16]

So the tropes of colonial jargon were prominent as the British imposed the most obvious measure of colonial control, the monopolization of the means of force, in the name of being a "friend" and "well-wisher," and Griffith patronizingly told the BaSotho that it would be a "good thing" for them.

In the next passages he refers to the Queen, a term that reminded the BaSotho of their voluntary adherence to the British and was friendlier and more personal than the term "Government," which he also used, as was common, to imply unquestioned authority. Griffith tried to suggest that disarmament was part of a favor the Queen was "willing" to confer because the BaSotho had placed their "trust" in her. He then tried to adopt the most prominent tropes of local discourse about social welfare, referring first in English to "Peace and Prosperity" and then repeating the local proverb in the name of Western "Civilization":

> You have a proverb of your own "Khotso ke nala" (Peace is Plenty) and this is what the Government is anxious to see in the country, in order that you may progress in Civilisation and Christianity, and that the resources of the country in which you live may be developed & improved and that you, and your children's children may long live in the land which your father "Moshesh" handed over to the Queen to take charge of for you.
>
> This trust Her Most Gracious Majesty the Queen will be willing to carry out for your benefit, & it will entirely depend upon yourselves whether she will be able to do so, by your being obedient to the Laws of the Land, and loyal to the Government.[17]

The BaSotho believed they had already demonstrated their loyalty by mustering troops over the course of the year to provide at least an appearance of support for the colonial government in the suppression of Moorosi's rebellion, but now they became worried that they would share his fate nevertheless. The Cape government did not appear to be acting in good faith with regard to rebels or loyals in the case of the BaPhuthi or BaSotho. On 24 December 1879 Griffith issued a notice "proclaiming a sort of amnesty to the Baphuthi rebels who are still wandering & hiding about the country in the neighborhood of the Orange River," but on 3 March 1880 Griffith notified the Resident Magistrates of the two southern districts of Quthing and Cornet Spruit that those BaPhuthi rebels who surrendered were to be sent to Cape Town "to be put on" public works there and elsewhere, that is, to be used as forced laborers.[18]

On 10 February 1880 Griffith wrote to Chief Masopha in the nearby Berea District, condemning him for actions that were clearly rebellious:

> I am very sorry indeed to see that you do not understand your position as a Chief under the government, your Magistrate was quite

right in calling upon you for an explanation and in pointing out to you that you had no right to assemble an armed meeting at 'Mbopa's village without first getting the permission of the magistrate to hold such a meeting.

In the case of the meeting held at the Chief Letsie's village, that Chief had my permission to hold that meeting, which is very different from your meeting which was held without the permission of any Government officer. There is no doubt about it that the object of your meeting at 'Mpoba's was in order to intimidate people from giving up their guns to the Government, and it is conduct like this of yours which is likely to bring trouble into the country and for which you will be held responsible.[19]

The dispensation of power in the colonial order was made clear to Masopha: he had lost his authority to call *pitsos*, and his people had already, even before the Disarmament Proclamation had been made, lost the right to bear arms. Griffith made clear his belief that Masopha was disloyal, openly accusing him of fostering rebellion.

Griffith's response to Masopha was more inflammatory than he realized, as he also wrote to Letsie about the incident and used it as a pretext to make a direct threat. Like most colonial officials, Griffith preferred to believe in the discourse of loyalty, in which so much was invested, but he also precipitously introduced, overtly, the threat of force, which put the lie to a pretense of consent to domination. Griffith told Letsie:

Herewith I send you a copy of a letter which I have written to your brother Masupha about his conduct in assembling an armed party at 'Mbopa's village for the purpose of preventing people from obeying the orders of the Government.

If I hear of any more such cases it will be my duty to ask the Government to send up a body of troops to support the Magistrates and protect the loyal people who wish to obey the orders of the Govt.[20]

In response Letsie sought the advice of a trusted missionary, Mabille, as he tried to maneuver in this game of power. In one of the messages conveyed through Mabille Letsie requested a delay in publishing the Disarmament Proclamation, to which Griffith responded: "I shall have no power or authority to delay the matter, my duty will be to obey whatever orders I receive from the Govt. upon the subject."[21] Griffith thereby absolved himself from responsibility by hiding behind the requisites of "duty" and "orders," by disclaiming any personal acccss to power, and by asserting the primacy of "the Govt," which would put the act "in force." In late February Griffith asked Mabille to inform Letsie that he had permission to hold a *pitso* but that it would be better to use the occasion to discuss Quthing land issues rather than guns:

> I did not see what use the guns were to them, but that with regard to the land there I could see that it would be of great benefit to them—that I was afraid they were grasping at a shadow and would lose the substance.[22]

Letsie was still trying to comply with colonial expectations of obeisance when he requested permission to hold a *pitso,* knowing the BaSotho would have answered his call to a meeting on his own authority in any event. At the same time, it is clear that underlying the hidden struggle over guns was a struggle over land. On 13 February Letsie wrote to the influential missionary Ellenberger, whose mission was located in the Quthing District, hoping for advice and support in opposing the colonial confiscation of Quthing. Letsie was not as careful to hide his sentiments from Ellenberger as he was from colonial officials, and his tone with regard to the colonial government was strident even while he addressed Ellenberger with respect. In this letter, written in SeSotho, Letsie informed Ellenberger that he had received a letter from the "Colonial Goverment [*sic*]" informing the BaSotho that the government was confiscating the Quthing District, which would be sold as farms, although the mission and its school would be preserved. Reiterating Ellenberger's right to the mission as conferred by Moshoeshoe and himself, Letsie invited the missionary to attend a *pitso* that would be held soon and asked Ellenberger to use his influence with the Cape government, because the confiscation of the land was "not in accordance with the *act* of *submission* and *acceptance* of Lesotho, which was accepted by the Queen."[23] Stating in SeSotho that "we cannot agree even the slightest with this [confiscation and selling of land in Quthing], which is thus"—and Letsie completed the sentence in English—"proposed by the Colonial Goverment as it is quite unjust." The use of English words in this SeSotho text underscored Letsie's understanding of a colonial discourse on politics that promoted the language of justice; moreover, his reference to an act that was "quite unjust" underscored his own indignation and outrage. He conveyed indirectly his perception of the colonial dispensation of the time through his choice of terms. Although he had already referred twice to the "Colonial Goverment," formal but misspelled, and once to the

"Mofumahali" (Queen), invoking the highest authority with reference to the original protection agreement, he then referred to the "Muso oa Boikarabello," or "Government of Self-Defense," to designate what the BaSotho intended to be a government of protection, a protectorate. Ellenberger reacted immediately by sending a long letter to Griffith, but it fell short of what Letsie intended, since Ellenberger requested that the land rights of his mission and congregation be preserved, with only a sentence devoted to the larger issue.[24]

Griffith must have suspected the motives of the French missionary, Mabille, who did not owe any loyalty to the British government, and chose to bypass him in his subsequent correspondence with the Paramount Chief. On 12 March he wrote directly to Letsie in reply to a letter from Letsie about land confiscation in the Quthing District. Letsie had requested that his letter be forwarded to "the Government," but Griffith replied that Letsie's letter contained "inaccuracies." Underscoring his words, Griffith told Letsie, these statements, "if not deliberately untrue are undoubtedly *perversions of the truth*."[25] Griffith stopped just short of accusing Letsie of lying, but he was determined to defend himself in the eyes of his superiors, to whom he sent both Letsie's letter and his reply. He conceded that he had implicitly threatened the loss of Quthing District to the BaSotho if they failed to assist with suppressing Moorosi's rebellion, but he refused to acknowledge the legitimacy of the BaSotho position that the converse would hold; that is, if they helped, they would retain Quthing. To Letsie Griffith used the tropes of colonial discourse in the hope that he would not have to call up the troops of colonial coercion. He employed a thick use of colonizing jargon: "lawful Sovereign," "loyal subjects," the "guidance" of "the Govt," and "the Same Queen." The language of imperialism was at his command, as were the troops of empire if needed.

Letsie then tried to go over Griffith's head by requesting permission to send a delegation of "trusty men" to Cape Town, which only antagonized Griffith further. Of course, Letsie had no way of knowing that Griffith had tried to protect the Quthing District for the BaSotho through his own correspondence with the Secretary for Native Affairs several months before. Griffith sent Letsie's letter to "the Govt" in Cape Town and promised to relay the reply, which he did on 3 April:

> I am directed by the government to inform you in reply to your letter of the 16th ultimo, upon the subject of sending a deputation

down to Parliament, that the government is intrusted by the Parliament with the administration of affairs and is responsible to Parliament for its acts, and one of those acts is the Proclamation having
reference to the surrender of arms.

Making clear the difference between Imperial rule and rule by the Cape
Colony, which he and Letsie ignored when it suited their purposes, Griffith wrote:

> The Secretary of State leaves the matter of disarmament entirely
> in the hands of the [Cape] colonial government, and you are ad-
> vised now as you have been advised before, not to listen to evil
> counsellors.[26]

In his letter Griffith conveyed, indirectly, the futility of sending
such a deputation without directly prohibiting it. However, he also provided Letsie with a means to save face with the "Govt," here spelled out
fully for once but in small letters as the "government." Only days later,
on 8 April, Griffith wrote to Letsie that "he had been directed by the
Government," this time spelled out and capitalized, to "inform" him
that "the Peace Preservation Proclamation for Basutoland has been
published in the Government Gazette of Tuesday the 6th Instant and
is therefore now law in this Territory." As required in the colonial dispensation of indirect rule, Letsie himself was to apply and enforce the
law. Feebly applying the tropes of "advice" and "loyalty," Griffith told
Letsie to "at once tell the people to surrender their arms" and that
"they must obey the law."[27] Letsie pursued a strategy of delay, and in a
barrage of messages Griffith told him that in British law the executive
could not overrule Parliament, that he could not delay the law, that
there were no excuses left for delaying compliance with the law, and
that he could not extend the time for surrender of arms.[28] Both men
were now playing a game of brinkmanship, and at this point Letsie
won: on 9 June Griffith wrote to extend the time for surrender of guns
to 20 July.[29] Griffith desperately wanted to win with words rather than
bullets, but the battle of discourse was over and the war of guns about
to begin.

Paramount Chief Letsie: Loyalist or Rebel?

Griffith's fears that the colonial position was indefensible not only in
principle but also militarily were not unwarranted. People who complied

with the Disarmament Proclamation and turned in their guns were given receipts called "tickets," the term by which they came to be called: *matikiti.* Yet these disarmed loyalists were then vulnerable to the armed rebels, and their guns were returned to them so they could fight with colonial troops against the rebels. Therefore, it was the initial act of turning in their guns that set the loyalists apart from the rebels. What role did Letsie, as Paramount Chief, play in this colonial drama? While Letsie sent in a few guns to the government and on the surface appears to have been a loyalist, his brothers, especially the powerful and popular Masopha, and his sons, including his heir, Lerotholi, became rebels. Yet Letsie's role was deceptive. According to Sandra Burman, who has presented the most detailed analysis of this period,

> Letsie was old, obese, sick and vacillating, much under the influence of Griffith and the missionaries, and unwilling to lead a revolt which, if successful, would have disastrous results for Basutoland. As Moshoeshoe's heir, his experience fitted him to understand better than most the inevitability of aggression by the land-hungry Orange Free State should Basutoland completely shake off colonial rule—and protection.[30]

In arguing this, however, Burman perpetuated the false image of Letsie contained in the colonial records that Letsie himself had carefully cultivated so that the British would not suspect his role in the rebellion. In June 1880 Griffith wrote to the Secretary for Native Affairs in Cape Town:

> I am afraid the Chief Letsie has neither the energy or the power over his people to grapple successfully with the present state of affairs and I am very apprehensive that he may be drawn into the vortex of disloyalty and discontent which at present exists in this Country in consequence of the enforcement of the disarmament policy.[31]

Letsie sustained his image as weak throughout the war. In September 1882 Joseph Orpen wrote that "unfortunately Letsie is very old, gouty, sick, weak, doubleminded, undecided and failing in intellect and full of procrastination."[32] Sir Godfrey Lagden, who arrived in Lesotho in 1884 and served as the British Resident Commissioner of Basutoland from 1893 to 1902 and subsequently wrote a history of the BaSotho, was more perceptive. In his two-volume history, published in 1909, Lagden noted:

> Letsie halted between two expedients; in turns he professed abject
> submission to the orders of Government and intrigued against it;
> his shifty tactics were so cunningly devised that he enjoyed the con-
> fidence of Government all the while that he encouraged resistance;
> but his irresolution conduced to weaken the national cause owing
> to the mistrust he engendered, so that a good many surrendered
> their arms and formed a corps of loyalists.[33]

Lagden was only partially correct, however. According to oral traditions, Letsie did enjoy the confidence of the government and made a
show of turning in his guns while secretly encouraging resistance. However, Lagden misjudged the level of communication and understanding
between the Paramount Chief and his people. The BaSotho were fully
cognizant of Letsie's double role, and those who became loyalists did so
as part of a preconceived plan agreed upon by the BaSotho as a whole.
Mosebi Damane, the noted MoSotho historian who learned about Ba-
Sotho history from his grandfather, a "Masopha man" and therefore a
rebel, explained:

> Some people think that Letsie was weak. For me, I think that Letsie
> was a great diplomat. And the fact that up to now his policy has
> not been understood, that is the measurement of the depth of his
> diplomacy. . . .
>
> You see, the old man had just died, Moshoeshoe. And, then
> upon his death he had left, to use Letsie's expression, he had left a
> snake in the house. During his time the snake was not there, you
> see? Moshoeshoe was independent, he was the king of Lesotho.
> But then just before he — he died, he brought the British in, you see.
> And then now Letsie had now to grapple with the situation that
> even Moshoeshoe would find extremely difficult, especially that the
> British looked down upon him. . . .
>
> So the government here thought Letsie was very stupid. And
> also they had done, they had left no stone unturned to make him
> stupid. . . . And then after all now you had an eye that had been
> injured. They called him a blind, a, one-eyed, they said he was
> stupid. . . .
>
> When the war started, Letsie listened to himself. . . . He felt if he
> revolted, if he joined Masopha, then, and they were defeated, then
> the British would say all right now you are finished, you have re-
> volted, you're finished, you are no more there. He should give them
> the impression that after all the revolt was led by his brother who's
> an upstart. At the same time, he used to have secret meetings with
> his brothers and Lerotholi to the fact that they should go on fight-
> ing against the Cape Colonial government.[34]

Other independent oral sources confirm this version of Letsie's position and the joint decision made by the BaSotho chiefs to have one party pretend to remain loyal while the majority rebelled. The agreement among oral traditions handed down from both rebels and loyals, which do not appear to have been coordinated, lends credence to the evidence of prior planned complicity between the two sides during the war. According to one of my interviewees, when the BaSotho were informed about the Disarmament Proclamation

> they met to discuss it. It was a meeting of the chiefs under Letsie. At that meeting two decisions were made. . . . They realized that if they were to be defeated the British would then take the country. But at the same time they realized if some of us would hand over the guns and the British defeat us, they would give the country to those that handed the guns in and we would live still as a nation in Lesotho. That is why two things happened at that meeting. It was decided that Jonathan Molapo—let me say Molapo, he was still alive, he died during the war—Molapo should hand over the guns, and Letsie, who was then the Paramount Chief, should hand over. And all others, no: Maama, Masopha, do you see it? Joel, all others should not hand over except these.[35]

Similarly, another informant told me that after the Disarmament Proclamation was introduced the decision about who should rebel and who should remain loyal was made jointly, under Letsie's direction:

> Then the King Letsie and his younger brother Molapo [demonstrated] the diplomacy of the BaSotho, which is spoken about. They said, as we are the heads of government, let us agree that the British may come to take these guns. But our younger brother Masopha and those boys of ours as well as the nation must refuse to have the guns taken. So we should agree to give up our guns. So Letsie agreed with Molapo to give up the guns. Now they said their aim was not to give up the guns. We should agree as if we are going together with the government. But it will be as if we are fighting against the government of the British. So there will be war. If we happen to be defeated, the British will leave us our position [throne, i.e., rule] because we agreed with them. Whereas, if we can defeat them, our boys will know who we are, and they will leave us our positions.[36]

The ruse worked. Griffith continued to believe in Letsie's loyalty even as he reported that Letsie's sons and brothers were disloyal. Two weeks before he denied to a European trader that trouble was brewing he had reported the reverse to the colonial government:

I beg to state that matters in this Territory are now in my opinion
of a most critical state. The sons of Letsie have thrown over their
father and have cast in their lot with Masupha who is now the
leader of all the disloyal people in this Territory.

The Chief Letsie informed me officially that he intended sending in his guns on Monday last—this he has not done & I have had
no communication from him since, but I have been informed that
his sons have prevented his doing so and that some of them have
gone so far as to threaten to kill the person daring to bring them
in.[37]

This letter confirms some aspects of the oral traditions about the
ploys Letsie used to allay British suspicions about his ambiguous role,
in this case stories about Letsie's attempt to confirm his loyalty by pretending to surrender his guns. Letsie did send either six or nine guns to
Maseru, and both the colonial administration and historians such as
Burman have taken this at face value as an indication that he was loyal
to the government.[38] The BaSotho, however, remember this incident
in a different light. Damane reveals that this was part of Letsie's strategy, which began when Griffith went to the Paramount Chief's home
in Matsieng to discuss disarmament. When Griffith arrived, Letsie
said:

> [H]e was not going to give an opinion because he must send some
> people to Mafeteng to collect Lerotholi to be present at the pitso.
> And it is said that this messenger was instructed to tell Lerotholi to
> drink brandy before he came. So he came in the afternoon. He was
> dead drunk. Okay, now Letsie, he says to Griffith, now look, you
> know my father had told me the regulation to the fact that brandy
> should not be brought into this country, now who has brought
> brandy, who has brought brandy, look at him. And then he [Grif-
> fith] was told, all right, when he, when he [Lerotholi] is sober again
> we shall continue the pitso on the following morning.
>
> So Griffith went to spend the night at Morija with the mission-
> aries. So, the following morning he came, and he finds he [Lero-
> tholi] was drunk again. Because early in the morning, they would
> say how he used to snore, you know, when he slept, Lerotholi. His
> father was listening; when he stops snoring he knew he was up, and
> they told him to go and drink again. So it was that time, the pitso
> ended this way: [Letsie said,] ah, but I'm willing to hand in my
> guns, but now you see the situation in which I'm in. This is my heir,
> he is very popular and is now under the influence of his uncle. I
> shall send in my guns to Maseru.[39]

And so the guns were sent to Griffith at the capital, Maseru. The guns were intercepted by the rebels, however, and according to oral reports this interception was arranged by Letsie himself. Damane says,

> Six of them were loaded on a scotch cart. But Lerotholi had arranged that they should be intercepted on the way. How could a man like Letsie only send six? He had more than six, but he only sent six guns. The British, the Cape colonial officials were bluffed you see. They thought he really meant it. He didn't mean it at all. He was just bluffing. So there it is then. He was on the fence all the time. At least *we* knew that he was not on the fence. He had courage, he was encouraging his brother and Lerotholi and his children to go on, and he himself, was of the same, giving the impression to Griffith that he was on his side. I think he was a great diplomat.[40]

Damane was perceptive when he pointed to the key evidence that Letsie was dissembling: "How could a man like Letsie only send six?" The Paramount Chief had the authority and probably the power to see that thousands of guns were turned in, and the guns in the hands of the people living with him at Matsieng alone surely numbered in the hundreds. Two other informants told the same story independently.[41] According to one, the interception of the guns was a way both to prove Letsie's innocence without actually losing the guns and to mislead Griffith into thinking that Letsie could not control the rebels. Thus, after the *pitso* with Griffith,

> The following day Letsie sent his guns to Maseru from Matsieng and chose old things and sent them to Maseru, and then Lerotholi took them on the way to Maseru, and Letsie then sent a message to Maseru: "I sent the guns, my son has taken them, he is disobedient. . . . I am old, what can I do." But it was all a prearranged thing. And then he said, "My people are also old, the young ones have gone with this young boy, there's nothing we can do."[42]

These oral traditions accord well with the written colonial record both in terms of the events remembered and of the effect the event had on the British interpretation of Letsie's role and authority. Griffith often alluded to his belief that Letsie was weak and subject to influence or control by others; it did not occur to him that this was what Letsie intended for him to think. Thus when Griffith reported the incident of the guns sent in by Letsie but recaptured by the rebels his words implied a belief in Letsie's ineffectiveness as a leader and figure of authority, necessitating preparations for the use of colonial force:

> I have the honour to forward herewith for the information of the Government a copy of a sworn statement made by "Mosemekoane Nchela" a special messenger sent to me by the Chief Letsie on the evening of the 8th instant to report that nine guns which he was sending in to be surrendered in compliance with the provisions of the P.P. Proc.[Peace Preservation Proclamation] had been forcibly seized by sons and other young men of his tribe & carried away.[43]

Letsie had sent a "special messenger" who had made a "sworn statement" to Griffith, indicating that Letsie wanted to ensure there was no ambiguity in the message, that is, that he had complied with the disarmament policy but that his sons and their followers had forcibly prevented his guns from arriving in Maseru. Griffith had recently ordered Letsie not only to comply but to enforce the compliance of his people, so it was necessary for Letsie to make clear the problem: he had no means to apply force, since he had surrendered his guns, while the rebels retained the means to resist disarmament by means of force, since they had retained their guns. Letsie could not, therefore, be expected to play the role of policeman if he was himself to be obedient and disarmed. Letsie was indicating not that he would not enforce compliance but that he could not; the colonial government had disempowered him. He could not be reproached, for he had demonstrated, literally, obedience and loyalty; now the responsibility for disarming the rebels was out of his hands.

The strategy of dissembling is clearly evident in these incidents. These deceptions required collaboration among many rebel participants, and the oral traditions indicate the conscious adoption of strategic deceit. Letsie carefully arranged and stage-managed his response to Griffith's visit to Matsieng to discuss the surrender of arms; the presentation of Lerotholi in an inebriated state, not once but twice, implicitly scapegoated European liquor imports as responsible for BaSotho drunkenness and disorderliness. The persistence of this oral tradition and its agreement with significant other aspects of the written record tend to confirm the accuracy of the oral report and certainly reflect BaSotho beliefs in the matter at the time and since regarding both Letsie's and Lerotholi's responses to the colonial order. The chiefs who coordinated the responses to the disarmament policy accomplished their purpose, as Griffith laid the blame for rebellion at the door of the subordinate chiefs and absolved Letsie on the basis of his weakness as a ruler:

> It is now my duty to bring to your notice that in consequence of the above proceedings the influence & authority of the Chief Letsie has been completely set at naught, and that the whole country is now in a state of chaos; I could almost say in a state of open rebellion although no overt act of rebellion has been committed. The principal rebel leaders are the Chiefs Masupha & Lerothodi; the latter being the eldest son of the Chief Letsie. These men have declared that they will not surrender their arms; that they intend to offer only a passive resistance until such time as the Govt take steps to enforce the P.P. Proc. either by sending in troops to support the magistrates or by sending Constables or Police to search for arms; that then in such a case they will resist by force of arms & will commence by plundering the shops & murdering every European in the Country as they know it will be the only chance they will have of doing harm to the whitemen.[44]

In attributing to the rebels the intention of "murdering every European in the Country" and "doing harm to the whitemen" Griffith may have been exaggerating and expressing his own paranoia, but he may also have been unconsciously revealing some of the BaSotho discourse of colonial rule. Far from accepting colonialism as natural or inevitable, the BaSotho had not succumbed to the hegemonic aspirations of their colonizers, and they knew the British were vulnerable to force.

Griffith needed to believe in the loyalty of Letsie because he never harbored any doubts about what he considered to be the treachery of his brother Masopha. As early as 8 March 1880 he wrote to the colonial government about Masopha:

> My own opinion is that he [Masopha] is never to be crushed, and that he will take every opportunity to plot intrigue against the Govt. & whenever he sees a favourable opportunity to do so, and can get support from any of his elder brothers, he will not hesitate to plunge the country into rebellion.[45]

Griffith also attempted to bring Masopha into line. He depicted the role of the colonial government as one of preservation, with Masopha portrayed as posing the threat of destruction:

> It is with great regret I hear that people are being eaten up [having their property confiscated] & killed for obeying the orders of the Govt & I cannot understand why you wish to destroy your tribe. . . . I still wish to preserve the Basuto from destruction.[46]

He then followed up with another letter containing direct threats to Masopha and a month later reported to the colonial government the names of the rebels. He explained his perspective on the broader issues at stake:

> It is very evident that the crisis through which we are passing is an endeavor on the part of some of the Chiefs to re-establish their arbitrary power and if possible regain their independence.[47]

The BaSotho believed, quite rightly, that the British Crown did not share the same interests and goals of the Cape Colony, and they persisted in seeking to bypass the Cape government through appeals to the Queen. Thus a number of chiefs, including Lerotholi, Joel, and Molapo, signed a petition that they directed to the Governor and High Commissioner in Cape Town. In response Griffith told them it would be forwarded to the Queen but that they nevertheless had to lay down their arms to show their loyalty.[48] By December Griffith had evidence that Masopha was seeking to arm himself, as President Johannes H. Brand of the Orange Free State had informed him that Masopha had requested permission to purchase ammunition in the Free State.[49]

Griffith indicated that as a result of the incident in which Letsie's guns had been waylaid and of the growing confidence of the rebels, government officers had been humiliated and needed to be vindicated to restore their authority. Thus the myth of Letsie's weakness and cowardice spread through colonial channels. As one informant explained, however, Letsie was running from the British, not from the BaSotho, which indicates that he feared the government and not his own people:

> Letsie started hiding now in various places in the country fearing that he would be arrested and so in many places you find a cave named after him—we have it here, just here. These were places where he touched when he was running away from the British government fearing that he would be arrested.[50]

If the BaSotho believed Letsie was afraid he would be arrested by the British, it can only be because they believed he was working against the British rather than as a colonial collaborator. Hence his supposed reputation among the BaSotho for being a coward stemmed not from a belief in his refusal to resist but rather from his participation in resistance and his fear of being caught.

Griffith certainly did not trust the BaSotho, and he was aware of the potential for conscious dissembling and deceit. He warned the Secretary for Native Affairs not to take BaSotho pronouncements at face value, explaining that the proceedings of the important national *pitso* on Saturday, 3 July, were deceptive in intent: "The Basutos are adepts in the use of language for the purpose of concealing their thoughts and intentions and therefore I hope you will not be misled by the speeches."[51] In his later account of this history Lagden explained the first *pitso* in October 1879 at which the BaSotho presented their responses to the disarmament policy and noted the intentional use of junior chiefs by the BaSotho to present the BaSotho case:

> Letsie and the principal Chiefs preserved a most significant silence upon the important subject that was harrowing the feelings of the nation. All persons conversant with natives read from that silence the warning that indignation lay behind it. By a custom commonly understood, junior Chiefs were put up to voice the public mind when their seniors found it expedient to be guarded in their utterances. The sentiments of the multitude were wrapped up in the following sentences extracted from a flood of oratory.[52]

The discourse of race and pan-Africanism was beginning to be sounded, as Tsekelo, a younger son of Moshoeshoe, said, "We are to be disarmed, not because we have done any evil, but just because our colour is black." Lerotholi made it clear that he would not give up his gun but also said that "my gun belongs to the Queen and that I will follow the Queen about with this gun wherever she goes, and I will stick to it." The following day Moshoeshoe's son Tsekelo voiced a hidden transcript of colonial rule. Tsekelo pointed out that "if the Government thinks that by taking away a few rotten guns it will prevent war, I do not agree; the real remedy is to take away all the causes of dissatisfaction that are likely to produce war."[53] The battle of words and discourses played itself out, then, not just in the private correspondence between Griffith and Letsie but also on the public stage, as the hidden transcript of resistance became part of the public transcript without ever breaking the silent code of conspiracy.

6

Hidden Discourse in the Public Transcript

Ceremony and Subversion

The formal *pitso* of 3 July 1880 was the stage on which the hidden transcript of resistance was performed publicly, but it was disguised in the discursive tropes of loyalty from the colonial repertoire. Griffith was right to trust his intuition that the speeches were meant to be misleading, even if he couldn't quite interpret them himself. Yet an analysis of the *pitso* speeches reveals the very strategies that so confounded colonial officials, who could not condemn the BaSotho for either what was said or what was not said. Lagden was wise to be alert to significant silences, but in the case of the *pitso* of July 1880 the BaSotho speakers, including Letsie, revealed a great deal about the hidden transcript of rebellion in the words that they did speak to the crowded assembly. In chastising Masopha the previous February for holding a *pitso* without obtaining colonial consent Griffith had made it clear that the BaSotho chiefs could not hold public meetings independently or privately, hidden from colonial scrutiny. Their only option for conveying public messages was in public *pitso*s attended by the colonial government, but they could disguise the real messages through spoken strategies of dissembling. Using the tropes of colonial discourse against itself, the BaSotho spoke of colonial rule as the "Queen's peace," an ironic reference to the so-called Peace Preservation Act.

The BaSotho had sent a delegation to Cape Town in the hope that they could speak directly to the Cape Parliament to convey the BaSotho opinion with regard to disarmament. There they were not allowed to speak for themselves, but their opinions were voiced by others, and they heard the issues and evidence discussed. They had convinced the

colonial government to delay enforcement of the new law until the return of these delegates, and this *pitso* was ostensibly held in order to hear
from them, although most of the contributions to the discussion were
made by others. The first speaker, Ramadibikoe, was one of the delegates who had just returned from Cape Town. He told the assembled
crowd that they had been able to see the Governor personally, that the
debate on disarmament had lasted three weeks, and that the final vote
was thirty-seven members of Parliament supporting the extension of
the act to Basutoland and twenty-eight opposing it. Perhaps the most
significant news he brought was that the delegates had heard the evidence read out in Parliament and that Griffith himself, without informing the BaSotho, had supported their position:

> Before we went to Cape Town we did not know that Mr. Griffith
> had interceded for us.—In the House of Parliament letters from
> the Governor's Agent, Mr. Griffith, and Major Bell were read: by
> those letters the Governor's Agent and Major Bell fought for us.
> Major Bell told the Government that he disapproved of the disar-
> mament; that he had himself granted 4000 passes to Basutos who
> were going to the Diamond Fields to get guns.[1]

He also told the BaSotho that the delegation had been told that "Her
Majesty would not interfere as we are part of the Cape Colony." The
BaSotho were well aware that their status under the government of the
Cape was not the same as it had been under the Imperial protection of
the Crown, to which they had originally submitted a dozen years before.

The next speaker, Jonathan Molapo, who was to become known as a
"loyal," pledged to support Letsie. Implicitly insulting "white men," he
addressed his words directly to Letsie:

> Peace is a young girl we have wedded against her own will. . . . We
> have enjoyed peace under the British Government; we have be-
> come rich and we are prospering in every way. . . . Mogato (Letsie)
> is the only one who has a right to speak. . . . Even if he wants us to
> do what is painful for us, we will follow him because his will is the
> will of God.—This matter is yours Mogato, the white men are
> yours.—Retain for us the lands, corn, prosperity and peace which
> is a nice thing.—We do not eat guns, they are pieces of wood.

The tropes of BaSotho discourses of power and local power were
used by speakers. Jonathan said to Letsie, "There can be only one Bull
and you are that Bull," and Mphoma, identified in the minutes as "an

influential man living in the Leribe District," compared British overrule to that of the Zulu king Shaka, to whom Moshoeshoe had sent tribute. The following speakers indicated loyalty not to the Cape Colony but to "the Queen," as British Queen Victoria was known in Basutoland, a distinction that would not have been lost on the audience. Another man from the Leribe District said, "Let the Queen watch over us, the Queen has not found any fault with us," and Lerotholi himself said, "The Queen is like heaven and earth, she is everything." He pointed out that the BaSotho had followed proper protocol: "[W]e presented our supplications through Griffith who is the door, we did not stray." Lerotholi said that the BaSotho would never have agreed to any colonial dispensation that involved disarmament, since this was the very reason they had rejected annexation to Natal at the time they were seeking colonial protection. Invoking the privileges due to loyal subjects, Lerotholi said, "[O]ur guns are the Queen's guns; it is with those guns that we destroyed Langalebalele & Morosi," a message reiterated by the next speaker.

Then Letsie's son Maama spoke, saying, "I have not been circumcised, my father preferred to send me to school that I may be enlightened," and "if I err, you must not think that I do it wittingly." He thereby implied that he considered the Western "school" education he received to be inferior to that he would have received at circumcision school; there is no colonial ideological "hegemony" evident in Maama's words. Then he condemned the disarmament policy and other aspects of colonial rule associated specifically with the Cape Colony as opposed to Griffith or the Queen:

> I feel dissatisfied because we have given ourselves to the Queen and I cannot understand what we have done to be punished.—I also feel dissatisfied because our deputation was not allowed to speak in the House of Parliament; when I appeal against any judgement I am allowed to speak myself to Griffith. Peace is a fine thing but God only knows about the death of every one. The question of guns is a very hard one & every one must speak for himself. We have not the shadow of a fault, we have confidence in the Queen. I was present when Langalebalele was apprehended and when Morosi was killed.

Maama has indicated his fear that the loss of guns would result in the confiscation of all the land and property of the BaSotho, and that at stake was not merely their right to keep their guns but rather their right to be heard and their very existence as a nation. Both those who became rebels and those who became "loyals" opposed disarmament but expressed loyalty to the Queen and to Letsie. Even those who counseled obedience to the law also voiced their dissent to disarmament. But there was a public acknowledgment that they would remain loyal to Letsie no matter what he did. As Mapeshoane, son of Chief Posholi, noted:

> When the question of guns was first mentioned, in the last Pitso at Maseru, Letsie said that it was too hard upon him; he then sent a petition to Government and also a deputation. . . . If Letsie takes the first leap we will follow & leap after him. . . .
>
> If a man takes clothing away from his wife, she knows that there is no more hope for her; but although it is the first time we hear of guns taken from a loyal Tribe, Letsie you are a subject of the Queen; you are the Queen's wife, pray for us.

Thus indicating that the BaSotho recognized that Letsie was not free to act of his own accord because Letsie was "a subject of the Queen," Mapeshoane nevertheless questioned the rationale for disarmament, and his words were heavy with irony:

> We never heard of a Tribe getting prosperous after the guns have been taken from it; you say that after the surrender of arms we will be prosperous? Are we not prospering. . . . Even the Bushmen had arrows but since those arrows were taken from them they have been destroyed.—We went against Morosi & Langalebalele; Langalebalele was disarmed & he is now prospering! (laughter).

The audience laughed because the Bushmen, or San population, had been almost exterminated, Langalibalclc had languished in prison on Robben Island, and Moorosi was quite dead after having been disarmed; none of them had prospered as a result of disarmament.

Significantly, all of the commoners (i.e., not chiefs) who spoke came from Masopha's district, and all opposed disarmament. One stated the loyalty of the commoners to Letsie because they knew he had not intentionally betrayed Langalibalele or Moorosi:

> We are your lice Letsie, although this day must divide us.—Langalebalele & Morosi are dead although, Letsie, you pleaded for them. Morosi's country is taken from you, and Austen is cutting it up into farms to be sold. If our guns are taken from us we will be killed.

The most eloquent of the commoners to speak, Ramatseatsana, the "favourite counselor of Chief Masopha," began by taking aim symbolically at Western civilization itself, indicating that he had not been taken in by the trimmings of Western culture and that neither he nor his listeners were controlled or constrained by a Western colonial hegemonic discourse embedded in everyday signs and practices. He began, humorously,

> My shoes pinch my feet. What is to be done when shoes pinch one's feet? I have been obliged to throw mine away. Every pair I buy pinches my feet.

The message and the humor were not lost on the crowd, and a "voice from the crowd" called out, "It is because you do not know your No. [number, i.e., shoe size]." Several speakers had underscored their support for Letsie by making reference to "God," which they knew would resonate with colonial officials. Ramatseatsana used this trope to open his criticism of the Cape government, saying:

> All chiefs are from God. . . . Ramabidikoe, you say that you went to Cape Town & we hear that you have not been allowed to speak in the House. You say that the Queen's answer was, that we were annexed to the Cape Colony & that she has no right to interfere. What we wanted, Ramabidikoe, was that if you failed in Cape Town that you should go to England. Letsie, show us how we will get peace.

The use of precedent in legal proceedings was as central to BaSotho law as it was to British law, and the BaSotho were adept at invoking legal agreements and precedents in making their arguments to the British. Letsie intervened at this point and interjected: "You all speak of matters of the past. At first I suspected that Griffith had suggested to Government that we should be disarmed." He has reminded the audience that historical agreements are important, even as he appeared to dismiss them, and that Griffith had not betrayed them after all, implying that a moderate approach to him by Letsie was now appropriate.

Two younger sons of Moshoeshoe (Sofonia and Tlalele) both pronounced their support for their brother, Letsie. Sofonia reminded the audience that there was a greater threat than either the British or the Cape Colony, and that was the Boers: "[W]hen the British Government consented to have mercy upon us & to help us, we were disgracefully beaten by the Boers, by those Boers we had always dispised [*sic*]. Our guns were useless." Guns alone would not be enough to protect the sovereignty of the BaSotho nation.

Then Masopha took his turn, and his greeting to the people placed him at center stage in the drama. Invoking an audience reply by saying "Greeting Bakwenas! Peace!" to which the crowd responded with cries of "Peace!" Masopha used the idioms of the indigenous discourse on power and authority to explain why he and the people, although loyal to Letsie, would not agree to disarmament:

> Chief Letsie, I stand up when I see you move: it is the custom to follow the chief; but the common people are like crows which roost in the galleries of different precipices & we know that a chief reigns by the people. If the chief does wrong he must not be followed; the voice which must be listened to is the voice of the people. Plead, Chief, plead for Peace that the people may thrash out their grain!

Masopha next had his son Lepoqo read from Mr. Sprigg's speech at the previous *pitso*, when he had announced the disarmament policy and had promised, "[T]he Government will not take your guns from you by force, there will be no bloodshed. They (the guns) will remain in your hands until you understand it is your duty to surrender them." Masopha then compared the abandonment of guns to the BaSotho adoption of trousers and ploughs in place of skins and picks; his point was that, as previously, any change should come willingly. Deploying the tropes of loyalty to the Queen, he also adopted a strategy of dissembling by pretending to fit the colonizers' image of the colonized (i.e., innocent by virtue of simplicity and ignorance), announcing:

> We are the Queen's people & we beg for mercy; the Queen is the sun that melts the frost fallen during the night. We will surrender our guns the day we understand the advantage of doing so, as in the case of the ploughs, &c &c.&c.—We beg for mercy, we do not conspire against the Government. One day we will understand & then we will give up our guns.
> We refused to be annexed to Natal, as in Natal a man had his right hand cut off (his gun taken from him).
> We are not insolent, but we are blind. The guns are ours but they belong with us to Government. Peace!

The audience again responded with the customary salutation "Peace!"

Tsekelo Moshoeshoe, who was close to his half-brother Letsie and often served as his amanuensis, spoke at length and strongly in support of surrendering their guns. However, he argued for compliance only on the basis of their duty to the colonial government, reminding the BaSotho that they were no longer their "own masters":

> You forget what you are; you speak as if you were your own mas-
> ters; you forget that you are the Queen's subjects. . . . Our duty,
> now, is to give up our guns: Let us surrender our guns!

According to Charles Maitin's official minutes, only a few voices echoed him with the words "let us surrender them." Then Ntsane Mo-shoeshoe, a half-brother of the Paramount Chief, spoke, referring to Molapo in a way that carried a distinct but hidden meaning for the Ba-Sotho audience, a way that was not likely to be understood by the colonial officials who were present. Ntsane spoke only briefly and referred to past events involving his father, Moshoeshoe, and Molapo, who was Letsie's full brother:

> Chief Letsie, my father Moshesh said to you: "my son remember
> that it is only by great perseverance that I persuaded the British
> Government to receive me with my people as British subjects; now,
> hold fast the peace I have got for you." When Molapo wished to be
> placed under the protection of the Free State government, he re-
> ferred the matter to Moshesh who sent him his seal as a sign that he
> approved of what Molapo wanted to do. But Moshesh said Mo-
> lapo may change but Letsie will hold fast the Peace I have fought
> for him. Letsie is the only one who has a right to speak in this mat-
> ter not the tribe. Molapo was a supporter of Letsie and he wanted
> to obey the law. Molapo now is dead but even Masopha has said
> that Letsie is the Chief.

Ntsane thus reminded the audience that Molapo had surrendered separately to the Orange Free State in 1865, an act that on the surface appeared to constitute betrayal of the BaSotho cause. But, as Burman explains, Molapo "subsequently claimed that Moshoeshoe had ordered him not to fight the Boers so that his country could be used as a cattle refuge, a place to grow corn, and a rallying point when the Boers tired,"[2] in accord with Ntsane's assertion that Moshoeshoe "sent him his seal as a sign that he approved." It was not by chance that Ntsane chose to refer to this historical incident, in which the BaSotho appeared to have split their allegiance, for the story reminded the BaSotho audience of 1880 that such a strategy had worked in the past and would work again. Since Ntsane then referred to Molapo's loyalty to Letsie and to Masopha's current declarations of loyalty to Letsie, he appears to be telling his Ba-Sotho audience that they could be loyal to both sides even after a split occurred between these leading chiefs. Molapo himself had died only days earlier, on 28 June 1880.

The messages were well disguised, but taken together they indicate a consistent hidden transcript. On the one hand, popular sentiment of both commoners and chiefs supported Masopha and resistance to disarmament. On the other hand, it was publicly recognized that Letsie was compelled to obey the law of the colonial rulers because of the persistent and greater threat of loss of sovereignty to the Boers of the Orange Free State. Therefore, the people were not to abandon their loyalty to Letsie even as they fought against the colonial government that he was compelled to support.

Finally, Letsie spoke, and his words were consistent with the hidden transcript of resistance. It is striking that he opened by engaging in conversation with Masopha and referred to another historical incident involving Lasaoana Makhabane, known as Ramanella, in order to speak obliquely to the issues at hand. A nephew of Moshoeshoe who had stolen some cattle from Natal in 1865, he was a subordinate chief living in Letsie's district, and Letsie had been called upon to rectify the situation to the satisfaction of British colonial officials.[3] To prevent war with Natal Letsie had returned the cattle and had paid an additional fine, thus taking responsibility for his subordinate but also shielding him from serious consequences. By referring to this incident, Letsie was by implication telling his people that he was able and willing in 1880 to do the same; if his people were to break the law, he would ultimately take responsibility and pay a fine on their behalf in order to shield them from colonial punishment. Using the forms and rhythms of indigenous discourses of power and authority, Letsie asked his brothers Masopha and Tlali, "[W]hat did I say to you when Ramanella had stolen some cattle in Natal?" to which Masopha replied, "You said that you love peace and that you liked to be ruled by the Government."

Letsie thus established that colonial rule was necessary in spite of the concessions necessary to maintain peace, which included taking disciplinary action against his own kin. But Letsie had to hide his meanings even more carefully than did the rebels, for his people could be punished if he was seen as disloyal:

> Are we disputing for the chieftainship? Griffith it is bad of you to
> have hidden from me that you interceded for us. When Moshesh
> went to meet Prince Alfred [to offer to become an ally or a subject],
> I refused to go with him; I said that if we wanted to be British sub-
> jects, that we were to be true subjects.

All of the previous speakers, including those who said they planned to defy disarmament orders, had also stated explicitly that they did not dispute Letsie's chieftainship, so Letsie's question was rhetorical. Letsie reminded the BaSotho that he had dared to defy his father in 1860, and yet no one, including Moshoeshoe, ever disputed Letsie's loyalty or the legitimacy of his chieftaincy. By implication Letsie communicated the message that he would not dispute the loyalty or legitimacy of the junior chiefs, including his sons, who might defy him. The audience was to understand that, unlike Griffith, Letsie had properly informed his subjects of his position and actions, and they all knew that he publicly opposed disarmament, having sent a petition and a delegation to voice his opposition. Although Letsie putatively supported compliance with the new disarmament law, he also publicly chastised two chiefs for their compliance, giving as his reason that they did so without consulting with him or waiting for him and then following suit. Then, as soon as he had asserted his preeminence as "the Chief," in the next breath he told Griffith he was powerless, saying, "I have no horns. Griffith! Yesterday I asked you to carry me on your shoulders." The statement was unambiguous: if he had no horns, he was not a bull and did not have the power of a chief, thus showing publicly that he had told Griffith he could not be held responsible for whatever happened; that responsibility fell on Griffith himself, who must carry Letsie on his shoulders. Letsie then informed the audience that he had intended to turn in his guns just before the extension of time was granted because he "was afraid to disobey the law," but he did not indicate that he supported the law itself.

Nevertheless, he then asserted: "Masopha, my brother, you are a courageous man," to which Masopha replied, "I am a coward." In spite of its apparent disjuncture the conversation appears to have been well orchestrated, for Letsie again addressed Masopha, appearing to publicly order him to fight disarmament while acknowledging his own compliance.

> You are courageous when I order you to fight. It is a difficult thing to give up our guns; Griffith, please, do not take our guns from us! But I have already given my gun to Seta, Tsekelo and [Dr. Eugene] Casalis who will take it to Griffith. Griffith, my father, you have heard that all say, that I am the Bull.
>
> My own gun I have already surrendered; I only mention my own gun because even my own son (Lerotholi) has turned against me. But a chief can do as he likes and I declare that I will surrender my gun. If the people were still mine I would say that all the guns will be surrendered. Mapeshoane has spoken well. O, my people my gun is going to the Government: All those who like me will follow my example. If a house is devided [*sic*] that house will not stand. Chief Griffith, will you not give us, as a guaranty a written

> document stating that after the surrender of the guns we will live as
> usual and that nothing will happen to us? For the Basutos guns are
> like their teeth. But now we can no longer pray for mercy, we have
> already pleaded and done all that can be done.

Letsie had finally raised the primary concern: could Griffith really
guarantee their land and livelihood if they were disarmed? So at the
pitso of July 1880 Letsie did not order his people to obey the Peace Preservation Act and surrender their arms; on the contrary, he appears to
have ordered the reverse, claiming he was unable to enforce compliance. No wonder that Griffith, who said that he had not been planning
to speak, seized the last word:

> This is the most important meeting which has ever been held since
> the Basutos came under the Queen, because to-day you will decide
> whether you are loyal subjects. You Basutos know how I like you,
> how I have trusted you, and done all I could for you during the ten
> years I have lived amongst you and if any man can say that I have
> cheated him or told him an untruth, let him stand up in this meet-
> ing and say so. Don't be afraid but stand forth and declare it. Since
> no one comes forward I must conclude that you agree that I have
> never told you an untruth or deceived you.

Concerned to establish the legitimacy of colonial rule, reflected in his
own integrity and embodied in the Queen, who he emphasized was "the
same Queen to whom your father Moshesh fled for protection and who
accepted you all as her subjects," he insisted the goal of disarmament
was to prevent bloodshed and warned in a counterproductive argument
that the neighboring chiefdoms of the AmaXhosa, AmaZulu, BaPedi,
and BaPhuthi, "with their chiefs have been destroyed through having
guns."

Griffith thus did not hesitate to reiterate the very threat that the Ba-
Sotho most feared, the threat of loss of their land and country, even as
he couched it in terms of loyalty. He told them that they should trust the
Queen, and their country would "never be taken away from you for any
reason except one, and that is for rebellion." Griffith still hoped that he
could use moral suasion and colonial discourse to bring about compliance with this colonial law of disarmament that was so obnoxious and
threatening to the BaSotho, but he was also alarmed by what he had
heard at the *pitso*. Griffith was not deceived: he told the Secretary for
Native Affairs in the cover letter to the minutes that "my own opinion is
that the Basutos as a tribe are averse to surrendering their arms and do

not intend to do so."[4] The hidden transcript of resistance, which had been played out on a public stage, could also be read by an astute colonial official who was to find himself powerless to prevent the collapse of colonial rule.

Letsie and Griffith: A Battle of Wits and Words

The aftermath of the *pitso* made clear that the BaSotho had understood the hidden transcript embedded in the public record, and resistance was soon afoot. On 5 July Austen sent a warning to Ellenberger that he had heard: "Masupha has retired to Thaba Bosigo, with all his men, & says if Govt. want the guns, they must come and take them." He added, "Please keep this quiet until after London Post, when I expect we will see what is the truth—I am very anxious to avoid a panic."[5]

Letsie clung to the public transcript of loyalty and obedience to the colonial order, and that same month Griffith reported this in terms that indicated Letsie had indeed employed the jargon of colonial discourse effectively. Griffith wrote on 22 July that Letsie had conveyed "grief," professed his loyalty, and said he was trying to rectify the situation.[6] But the government was taking no chances, as it turns out. Three weeks later Austen wrote to Ellenberger, saying that he believed Letsie was deceiving the "Govt,"[7] while the pressures placed on Letsie by the colonial government were direct and unambiguous: they ordered him to arrest his brother Masopha.

Griffith's frustration with Letsie is evident throughout his correspondence both with Letsie and with his superiors in Cape Town. When the government was attempting to enforce disarmament, Letsie wanted to know just how far the government would go in terms of mobilizing military force. On 31 July 1880, in a letter to Letsie marked "confidential," Griffith dissembled, conveying the public transcript while suppressing the hidden transcript of the colonizers.

> I am surprised to hear you ask me whether it is true that Colonial troops are on their way up because I told you by your messenger "Mohlepe" that troops were coming up to support the authority of the government and also to give you confidence and support in carrying out the orders of the government.[8]

Griffith also used the opportunity to order that Letsie should occupy the old and formidable mountain fortress of Thaba Bosiu to prevent its use by the rebels. It was from there that Letsie's father, Moshoeshoe, had protected his people and constructed a nation beginning in 1824, and the large, well-watered, flat-topped mountain fell into the district of Letsie's rebellious brother Masopha, providing a base from which he could withstand colonial forces much more effectively than had Moorosi in the south of the country. Lagden later believed this had been part of a deliberate strategy of Letsie, whose foresight had led him to leave Masopha at the doorstep of the nation's stronghold while keeping his own residence at the relatively open village of Matsieng in the lowlands farther south, where he could not be suspected of conspiracy.[9] With war threatening, Griffith wanted Thaba Bosiu in the hands of "loyals" rather than rebels. He insisted that Letsie prevent Masopha from fortifying Thaba Bosiu:

> This is the matter that will destroy this country unless you take steps <u>at once</u> to stop it and the best plan that I can suggest to you is for you to go and occupy Thaba Bosigo yourself—You will then be able to prevent any one else taking possession of it and you will also then show that you are the Chief of the Basutos and the successor of Moshesh.
>
> If you do not at once act in this matter (before it is too late) I cannot hold out any hope of saving yourself and country, but if you act with energy and determination then I can still hold out hopes that peace and prosperity may still continue.[10]

Letsie replied that he would go to Thaba Bosiu, but Griffith had also ordered Letsie to arrest various named rebels, which he declined to do.[11] While Griffith had informed Letsie prematurely that troops were "on their way up," he now wrote that the troops would not be mobilized unless Letsie's own forces proved inadequate to put down the rebels. Griffith couched his new message to Letsie in terms of the colonial pretense of indirect rule by falsely implying that the rebellion was directed against Letsie and the colonial government was only there for his benefit:

> I told Ntho to tell Letsie that the [colonial] troops would stand still and do nothing until we saw that the rebels had mastered him and then if he wanted support we would do our best to assist him.[12]

With this, Letsie now had written confirmation of his orders and of the government's intentions to use military force to impose disarmament, which exposed the real locus of power to his people and absolved him from responsibility. Letsie was threatened implicitly that his people would be destroyed should he fail to act as the colonial power intended:

I have received your letter dated yesterday written for you by Nehemiah in which you tell me that you are going to Thaba Bosigo on Friday.

I am very glad of this, and I hope you will have a strong heart and act like a Chief, and put a stop to all this disturbance *(moferefere)* that is going on in the country.

The Government is looking to you, and expects you to act like a man. We don't tie your hands in any way, but give you full power to act as a Chief going to war. Take your shield with you, & show the people that you are in earnest.

You have always said you are a loyal subject of the Queen, well, now is the time to show it by actions as well as by words, and by doing so [you] will save the people from destroying themselves.[13]

Once Letsie was on Thaba Bosiu Griffith again ordered him to arrest his brother Masopha and bring him for trial, but Griffith must have known that this was unlikely, since Letsie could not have ascended the mountain fortress without Masopha's consent. Nevertheless, he presented the case as if Letsie were still in charge and employed the jargon of loyalty and duty once again, with the military threat again expressed only indirectly:

I am glad to hear that you have succeeded in getting on to the top of Thaba Bosigo, and I hope you will remain there until the disturbance is over, and that you will destroy the fortifications which have been built by Masupha.

I am also directed to order you to apprehend the Chief Masupha and send him in here a prisoner in order that he may be tried if found guilty.

There can be no peace in this country until Chiefs like Masupha and others are taught to obey the law. . . .

The Government does not wish to bring any troops into this country as long as you are able & willing to do your duty as a Chief and a loyal subject of the queen. I therefore call upon you to do your duty.[14]

In retrospect, Lagden was more astute, recognizing the evident complicity between Letsie and Masopha:

At last Colonel Griffith persuaded Letsie to make a pilgrimage to Thaba Bosiu to coerce Masopha. It was hailed at Cape Town as a sign that the tide had turned, but was a farce. He paraded up the mountain with 1,000 men and down again, seizing the opportunity, it is believed, to privately acquaint his rebellious brother and sons with the success that had followed his efforts to play off the white people against each other; he was able to tell them the Home Government were not unsympathetic and the Cape people making Basutoland a party question. It was all true, yet deplorable that a savage tribe should hold the balance in such a way.[15]

Griffith repeatedly tried to get Letsie to hold Thaba Bosiu and arrest Masopha, and there is an increasing tone of desperation in his orders to the Paramount Chief:

> I have received your message by Sofoniah Moshesh and I have directed him to tell you that on no account are you to leave Thaba Bosigo, but that you are to send and collect all your people to come and support you there—if you leave now Masupha will consider that he has gained a victory over you and will be more unreasonable than ever, therefore I cannot approve or consent to your leaving Thaba Bosigo—it has also come to my knowledge that as soon as you have it is Masupha's intention to eat up all the remaining loyal people and also close all the roads from this place to Thaba Bosigo.[16]

Thinking he was now on the verge of victory, Griffith gave Letsie direct and clear orders and again raised the specter of the arrival of colonial troops as an implicit threat should Letsie's loyalty falter. Letsie was to arrest both his brother and his son, with Griffith offering leniency only to the latter and merely promising to spare the life of the recalcitrant Masopha:

> I am directed by the Government to convey to you the following instructions—namely that you are to inform Masupha that he is to surrender to you unconditionally for trial, his life being promised him, that the people with him must lay down their arms and that fines will be imposed upon them according to their rank and position in the tribe—If Masupha does not agree to these terms then you are to keep possession of the mountain until a force of Colonial Troops can arrive to support you.
>
> With regard to your son "Lerotholi" the Government says his case can be dealt with by a fine upon your giving a guarantee for his good conduct in the future.[17]

Finally, two days later Griffith reluctantly gave Letsie permission to descend the mountain after Letsie told him his life was in danger.[18] Griffith was disappointed and wrote to Cape Town that because of "the weakness of the Chief Letsie" it was futile "to depend upon him to punish 'Masupha' or even to destroy the defences which have been erected at Thaba Bosigo."[19] Letsie then descended the mountain without extracting any concessions from the rebels, and the rebellion continued. Griffith's tone became more strident:

> I am directed to inform you "that he that is not with us is against us," and therefore you must not expect the Government to do everything for you, if you do not support the Government—why don't you do something by collecting your loyal men and defending yourself against the rebels—the time for talking is past and you must now act like a man and do something which will enable the loyal people to place confidence in you and in your professions of loyalty.[20]

Griffith was no longer deceived or clinging to false hopes. As colonial troops moved up from the south he insisted that Letsie leave Matsieng and join him in Maseru to show his loyalty and finally expressed his own suspicions to Letsie himself:

> [M]y only advice to you now is that you make haste and come here to me and I will take care of you—If you remain at your place when the troops move up to Morija why then you will have to put up with the consequences because if the rebels go to your place the troops will follow them there.
>
> This is the only advice I can give you and I repeat that if you are really loyal to the Government then show your loyalty by coming here and then all the people in Basutoland will see on what side you are, whereas by remaining among the rebels many of your best friends are doubtful about you and I am amongst the number.[21]

Letsie replied that he would remain at the capital at Matsieng, but he continued to profess loyalty in a letter Griffith forwarded to the Secretary for Native Affairs, explaining that he was enclosing

> a copy of a letter which I have received from the Chief Letsie, relative to the difficult position in which he has been placed since the outbreak of the Rebellion etc, and earnestly requesting me to communicate to the General in Command of the Troops his resolution to remain at his own village & that he will hoist a white flag over his house to show that he is a loyal man.[22]

War and Negotiation

The costs were higher than either side anticipated, and the course of the war was more painful and more damaging than the BaSotho had hoped for when they adopted their strategy of taking both sides in the war. By August the British magistrates had lost their authority and could not enforce the law, and rebels were confiscating, or "eating up," the property of those who had turned in their guns and were therefore identified as "loyals."[23] A long letter from Griffith to Letsie dated 5 September 1880 outlining the necessity for his people to submit to the laws and to disarmament was fruitless. Troops crossed the border, and military engagements began on 13 September 1880.[24]

The war had its human side, which posed a dilemma for those who led the fight on both sides. Prior to the war the rebel Lerotholi was on familiar and friendly terms with Arthur Barkly, the magistrate in his district of Mafeteng. When Barkly had word of the approach of the first colonial troops to enter Basutoland, he rode out with a contingent of BaSotho police and encountered Lerotholi and three hundred armed BaSotho about two miles from his headquarters.[25] Using a messenger, Lerotholi notified Barkly that he was personally leading his troops, asked to speak with him personally, and inquired whether Barkly would fire on him. Barkly later explained that he had agreed to talk, but then from Lerotholi "the answer came that he would do so if he could, but was prevented by his people." Barkly rode toward Lerotholi with two men, a "white volunteer" and a MoSotho policeman who was a relative of Lerotholi.

> As I came up I saw a queer spectacle. Lerothodi dismounted was engaged in a violent struggle with two of his men, who were forcibly holding him back. I shouted to him, and he waved his hat to me, but as I rode on they all prepared to retreat, so I stopped and told Dechaba (the chief constable) to ask what on earth they were afraid of. "Of Morena's (the chief's) revolver," replied the heroes. Accordingly I divested myself of this deadly weapon, dropped my reins, and rode in among them unarmed, with my hands displayed to show that "there was no deception." Lerothodi then shook off his brother who was detaining him, and came up to me with proper salutations, calling me his father and his mother and so on, after Basuto fashion. I shook hands with him, and said that out of friendship for him I had come to try and save him from utter destruction if possible, and told him that nothing could delay or stop the march of the Cape Mounted Rifles, whatever he might think, and that if he attempted it he would simply be sent flying (which occurred accordingly, five minutes afterwards). I then suggested that he should withdraw his men and surrender to me *pro forma* as proposed by Mr. Sprigg. When I would inflict such fine as I thought proper, and refer the sentence for confirmation. He said he would do this if I

would stop the "policies," which of course I could not do, a fact of which he was perfectly aware.[26]

Both Barkly and Lerotholi were fearless in the face of war. Lerotholi's men valued his leadership on the field so highly that they had not dared to risk his life at the hands of an armed colonial official whom they did not know as well as did Lerotholi. Lerotholi himself jumped on one of his own men who fired over Barkly's head after he had turned to ride away. Barkly later wrote, "I must own, however, that I did not expect to get back alive to my men." Both men respected the conventions of diplomacy and the conventions of war, neither of which permitted shooting a man in the back as he rode away from a diplomatic foray.

Lerotholi's troops repeatedly attacked Barkly's headquarters at Mafeteng, which the latter successfully defended, although it was often besieged, through the war. This required a concentration of troops there, hindering war efforts elsewhere even after the British brought in reinforcements under Colonel F. Carrington. A force of sixteen hundred men under Commandant Gen. C. M. Clarke tried to relieve Carrington and his men besieged at Mafeteng but lost thirty-two dead and ten wounded in an attack by BaSotho cavalry, demoralizing the colonial troops, who were largely volunteers.[27] Government headquarters at Maseru were also defended with a concentration of colonial troops, who were not as successful. BaSotho rebel troops directed by Masopha on 10 October burned the major buildings and engaged in man-to-man fighting but in later assaults encountered stronger defenses.[28] Lagden wrote:

> As the year closed the position was that the Basuto, in spite of the large army in the field against them, were still in possession of practically the whole country. They had worried and despoiled their "loyal" brethren of all their cattle and belongings. Jonathan the "loyal" leader was driven from his stronghold at Tsikoane and forced to take refuge in the camp of the Magistrate at Thlotsi [next to Leribe] under guard of a regiment of [burgher] volunteers.[29]

The arrival of Sir Hercules Robinson in Cape Town to replace Acting High Commissioner (Governor) George Strahan in January 1881 marked the beginning of an attempt at negotiations. A Member of Parliament from Aliwal North who sympathized with the BaSotho position, J. W. Sauer, helped the BaSotho chiefs petition for peace, and the BaSotho managed to harvest their crops during the brief armistice. Failure, however, was a foregone conclusion, since the BaSotho insisted on retaining both their guns and all of their territory.[30] The Cape government similarly made no concessions in its response. Offering terms that had to be met within twenty-four hours, it insisted on unqualified BaSotho submission to Cape government and laws, the immediate surrender of arms, payment of a fine, and Cape parliamentary control over the decision about the use and dispensation of the Quthing District. It offered amnesty to everyone except Masopha, Lerothodi, and Joel, whose lives would be spared but who were to stand trial.[31]

The amnesty terms were generous, as the Cape had suffered significant losses, and colonial governance had suffered a significant loss of prestige. Not only was Hamilton Hope, the Resident Magistrate, killed in the Griqualand East uprising, which had been provoked by the Gun War, but so was the magistrate for the southern district, John Austen, in a particularly sordid affair:

> Of the magistrates, Austen was killed, an event which occurred at the end of January 1881 in a badly planned sortie against rebel Tlokwa who had fled over the Drakensberg from the Transkeian territory. No doubt inspired by the example of the colonial troops' mutilation of Moorosi's body in 1879, the Tlokwa decapitated Austen's body and sent the head to Letsie as a peace-offering for a past attack on Thaba-Bosiu in Moshoeshoe's time.[32]

Eventually, Griffith employed Letsie to initiate a correspondence with Lerotholi, with the French Protestant missionaries taking a hidden hand in the negotiations, as Griffith was aware. On 17 April 1881 Lerotholi, acting on behalf of the rebels, met with Griffith, who was acting on the High Commissioner's orders, near Maseru. There Lerotholi accepted arbitration by the High Commissioner and agreed to end hostilities, but not to disarmament, to which he knew his people would not agree.[33] On 29 April 1881 the High Commissioner, Sir Hercules Robinson, announced his terms of settlement, referred to as an "Award": in principle disarmament would be enforced, but in practice the BaSotho would be allowed to own and keep guns on condition of registration and the annual payment of a license fee of one pound per gun. Compensation was to be paid to BaSotho "loyals" and European traders, the BaSotho collectively would pay a fine of five thousand cattle, amnesty would be granted to all, and no territory would be confiscated.

It is hard to imagine better terms to be offered to the BaSotho under the circumstances, and Letsie, Lerotholi, and the majority of the nation accepted the terms and immediately paid three thousand head of cattle to demonstrate their intentions. But the process dragged out because Masopha remained unwilling to accept colonial rule on any terms, and an inheritance struggle over the chieftaincy in Leribe District between the legitimate heir, Jonathan, and his half-brother Joel persisted, resulting in outbreaks of violence for the next two years.

A change of government in the Cape Colony put J. W. Sauer into the position of Secretary for Native Affairs, and his previously demonstrated sympathy for the BaSotho seemed to bode well. Thomas Charles Scanlen also replaced Gordon Sprigg as Prime Minister, but the new government remained committed to the terms of the settlement. Griffith, however, was mortified that his authority had been so undercut by events and, in a long letter to the government, wrote that because he had represented the government against which the Basuto rebelled his usefulness to the government now was greatly impaired. He was granted his request to be relieved from his position, and, perhaps not surprisingly, the new Cape government sent Joseph M. Orpen to replace him. Orpen's earlier sympathy with the rebel causes of opposing disarmament and land expropriation subsequently undermined the colonial position and the colonial authority he was sent to reestablish.

Orpen was faced with a formidable task at an inopportune moment, expected to reimpose colonial rule even as proposals were being presented in the Cape Parliament for repeal of the Annexation Act by which the Cape had assumed control over Basutoland a decade before. Sauer had just spent three months in the country holding meetings to try to persuade the BaSotho to comply with all the terms of the settlement "Award" but had not succeeded, and he, like Griffith, left at the end of August. When Orpen was introduced at his first *pitso* as Governor's Agent, he was met by a strident and poignant speech by Tlali Moshoeshoe, a younger half-brother of Letsie who had been serving as a policeman when the war broke out and who had followed orders to report to Maseru. There by default he became a "loyal," defending colonial government headquarters. He presented the grievances of the "loyals" who had suffered loss of property and life and had yet to receive any compensation.[34] Nevertheless, Orpen now had not only Letsie's cooperation but also Lerotholi's. Three weeks after his arrival in September 1881 Orpen was able to report that Letsie was enforcing the restoration of stock, fields, and villages to the "loyals," although there had been no such progress in the area around Thaba Bosiu still controlled by Masopha's men.[35] A week later Orpen wrote that although resistance around

Masopha was "still strong," nevertheless, "it is sapped & diminishing & I have no doubt it will be overcome."[36]

But the intransigence of Masopha persisted, frustrating Orpen's attempts to restore colonial rule and law. By November he was warning the Cape government that he thought the Imperial government should declare itself willing to send support troops if necessary, and the Orange Free State should be pressed to help maintain order along the borders.[37] The Cape government responded by requesting Her Majesty's government to restore order and assume responsibility for colonial rule in Basutoland, but the request was declined. London also rejected the Cape government's preparations to repeal the Annexation Act. In January 1882 Letsie prepared to move troops against Masopha at Thaba Bosiu, which colonial officials had been urging all along, but both he and Orpen concluded the time was not auspicious because Masopha still retained too much popular support. Letsie feared treachery: "[H]e heard a whisper there was a proposal to murder us by surprising our encampment as soon as Lerothodi moved towards the cattle" in any attack against Masopha.[38]

The Cape Colony continued to pursue seemingly contradictory policies. Overconfident of success, it had allowed all colonial troops to be withdrawn except the Cape Carbineers ; now Letsie was expected to achieve militarily what the Cape forces had been unable to do: subdue Masopha.[39] But when London refused to allow the Cape government to abandon Basutoland and cancel the Annexation Act, the Cape offered a new proposal, which was accepted by the Queen's government: to enforce militarily submission, disarmament, and the expropriation of the Quthing District for distribution as reward to colonists who enlisted to fight.[40] A new deadline of 15 March 1882 was set for compliance with the terms of the "Award" that had been offered by Sir Hercules Robinson, but in the end the settlement offer was canceled because of noncompliance. The announcement of the cancellation was constructed in such a way as to ensure even greater intransigence on the part of the BaSotho, who were still facing their worst fear, loss of territory, which threatened their survival as a nation. Orpen's letter to "The Paramount Chiefs Letsie Moshesh, Lerothodi & Joel," dated 15 February 1882, began with the language of diplomatic protocol:

> I have the honor to inform you that I have been requested by the Government to communicate to you the agreement which has been come to between the Imperial & Colonial Governments with regard to matters in Basutoland.[41]

Orpen, self-styled friend of the BaSotho, continued in the most formal language to lay out the terms dictated through him from his superiors:

> The refusal of Chief Masupha and others to fulfil the terms of the Governor's Award has led the Imperial Government to consider that the position of affairs is now so changed that the Imperial Govt. will now permit that the land of offenders may be confiscated and the Colony shall if necessary use force to punish all those who do not obey its authority.

After explaining the provisions Orpen reiterated:

> The Colonial Government thereto authorized by the Impl. Govt. will there undertake to enforce law in Basutoland North of the Orange River and where there is resistance to authority it will have the liberty to confiscate the land of those who remain in rebellion, but due regard will be had to the rights of all who respect authority & law.[42]

On the same day, indicating his sense of urgency, Orpen voiced dismay and set forth his reasons for "grave apprehensions" in a five-page telegram to the Cape government.[43] Letsie himself wrote directly to the High Commissioner to express the same sentiments and plead for more time. As translated for the High Commissioner, the letter from Letsie stated that "this work could never be carried out by a people whose heart is despairing and who are only looking for death for we understand that if we do not fulfill the award by the 15th March the country south of the Orange River will be taken by the Colony and perhaps also more country may be taken."[44]

Robinson finally recognized the conundrum that prevented a resolution of the BaSotho rebellion. Following the pleas of Orpen and Letsie, on 6 April 1882 he issued a new proclamation that repealed the Disarmament Act. This was his prerogative as the representative of the Imperial government because the terms of Responsible Government status that had been granted to the Cape Colony ten years before had included a provision that all legislation was subject to approval in London.[45] This left unresolved, however, the colonial status of Basutoland, for which the Cape government no longer wanted responsibility. The next actions of the Cape Colony created problems for the BaSotho nation for years to come. In a misguided effort to be helpful Gen. Charles Gordon (who previously had served in China, earning him the moniker

"Chinese Gordon," and later lost his life in Khartoum waiting for reinforcements and relief that never arrived) accepted an invitation to
come to the Cape Colony and help resolve the crisis. Appointed as Commandant General of Colonial Forces, Gordon toured the eastern districts of the Cape Colony and presented proposals for administration
of the Transkeian Territories and for resolution of problems in Basutoland. He was widely condemned by Cape and Basutoland authorities
for entering into unauthorized correspondence with unofficial persons
in Basutoland, including missionaries and Masopha, whom he claimed
to admire, but when Sauer went to Basutoland in September 1882 to try
to effect a resolution of the continuing resistance from Masopha, he
took Gordon along. There, before meeting Masopha, they encountered
Letsie, whom Orpen described at the time as "very old, gouty, sick,
weak, doubleminded, undecided and failing in intellect and full of procrastination."[46] The colonial officials all found themselves working at
cross-purposes. Gordon, initially supportive of Orpen, turned against
him. He made his sympathies for Masopha evident just when Sauer had
finally succeeded in convincing Letsie and Lerotholi to mount armed
forces for a military operation against Masopha in his stronghold at
Thaba Bosiu.

A debacle ensued. Gordon's presence on the mountain forced Lerotholi to delay action for a day, a delay Masopha had ensured by keeping Gordon waiting for a day before meeting him, knowing that the entire military expedition against him might have to be canceled as a result
of a brewing storm that would swell the rivers with rain. While Masopha
dissembled with a show of interest in Gordon's proposals, which were
explicitly contrary to the orders Gordon had accepted in writing (a pre-
caution taken by Sauer, who rightly distrusted him), Lerotholi fumed,
and Sauer had to send a message to Gordon to get off the mountain immediately before it was attacked. Gordon in turn sent in his resignation
before even leaving the mountain, unaware to the last of how he had
been manipulated by Masopha, for whom he had expressed such admi-
ration.[47] Masopha was unaffected by Gordon's flattery, which he had deployed as a means to effect conciliation, and instead was bolstered in his
self-aggrandizement as equal in status and importance to Letsie. Lagden
seems to be correct in his assessment of the significance of this fruitless
meeting between two men of strong ego, Gordon and Masopha:

> The line taken up by General Gordon in his mission to Thaba Bo-
> sigo was to play upon Masupha's vanity, exalting him in rank above

his fellows and his Magistrates. It was bound to fail. Masupha was cautious in his utterances and talked about the weather and crops. It had the effect not only of disparaging the Governor's Agent [Orpen] and defeating Mr. Sauer's coercive plans but of weakening Letsie's paramountcy and infuriating Lerothodi who, as heir apparent, viewed with ill-disguised concern the growing ascendancy of his uncle Masupha; it contributed in fact to a rivalry between uncle and nephew that never died down.[48]

Gordon departed, resigning his post before he even left Basutoland and leaving the colonial government more despised and disrespected than ever in the eyes of the BaSotho chiefs and people. Masopha stayed on the mountain.

Rifts in the Nation: The Leribe Inheritance Struggle

Masopha's recalcitrance was not the only obstacle to a peaceful resolution of the Gun War. When Letsie's brother Molapo, who presided over the Leribe District in the north of the country, died at the beginning of the rebellion, an open conflict developed between two of his sons, half brothers Jonathan and Joel. Before his death Molapo had declared his intentions of obeying the new disarmament law in spite of his objection to it, but, as Burman points out, he had recently suffered from paralysis in his old age and carried little weight politically.[49] After he died his legitimate heir, Jonathan, gravitated to the same position. Letsie, in consultation with his senior chiefs, had designated to Jonathan and Joel the roles of "loyal" and "rebel," respectively. Had the conflict not been drawn out, and had "loyals" been protected from later depredations, the return of their villages and property, which Letsie and Lerotholi had personally overseen, might have limited the damage to the nation caused by the war. But Joel took advantage of his more popular position as a rebel to press his challenge to the inheritance of his father's position and property, and fighting broke out sporadically between the two sides following the formal cessation of hostilities in 1882; indeed, these conflicts persisted for three more decades.

In the case of Molapo, Moshoeshoe's second son from his first wife and therefore Letsie's full brother, the inheritance of the Leribe chieftaincy was complicated because the first son of Molapo's first house, Joseph, was mentally incompetent. When this had been discovered, Moshoeshoe had contrived a union between Letsie's daughter Senate with

Joseph without payment of bridewealth. She could then bear a son who could be legally recognized as the heir to her father, Letsie's house, since the rights to the children of the union had not been transferred to Molapo's line of descent through a payment of bridewealth by Joseph.[50] The son born of this union, Motsoene, was declared by Moshoeshoe to be Letsie's heir, but he, like his biological father, proved to be of diminished capacity in mind.[51] Jonathan's inheritance was clearly legal, since he was Joseph's younger full brother and a son of the first wife in the first house of Molapo, and Joel's grounds for disputing that inheritance were specious.[52] However, Joel, first son of Molapo's second wife and second house, was older than his senior half-brother Jonathan, and he tried to make the legal claim that in the event of the incapacity of the senior son of the first house, in this case Joseph, the inheritance should fall to the first son of the second house (himself) rather than to the second son of the first house (Jonathan). It was only his popularity as a rebel that won Joel support rather than any legitimate legal claim to the inheritance of his father, Molapo.

As the settlement of the Gun War was being reached in mid-May 1882, it was urgent for Letsie to enforce the compensation and restitution to the "loyals" to mitigate any harm that had been done and thus ensure the future unity of the nation. Lerotholi joined him in this effort, explicitly taking a position contrary to Masopha, with whom he had been allied during the war. However, the distrust and despair of the "loyals" is in large part explained by their continued vulnerability to Joel's continued attacks against their homes and lives in the Leribe District in his pursuit of his personal agenda of seizing his father's inheritance.

The unresolved feud between Jonathan and Joel kept the country on the brink of disaster in 1882 and 1883 and had a decided influence on the final resolution of the colonial status of the country. December 1882 brought a renewed outbreak of violence between Jonathan and Joel. After a skirmish during which sixty of Joel's forces were killed and Jonathan prevailed, Orpen held a trial in Leribe, but, as Lagden wrote of the affair, "the feud slumbered; the district remained in a state of anarchy, the late combatants watching opportunities to plunder and kill defenseless people found on the border lines."[53] For the country as a whole this fight was the final disaster. As victims of the conflict fled into the Orange Free State with their herds of cattle, Free State farmers found themselves in the middle of the fighting, and their president, J. H. Brand, urgently insisted to the Cape government and to the High Commissioner that they fulfill their agreement of the Treaty of Aliwal North of 1869 to control the frontier.

Faced with an international incident as a result of the Leribe fighting, in January 1883 Robinson called a special session of the Cape Parliament. On 16 March 1883 Scanlen and Sauer went to Basutoland and at their first public meeting announced the replacement of Orpen by Captain Matt Blyth, who had had administrative experience in Griqualand East and the Transkei. Two weeks later Scanlen gave Letsie proposals for new constitutional arrangements that included a BaSotho council that would be able subsequently to alter provisions of the new government administrative system and that would leave all internal affairs to the chiefs except court cases involving Europeans and murder cases on condition that justice and humanity be upheld. Less than a month later, on 25 April 1883, Captain Blyth held a national *pitso* to hear BaSotho responses to the Scanlen proposal. Letsie accepted, but Masopha, Ramanella, and other chiefs were absent, signifying their rejection. This was followed days later by another outbreak of violence in the Leribe District. Joel, assisted by Masopha, attacked Jonathan, who fled to the Hlotsi camp while his people took refuge in the Orange Free State with their cattle and Joel burned down their villages. President Brand of the Orange Free State refused Blyth's request for permission for Jonathan's people and cattle to stay in the country pending negotiations. The Cape government, in a minute by Scanlen to the High Commissioner on behalf of the ministers, declared that the relations between the colonial government and Basutoland would not be continued and that the Queen's government should prepare to prevent "serious complications" upon the withdrawal of authority from Basutoland.

In Cape Town the Queen's representative at the moment was the Acting High Commissioner, Sir Leicester Smyth, since Robinson had gone on leave to England, where he was consulted by Lord Derby, the British Secretary of State. Following this consultation, on 14 June 1883 Lord Derby sent the government's reply to the Cape Parliament, which refuted all of the assertions on the parts of the Cape Colony, the BaSotho, and the Orange Free State that the Queen's government had any obligations at all to resolve their conflicts but offered conditionally to attempt to do so. Each of the parties was asked to agree to minimal conditions: the Orange Free State was to help maintain border control; the Cape Colony was to pay customs duties for goods entering and leaving Basutoland into Basutoland revenues; and the BaSotho were to accept and obey British government and laws. In its offer the British government gave no commitment to any future obligations to remain or continue its intervention, which Lagden scathingly characterized as a repudiation of the provisions of the Treaty of Aliwal North.[54]

In the meantime the dispute in Leribe continued. Caught in the middle, in May Jonathan's people were driven back over the border and out of the Free State by Free Staters, while Joel's people continued their depredations and murders. John Widdicombe, the Anglican missionary, pointed out that it was during this fight that Joel lost his popular support because he burned not only the village but also the stone house of his deceased father, Molapo, which the BaSotho found repugnant. Widdicombe further noted that from that moment Letsie began to show his preference for Jonathan.[55] At a national hearing in early May Letsie formally declared Jonathan to be the legal heir of Molapo in Leribe.[56]

Nevertheless, colonial officials found themselves confronted with the Leribe conflict for the remainder of the year, even as they dealt with larger issues. In October Blyth wrote to the Resident Magistrate in Leribe, Major Charles Bell:

> It is with much regret that I learn that matters are in such an unsettled state and I need not press upon you the importance of your urging upon Jonathan & Joel the necessity so far as their own real interests are concerned of remaining quiet.
>
> In the present state of Basutoland there is but little doubt that should disturbances break out in the Leribe Dist. there will be a general war throughout the country. . . .
>
> I have before this urged you to give all the support in your power to the Chief Jonathan who by his loyalty to the Govt has been placed in his present position and I can only repeat these instructions. Not only must it be remembered that the grave crimes committed by Joel & his people remain unexpiated, but the interests of the Govt demand that every effort be made to prevent a renewal of hostilities and the possible destruction of Jonathan.[57]

A month later Blyth warned Bell:

> It appears to me that when Joel considers it his interest to do so he acknowledges Letsie, and when he gains nothing by it, he ignores him. . . . I hardly consider the manner in which you address Joel, as "my good friend" and "my friend Joel" as a proper one when writing to him on official matters. As a Govt officer you are aware that Joel was an accessory to the brutal murders of old men and women

and the mutilation of a boy, also he was a direct actor in the shameful ill treatment of women at the Leribe.[58]

The turmoil created a crisis that could have broken the nation apart. In a moment of desperation Letsie actually wrote to Blyth stating his plan to abdicate the paramountcy at a *pitso* if Blyth approved. Furious, Blyth angrily rebuked him even as he gave him permission to abdicate, for, he wrote, "anything is better than this present way of going on."[59] Confusion reigned. Letsie somehow came into possession of two letters reputed to have been written by President Brand of the Free State, and, after checking with the president, Blyth had to inform Letsie they were fraudulent.[60] Blyth found himself countering false rumors that the Cape Colony had been empowered to send in Imperial troops.[61] In September 1883 the Cape Parliament passed the Disannexation Bill.

The ball was now in the Queen's court. Blyth had mastered the discourse of British colonialism, designed to mask incivilities in the imperialism project both at the time and for posterity. Appealing to the very real BaSotho sense of loyalty to nation, Blyth attributed to the Imperial government sentiments of sincerity and earnestness in its attention to "peace," "welfare," and "safety" in colonial Lesotho. After a series of letters were exchanged, on 24 November 1883 Her Majesty's government sent a telegram to Cape Town to be transmitted to Letsie and the BaSotho, inquiring,

> Do you desire to remain British subjects under the direct Government of the Queen, and if so, do you undertake to be obedient to the laws and orders of Her Majesty's High Commissioner, under whose authority you would be placed, and to pay a hut-tax of ten shillings in aid of the administrative expenses[?][62]

The message ended with the admonition that "Her Majesty's Government cannot take over a divided people." On 29 November 1883 a national *pitso* was held by Blyth at Maseru to deliver the message to the nation and allow deliberations. The next day he sent a message back to Cape Town that most of the chiefs had signed a document declaring their desire to remain British subjects under the Queen but that Masopha had not attended. Three days later Letsie sent a message to the government, pleading,

> Abandon me not, even although Masupha refuses to follow me. Abandonment means our complete destruction. We do not want

our independence. Listen Queen, to my earnest prayer; I and my people will follow faithfully wherever you lead.[63]

Masopha held a *pitso* at which he declared he did not want rule by the British or a magistrate but rather complete independence, but in Britain the Secretary of State yielded and conceded to grant Imperial administration to Basutoland in spite of the division caused by Masopha's intransigence. An Order-in-Council granting the Queen's consent to Cape disannexation and the assumption of direct Imperial control, with all powers vested in the High Commissioner, was promulgated on 18 March 1884. Letsie's strategy had succeeded, and it appears that Letsie had remained faithful to the BaSotho after all.

Why had the BaSotho fought with such unremitting determination? Beneath the rhetoric about guns lay a local discourse about colonial rule that understood it to entail a loss of liberty as well as land. For the BaSotho the stakes were nothing less than everything. The Gun War was fought over the same issues of land and liberty that had marked southern African history for more than two centuries. When rhetoric and the deployment of tropes of colonial discourse failed to achieve success through diplomacy, the BaSotho employed silent and coded discursive acts and messages and resorted to their guns, and in their victory over the Cape Colony they retained their land, their cattle, and their children.

7

Lerotholi and "Masopha's War"

The Colonial/Civil War of 1898

The Basuto are in a bottle and should not get out of it.

The resumption of direct British Imperial rule over Basutoland in 1884 prevented the alienation of land in Lesotho for white settlement and allowed the BaSotho to keep their guns, but administrative goals and strategies remained largely the same. A typical British policy of indirect rule was implemented through increasing reliance on chiefly authority under the watchful eyes of the new British Resident Commissioner and his District Commissioners. Politically, British colonial officials directed their attention to subduing the still restive Masopha and asserting the dominance of the Paramount Chieftaincy toward the end of achieving a greater centralization of authority. This would only be achieved by eventually resorting again to the force of arms, in 1898, after rhetoric and diplomacy had failed.

Effective colonial rule was reestablished after the end of the Gun War when Col. Marshal Clarke, RA, set out from England in January 1884 to take up his new appointment as the British Resident Commissioner in Basutoland. He took two officers from England to serve under him: Sir Godfrey Lagden himself, appointed to the posts of Secretary, Accountant, and Assistant Commissioner; and J. C. Macgregor, appointed as Police Officer and later Assistant Commissioner.[1] Lagden described the surprise of the BaSotho that their arrival on 16 March was so unceremonious, but the next day they went with Lerotholi to hold a *pitso* at Maseru, where they were welcomed by all the chiefs except Masopha

118

and Ramanella and their rebellious followers. From this moment Lagden became a reporter of events he not only witnessed but directly influenced and for which he was held responsible as a colonial official. Nevertheless, his observations, upon which historical inquiry inevitably depends for this period, were generally acute, and even when faulty his reports reflect accurately the impressions that shaped the decisions he made and in turn influenced history. His two-volume history was written with the benefit of hindsight for publication but for the most part reflects the contents of the annual published Colonial Reports for which he was responsible during his many years in office and that contain the contemporaneous accounts of himself and his District Resident Commissioners. In his later, published work Lagden assessed Basutoland as it was on his arrival in early 1884:

> At heart the nation as a whole, though shy, was willing to be governed mildly and anxious to progress. But the success of Masupha in defying authority was a serious bar to unity. He was able to centralize disaffection and detach a strong body of ardent rebels who kept alive opposition to any form of government and hatred of the loyals. In this attitude there is reason to believe he received the moral countenance of the Paramount Chief Letsie whose secret purpose it was, while affecting to condemn his brother, to gain protection without forfeiting independence.[2]

Some of the former rebels, including Masopha's following, kept alive hostility toward the BaSotho who had fought on the side of the colonial government during the Gun War because they wanted to keep the booty of land and cattle that they had confiscated from the former "loyals." Although Joel, like Lerotholi, did break from his uncle Masopha and join Letsie in declaring acceptance of the new Imperial dispensation, his popularity and political base had been artificially strengthened by his role as a rebel, and he wanted to retain the political leverage he had gained over his senior brother Jonathan to press his claim for the Leribe chieftaincy. The "loyals," whose homes were in the central Berea and Thaba Bosiu districts, were at continued risk from the depredations of Masopha's intrusions, and those whose homes were in Leribe remained physically vulnerable to Joel's attacks. However, the junior sons of Moshoeshoe, Letsie's half-brothers George Tlali Moshoeshoe and Sofonia Moshoeshoe, both accepted land from the government in Griqualand East outside of Basutoland, where they settled permanently and their descendents can still be found today.[3]

It is not surprising that the Leribe dispute festered. As Burman's evidence shows, on his 1882 trip to Basutoland in the company of General Gordon, Sauer had inflamed the situation in Leribe by offering Jonathan's lands to Joel as a bribe if Joel would support Lerotholi against Masopha, while at the same time he promised Jonathan a fair resolution of their inheritance dispute.[4] After the arrival of Clarke and Lagden in March 1884 initiating direct Imperial rule, the conflict between Jonathan and Joel flared up again immediately. Days after the first *pitso* was held the new colonial officials were handling their first crisis. In the outbreak of fighting thirty-nine of Joel's troops were killed, as were several of Jonathan's. Refugees swamped the Orange Free State, causing a strong rebuke from the Free State president yet again, and Clarke sent Lagden to intervene physically between the two fighting forces and recall the refugees from across the border. Clarke then arrived to hold an investigation, accompanied by Lerotholi, who was representing Letsie. Lagden described the scene, one of the earliest of his colonial career in Basutoland, in which Molapo's senior but mentally infirm grandson, who had been bypassed as heir by all parties, waved a gun in the court until it fired and a bullet struck one of Jonathan's men. The upshot was that the court declared Jonathan to be the principal chief, heir to his father's position, reaffirming the judgment of Letsie the previous year, with Joel restricted to a subordinate position and strictly defined territorial boundaries.[5]

Residual conflicts also caused sporadic disturbances in the south of the country, as Lagden explained. Letsie decided to "place" one of his "rebel" sons, Nkoebe, with a rebel following, in the Quthing District. Establishing a son as a subordinate chief allowed a Paramount Chief to extend his control via family members, as his son was thereby given authority over any people and subordinate chiefs already in the area. This process was disruptive in any event and became more so with the increase of population and overcrowding that had become evident by the end of the nineteenth century. In this case Nkoebe was "placed" over a predominantly "loyal" population and by this process acquired jurisdiction over them. Clarke decided it was better to acquiesce to the Paramount Chief's decision with regard to his son rather than assuage the fears of the local "loyals" and confirmed the appointment, which inevitably led to local conflicts.[6]

Not surprisingly, sporadic conflicts arose in the area of Masopha's chieftaincy, as Masopha encouraged fighting between the sons of his two brothers, Letsie and Majara (then deceased), who were residing in his district.[7] Lagden refrained from taking credit for his role in reining in violence and disruptive elements, but his influence was obvious. Explaining the shift in Masopha's attitude, he noted that a series of fights between Masopha and his former ally and nephew, Ramanella, had unexpected positive consequences. After a particularly violent incident, in which some fifty combatants died, both chiefs sought the support of the colonial government. This led to formal arbitration in the colonial court system, and both sides accepted the verdict; the rule of law had been reestablished in the most volatile part of the country. For Lagden, the significance was enormous:

> A just and impartial decision accepted by both gave the impression that there was now in the country a Court of Final Appeal which had no soldiers behind it but, what was stronger, the force of public opinion.[8]

As a result Masopha finally requested that a colonial magistrate be assigned to his district. Lagden was sent to fill this position temporarily and in four months established the "machinery of government"; with great satisfaction Lagden reported that Masopha had attended the first "native Parliament" held by the Resident Commissioner. Masopha landed in trouble again in 1887 after his heir, Lepoqo, died of alcoholism, but Masopha's attack, again on Ramanella, in a land dispute, backfired. Twenty people died "and so roused the anger of Letsie that he took the field against Masopha with such effect that the latter clamoured for protection from the Resident Commissioner who adjudged the case and fined him 1,000 head of cattle which he readily paid."[9] Subsequently, the BaSotho enjoyed a period of real, if short-lived, prosperity, and the popular preference for agriculture and trade to warfare was not lost on the chiefs. But the crises of drought and devastating cattle disease that ensued in the mid-1890s presented a challenge for Lerotholi when he succeeded his father as Paramount Chief upon Letsie's death in 1891. An expanding population intensified the pressure on land resources and sparked feuds over land rights, highlighting once again the conflicts over jurisdiction and power that undergirded colonial rule in Lesotho.

The Prewar Climate: Contests of Power and Authority

When he became Paramount Chief in 1891 Lerotholi's position was ambiguous, as he often acted in his own personal interests in land disputes and took advantage of government support. His allegiance to his people and to Lesotho as a nation was never in doubt, but his relationship with the colonial government wavered frequently, and in the letters from Lagden to Lerotholi in the years leading up to the 1898 war the evidence of implicit colonial coercion is clear. The threat that hung over the heads of the BaSotho was the aggression of the Orange Free State, and Lagden used this threat explicitly time and time again. More than once Lagden reminded Lerotholi that the fate of Africans who had come under white settler rule elsewhere in South Africa was worse than what the BaSotho had experienced and that the BaSotho were relatively privileged in this context. This had provided the BaSotho chiefs and people with the overriding incentive to choose to remain under British imperial rule in 1884, but the divisions that had remained at the end of that conflict had never been entirely resolved by 1897, the eve of the brief "war" in which the dispensation of power between the colonial government, the Paramount Chieftaincy, and subordinate principal chiefs was once again openly contested.

Lagden had already come to know Lerotholi by working with him to resolve disputes, however, since, as heir to the paramountcy, Lerotholi had often represented his father at meetings before Letsie's death in 1891. One incident in particular may have taught Lagden and Lerotholi to trust one another in moments of crisis. During one of the sporadic outbreaks between Jonathan and Joel Molapo in 1890, Lagden was serving as Acting Resident Commissioner while Sir Marshal Clarke was out of the country. He and Lerotholi, who was serving as de facto Paramount Chief during the last months of his father's life, had gone to Leribe together to hold court. There both Jonathan and Joel had arrived with their followers, fully armed, for the open-air court session that was to hear and decide their case. The moment as described by Lagden was dramatic and poignant:

> Whilst so engaged listening intently to a witness and absolute silence prevailed, a gun accidentally discharged so alarmed the armies that, fearing treachery, they flew in a panic to their horses saddled near by. It was an electric moment and if the camera had been brought into requisition it would have revealed, standing on the spot where a minute earlier some 12,000 armed warriors were squatting, only the Chief Lerothodi with his hands on the shoulders of the Acting Resident Commissioner as if to protect him from violence, and one solitary Mosutu lying dead at their feet from shock.[10]

Lagden, who assumed the position of Resident Commissioner upon Clarke's departure in mid-1893, had reason to believe that in moments of crisis he could rely upon Lerotholi.

As Resident Commissioner Lagden preferred moral suasion to force, making a virtue of necessity, but he was not above employing implicit threats to achieve colonial law and order. Lagden's letters to Paramount Chief Lerotholi and the other principal chiefs in 1897 made evident the message that a worse fate awaited the BaSotho at the hands of the Orange Free State government should they reject British colonial rule:

> I daresay you think that you are secure and can defend your-selves. This is the common error of ignorance and pride. The Ba-sotho little realize how helpless they are were it not for the hand of this Govt which protects them and has generously carried them for so many years with patience and liberality which no other tribe now enjoys.[11]

The enforcement of colonial rule rested on the shoulders of a hand-ful of magistrates, now called District Commissioners, bolstered by a tiny police force, and whenever trouble resulted in violence Lagden's frustra-tion with the limits to colonial power were evident. Of necessity he pre-ferred that the hand of colonial rule remain as invisible as possible and that the task of enforcement fall to the chiefs. When the chiefs them-selves were the source of any conflicts that flared into violent outbreaks, he was reliant on the Paramount Chief to implement colonial law. The Paramount Chief's power rested on the influence he exercised by virtue of his office and the authority attached to it as well as the respect ac-corded it by the population at large rather than force of arms. When sub-ordinate chiefs chose to fight, they marshaled support from the people who fell under their jurisdiction and who owed their homes and liveli-hoods to their chiefs; mustering troops in order to fight a popular subor-dinate chief thus put the Paramount Chief's own popular support, and power, at risk.

Diplomatic exchanges during 1897, before the 1898 conflict, reflect attempts by Lagden and by Lerotholi each to place the burden of restor-ing and maintaining order and the rule of law onto the other so as not to risk their own perceived moral authority, upon which they relied so heavily. With rinderpest killing their cattle and drought killing the crops, famine was becoming widespread, and people found it impossible to pay the hut tax in kind or in cash, exposing the harsh realities of colonial oppression to all BaSotho. The Resident Commissioner sounded an alarm in a letter to Lerotholi after he heard a report that some of his sons, including Letsie II (called Letsienyana), had been heard "talking loosely about shooting the Gov't."[12] The language of violence and the suggestion of anticolonial rebellion seemed to throw Lerotholi into a panic, and he replied to Lagden immediately:

> Chief you frighten me if you talk about the matter of shooting the Government. Its a thing that is not right to speak of. Where can a person get such power from?
>
> I am glad that you say you are going to Mafeteng and will call Letsie and you will see him for yourself that he is a person whose head is not right.[13]

Lerotholi also sought the direct intervention of the Resident Commissioner to settle the festering land dispute between Leshoboro Majara and Thebe Masopha in Masopha's district. Just as his father had resisted colonial pressure to impose British colonial will over his people by pleading powerlessness, so too Lerotholi continued to insist to the colonial officials that he was powerless to exercise any authority over his brothers and other chiefs and that it was unreasonable to expect him to do so. But Lagden held to the line that Lerotholi's position as Paramount Chief by definition conferred power as well as authority, ignoring the fact that Lerotholi had no means to enforce his decisions if they were resisted or ignored and ignoring the possibility that Lerotholi himself might not want to impose Lagden's orders. The jargon and discourse of colonialism prevented Lagden from acknowledging the reality of Lerotholi's toothless position as long as he lacked the support of subordinate chiefs and popular support for any measures either Lagden or Lerotholi sought to implement. True to the language of colonial rule, Lagden told Lerotholi:

> It is useless to enter into any discussion as to your not being Paramount Chief which is beyond question as you know quite well, and as I have already frequently said, there is nobody who can question your entering [exercising authority in] any district where the peace of the country is concerned.[14]

In response Lerotholi insisted to Lagden that Masopha was ignoring him and that authority had been effectively divided between Letsie in the southern districts, based at Matsieng, and his powerful uncles Masopha and Molapo, who held the central and northern districts of the country:

Chief I repeat and say that this name by which its said I am paramount Chief its only a name it is not so with the Basuto, they do not admit that I am chief; why I say so is because I hear all matters from you, there is not one who could stand up and say he ever sends matters to me—And in this I blame the Government. I say it's the Government that does not strengthen me, you the Resident Commissioner my chief who has been sent to be the caretaker of this country, you do not show the Basuto my greatness. . . . Beginning at Seakha the day you said we were natural enemies, until this day I have ever been alarmed at your words.[15]

Some subordinate chiefs showed their lack of confidence in the Paramount Chief's authority and efficacy in settling disputes, indicating their awareness that real power lay elsewhere—with the Resident Commissioner. Evidently worried that land disputes would persist without a clear record of entitlements, Leshoboro, one of the litigants in the land disputes in Masopha's district, wrote directly to the Resident Commissioner to ask that books confirming boundaries be read in court.[16] Although Lerotholi had gone personally to the district to pursue a settlement of the dispute, he explained to Lagden that the tensions had remained unresolved and both sides were armed.

Chief I say that as government has been disregarded and I have also been disregarded in the same way. Now, I together with my father's councillors say we cannot die through Masupha's fault.

In his letter Lerotholi indicated that he had consulted widely with the appropriate high-ranking "councillors" of the nation before he had written to Lagden: "I together with my father's councillors." Collectively, in stating that "we cannot die" these powerful BaSotho men were stating explicitly that they would not allow their country, the nation of Moshoeshoe and his followers and his sons, to perish. They feared that if Masopha remained uncooperative and the nation remained divided, the BaSotho would be incorporated into the Orange Free State and cease to exist as a nation.

Lerotholi wrote that he intended to use military force against the disputants, and "even if I should die I will have died for Government with which my father left me."[17] The Resident Commissioner immediately replied: "We don't want more bloodshed."[18] Lagden wanted Lerotholi to settle all disputes without resorting to force or the threat of force, which remained the monopoly of the colonial government and the source of real power.

Lerotholi replied to Lagden with a revealing discourse on authority and in a tone that showed his own authority:

> Now chief although you say you do not like more bloodshed, I too say that I am afraid chief that blood be shed. But as you have already been disregarded will not those who placed you as the guardian over this Country come and dispute your position which has been disrespected? . . . I fear that if the Government should come and dispute you the Govt. Representative, I know of a truth that the Government will take this country. . . .
>
> Chief it is best now that you allow me to fetch Thebe by force. Chief my grandfather said he was leaving us in a peace and I am left with the peace. Chief even if you were to hear them say this or that I am standing here where I'm standing and I will not depart from here from Government I am a man of the Government, I will die with the Government where it dies.[19]

Lerotholi was determined to defy Lagden if necessary in order to achieve a settlement of the land disputes by force, but he provided Lagden with a face-saving ploy to avoid incurring the wrath of the British government. He implied to the Resident Commissioner that he should tolerate this decision of Lerotholi and the nation's "high councillors" because the Resident Commissioner's position was subject to higher British authorities who might "dispute" Lagden's decision, whereas he and the other senior chiefs had, in Lerotholi's view, a direct tie to the Crown, which they intended to honor and protect, even if it required their defiance of the Resident Commissioner.

The Resident Commissioner's reply seems to suggest he understood the underlying message, but, choosing his language carefully, he suggested that he was already following a prescribed course of action in his dealings with Lerotholi, and he wanted Lerotholi to know this:

> I cannot tell you to go aside and commit the country to bloodshed. My duty is to advocate settlement of matters by all possible means other than force.[20]

Two months later Lagden repeated to Lerotholi words of the High Commissioner that contained the same restraining message:

> You should lose no opportunity of impressing upon the chiefs that Her Majesty's Govt will not tolerate repeated breaches of the peace. If they choose to fall to fighting among themselves, the inevitable result must be that they will lose the large measure of independence which they at present enjoy. There is a simple choice before

the Basuto nation either to obey your counsels as the representative of the power which protects them & live in peace among themselves or to be reduced to the condition of a subject nation.[21]

In early October Lerotholi went personally to harrow four contested fields claimed by Masopha and explained subsequently to the Resident Commissioner that he was enforcing a court judgment in doing so:

> They were disturbing the peace and despising the Queen's judgements together with those of mine. For these reasons I went and harrowed these four fields. . . . My opinion was that if Masupha comes and fires at me I will have patience until he fired ten shots and then after that I would defend myself. What I want is peace and to preserve it and to carry out the law. Now I have carried out the law.[22]

Lerotholi explained to the Resident Commissioner that he was holding firm in his dealings with Masopha to protect "the law and peace which Masupha wants to break" and noted, "[I]t is he who is going about with guns which are seen by everyone."[23] A court decision had previously ruled against Masopha's claim to this land, but in response to Lerotholi's action Masopha wrote to Lerotholi, his nephew, ironically:

> Chief I have heard that you have harrowed my garden at Madisanyane's, but I say to you my Child I thank you for harrowing this garden for me because you knew that I am old. But I say you should have told me when you went to harrow, so that I would have been able to thank you, but know that the garden is mine I thank you for having worked it for me.[24]

Lerotholi had what he wanted when he received a letter from the High Commissioner that upheld his position, and he wrote to Lagden that he wished to read the letter at a *pitso*. He had already informed Masopha about its contents and warned him that if he violated the court-ordered boundary "we will lose our independence, and that no more blood is to be shed."[25] Masopha disputed Lerotholi's act in giving one of his fields to two other men and wrote him that if Lerotholi's people did not vacate the disputed lands, "I will in reality fight with them."[26]

Lerotholi had fruitlessly tried to warn Lagden of deepening problems caused by the lack of effectiveness of central authority, which he blamed on Lagden's refusal to countenance stronger measures to suppress violent disputes. Lagden seemed oblivious to the emerging crisis of authority and focused blame on Lerotholi personally:

> I see as if it is Brandy that is King. Your father told you to choose between chieftainship and brandy and you appear to have chosen. As for me, I may have patience with stupidity but with Brandy No.[27]

As during the Gun War, the crisis of colonial rule, or perhaps of colonial impotence, was only given serious attention when the resulting violence spilled over the borders. Once again a small event triggered an international incident that Lagden and his superiors could not ignore, and he immediately wrote to Lerotholi:

> Your letter about Masupha's hut Tax and about Moeketsi has just reached me. And I reply quickly that you can if you wish send one man to listen to Moeketsi's case at Ladybrand. He should be here tonight and can get a letter (which will be his pass).[28]

A "Colonial War"

The actual incident that set off the struggle between the British and the BaSotho involved Masopha's son Moeketsi. Moeketsi and his cohorts had crossed the border into the Orange Free State to catch a man who had run off with another man's wife, and when they caught him they assaulted him and, according to some reports, castrated him.[29] The Free State captured Moeketsi before he made it back across the border, however, and threw him into jail. Moeketsi then escaped and fled across the border, and the event ballooned into an international incident. The government of the Orange Free State insisted that the Basutoland government hand him back, but first the latter had to apprehend him itself. Masopha refused to turn Moeketsi over to the colonial authorities in Basutoland, inspired, it is said, by his defiant wife.[30] At this point Lagden turned the responsibility for apprehending Moeketsi over to Lerotholi, who as the Paramount Chief and the arm of the government had the duty to uphold and enforce the law.

Lagden's letters reveal that Lerotholi was reluctant to intervene, and it is evident that his reluctance resulted from popular support both for Masopha and for protecting his son from the long arm of Free State law. As a result Lagden was forced to use threats of Imperial military intervention to coerce Lerotholi to take action. Calling Lerotholi "the Chief

Great Policeman," Lagden reminded Lerotholi that the British protected the BaSotho from the Boers:

> I received your letter this morning about Moeketsi. For years we have been fighting your battles for you and preserving you, but it has been easier because you (plural) have avoided foreign complications. Sir Hercules Robinson when he sent to your father Letsie by [messengers] Seeiso and Ntsane said "Tell Letsie that the Basuto are in a bottle and should not get out of it." Now Moeketsi has gone and jumped out of the bottle. He violated the border and took violent action in a foreign state, seizing and beating people, for which he was arrested and tried and convicted. He escaped with a common man, a notorious horse thief named Maboka. Had this horse thief escaped alone he would have been arrested and sent in by the first chief who saw him. Are we to make an exception for Moeketsi. Are matters to be spoiled for him. Is it Government who has forced this matter on or is it you Basuto. You tell me Masupha says he will fight for Moeketsi. Well, where is this to end? I say you will be supporting a bad cause if you sacrifice the nation because of a man who went out of his way to bring trouble on you.
>
> Maboka the one who escaped with Moeketsi is a Free State subject and according to existing treaty is extraditable. Moeketsi, being domiciled in Basutoland is liable to be tried in Basutoland under our law. There is the matter. It is for me to speak to you the Chief Govt Policeman and not to Masupha.[31]

Although both sides of the correspondence between Lerotholi and Lagden are not extant, Lagden's letters reveal events as they transpired, his assessment of the circumstances and people involved, and even Letsie's motivations. Lerotholi immediately asked Lagden to give him direct orders, but Lagden did not recognize this as Lerotholi's attempt to shift the responsibility, and any future blame, away from himself and onto the shoulders of the colonial government:

> By Ntsane you ask for orders:—Moeketsi and Maboka should be produced at Court with messengers in the ordinary way like other cases and not with demonstration. . . . Moeketsi being a Basutoland subject should be heard and dealt with here in Basutoland. The law does not order me to hand him over to the Free State.[32]

Lerotholi continued to press for information and orders, which exasperated Lagden even at this early date. Lerotholi was evidently wondering if he was really going to be required to arrest Masopha's son, which would cause deep popular resentment, but Lagden appeared to think he was merely inquiring about the involvement of the Orange Free State government, which was an aggravating factor as far as popular opinion was concerned.

The international dimensions of the case preoccupied Lagden and caused his growing sense of urgency as the days passed. On 5 December he wrote to Lerotholi:

> I then told you that I was having a misunderstanding with the O. Free State because they have called for surrender of Moeketsi which I had refused to order.
>
> Today I hear that the President has opened communications with the High Commissioner on the subject.[33]

Evidently, the correspondence was almost daily: two days later Lagden wrote Lerotholi to explain that the extradition treaty with the Orange Free State dated from 1887, according to which the High Commissioner, Sir Hercules Robinson, and Orange Free State President Brand agreed that "men were not to be given up from their own [home country] domicile but could be tried there," which explained why one escapee, Moeketsi's companion, would be extradited home to the Free State but Moeketsi would remain home in Basutoland for trial. Lagden's tone betrays his frustration:

> I don't know why all the fuss and obstruction is being made today. . . . I have already given you my pledge that I cannot surrender Moeketsi. Does not that pledge make the matters easy.[34]

After another two days Lagden wrote to Lerotholi:

> As matters now stand it looks as if your people had made a raid into the Free State and acted unwisely and violently there and had stolen a man from their prison which is Maboka. It is my duty to place this before you in a clear light because it looks, and will be understood, unpleasantly. Why I say it is your people is because it is not an act of stupid people but has been headed by the son of one of your chiefs and therefore it appears in a more serious light.[35]

Lagden was concerned about two precedents counter to the law that might be set if Moeketsi were not arrested and tried. First, he feared that the chiefs would believe that they and their families were above the law and could act with impunity even in the commission of serious crimes. Second, he was worried about how to counteract the growing problem of runaway wives and the legal problems it caused when they fled from their husbands and sought refuge across the border in the Orange Free State, without encouraging illegal countermeasures. The seriousness of this particular incident was underscored by the punishment by castration of the man involved in running off with the woman, although most of the sources obscure this aspect of the case. While the punishment itself was a criminal act, it brought attention to the practice of BaSotho men taking the law into their own hands when it came to disciplining runaway wives. Lagden had evidently been looking the other way for a long time when BaSotho men disciplined runaway wives, but since this had become an international incident with criminal aspects and legal repercussions, he had to address the issue directly. Not wanting to alienate Lerotholi and the chiefs more than necessary, he therefore found himself openly expressing his sympathy for BaSotho men who were dealing with the problem, as they saw it, of runaway wives:

> By this I understand that the whole course of the law is to be stopped and things work backwards because of a woman.
>
> However much we may regret the weak ways of women & of men who go wrong with these we should be careful not to let them spoil larger matters.
>
> I have already told you that in this matter of women running over the border I am with you in this grievance and am seeking ways to help you.[36]

Lagden recognized that Lerotholi might need to be able to bolster his position relative to the other powerful men in the country with a clear demonstration of the support of the Resident Commissioner for his actions:

> It would be well if you read this letter to your brothers and uncles in order to show that I have no harsh thoughts but that my sympathies are with you, and that my desire is to guide you along a lawful way.[37]

Lerotholi did share all of the information, and therefore presumably some of the correspondence, with his principal counselors from whom he sought advice. In answer to a query Lagden wrote:

> In reply to your question by Mothebesoane as to whether if Maboka runs away you will be responsible, my answer is, Yes, you are the Paramount Chief and the one to whom Government speaks.[38]

This comment indicates that Lagden was aware that Lerotholi and the principal men in the country were exploring the dispensation of power and authority under colonial rule. They wanted to know the extent to which Lagden privileged Lerotholi as Paramount Chief in granting him the authority to act and in holding him responsible for the actions of his people. Lagden realized that all the chiefs also questioned the degree of Lagden's authority because they were acutely aware that Lagden himself answered to a higher authority, Her Majesty's government. Three weeks into the growing crisis he wrote to Lerotholi:

> It is for a long time at important Pitsos that I have been advising the Basuto not to tempt too far the patience and forebearance of Her Majesty's Government. My advice to you (plural) has always been—Take care of the law without which you cannot live, and carry it.

Informing the Paramount Chief that the High Commissioner had confirmed Lagden's promise not to extradite Moeketsi to the Free State, he reiterated: "[M]y demand that the two persons already named should be brought to me must be upheld." Underscoring his authorization, Lagden added that "His Excellency orders me to impress strongly upon you and the chiefs that he is *determined* that the law shall be respected without delay."[39]

But Lagden's words seemed to fall on deaf ears. Angry at Lerotholi's failure to arrest Moeketsi and accept responsibility for the action, which he had publicly bolstered, Lagden accused the BaSotho chiefs of being ungrateful and presumptuous:

> In your letters lately you have said your chieftainship has been despised and that you are standing alone in your opinion about the law and you ask for advice and orders because Masupha is seeking your place.
>
> I do not know how to give orders to a man who says he is standing alone. In thus expressing yourself you are making a confession of weakness and it would seem that although Government placed you in the position of Paramount and supported you in it you may have lost the power of that position.
>
> It appears as if the chiefs, instead of valuing the many privileges accorded to them and appreciating the position allowed them of being policemen to carry out the orders of the law, have now assumed the position of law-givers and desire to take the place of Government thinking in a thoughtless way that generosity to them meant weakness.

Lagden then invoked the authority of the High Commissioner, saying, "[H]e does not admit the possibility of your disputing his obligations by delay and irritation nor does he approve of either myself or Magistrates being put off by vexatious talk and delays."[40] Lagden further insisted that Lerotholi carry out his duties as Paramount Chief, and he restated colonial recognition of Lerotholi's rights and prerogatives as such. On 24 December he wrote:

> I have already explained what the law requires and informed you that it is for you as Paramount Chief of this country to carry it out. I have also told you of the High Commissioner's orders. If you are determined to carry the law and have called your brothers and people to follow you, you have done what is your duty to the country.[41]

At this point, however, a new concern appears, as Lagden began to worry that the colonial administration might be vulnerable in the event of a rebellion, and he asked Lerotholi not to call the men from Maseru to provide customary labor in the fields because that would leave the capital in an "unprotected state."[42]

The crisis came to a head in January. Lerotholi called out armed men to take up key points surrounding the fortified spot of Masopha not far from his village near Thaba Bosiu. In the initial troop movement and positioning the two sides engaged in fighting, and several men were killed. At this point an extraordinary rash of letters indicated urgency verging on panic on the part of Lagden. But, on the brink of war, Lerotholi bided his time until he got what he wanted: direct orders from Lagden. With trouble looming, Lagden tried again to invoke the authority of the High Commissioner to propel Lerotholi into ordering his troops, now on the scene, to take whatever further action was required to arrest Moeketsi:

> I have informed the High Commissioner of all you have told me. He answers me saying Lerothodi has begun well. Let him finish it quickly and bring Moeketsi as ordered. The High Commissioner is with you but do <u>not delay</u>. Let no walls stop you.[43]

While Lerotholi was there commanding the troops the messages between Lagden and the Paramount Chief were frequent and evidently sometimes crossed each other. Hence the next day Lagden found himself writing the same thing, this time at greater length, deploying laden tropes of loyalty and invoking the Queen directly:

> I have already said to you that you and your people being the Queen's subjects and you being working in the Queen's name and being the Queen's messenger have been fired upon and some of these subjects of the Queen have been killed. Masupha has been

fighting against the Govt, the High Commissioner—and the Queen—You have so far been trying to do your duty and have been doing it. It is not the nation who is fighting the Queen. It remains for you together with the nation to show that you (pl) have nothing to do with Masupha's action and that you will do what is ordered . . .

If the law and the Queen's authority are to be upheld by the nation there are no walls can stop them. P.S. In what way do you ask me to help you more than I have helped you?[44]

In his retrospective history Lagden demonstrated his sensitivity to rhetoric and the language of metaphor commonly used by the BaSotho. The tone of his next letter is deliberately if artificially intimate in tone, a far cry from the previous few missives. This switch to greater cordiality was evidently prompted by Lerotholi's own use of a reference that could be expected to elicit European sympathy: prayer. Lerotholi also positioned himself as a defender of the Queen, and Lagden picked up on this appeal to loyalty when he wrote that in defying the law Masopha had "fired upon" the Queen herself. Moreover, in what was meant as the greatest compliment imaginable from a British colonial official to an African chief who fell under Imperial rule, Lagden positioned Lerotholi as the Queen's representative and as being, metaphorically, Her Majesty, since he wrote that when Lerotholi was fired upon, the Queen was fired upon:

I quite agree with the way you answered those of your brothers who asked you to pray for Masopha. You said if they are praying let them bring Masopha to you. You said well.

I am not able to forget that the Queen has been fired upon when you were fired upon and that it is a very serious matter which talking of does not heal.[45]

This was evidently the turning point, when the "conversation" between Resident Commissioner Lagden and Paramount Chief Lerotholi turned to practical plans for the use of the gathered military force to seize Moeketsi from his father Masopha's protection. On 10 January Lagden wrote to Lerotholi that he had "informed the Magistrate of what you are doing and how you are acting under orders and that the Government is with you." Lagden declined to communicate further with other chiefs, leaving that to Lerotholi.[46]

Almost all of his subordinate chiefs had responded to Lerotholi's original call for military forces, so that during the days of waiting and correspondence in January he had some ten thousand armed men from every district of the country facing a similar number defending Masopha. Jonathan Molapo had initially showed support for Masopha but withdrew his men when the siege of his stronghold began. Lerotholi's junior half-brother Maama, who had had ambitions of inheriting the Paramount Chieftaincy on their father's death, refused to allow his men to support Lerotholi, but neither did he send support to Masopha. Then a standoff ensued that lasted for three weeks. Lerotholi did not want a British invasion, but he also did not want the BaSotho to think that he was acting of his own accord. He asked for, and received, direct orders in writing so that he might demonstrate his dilemma to his people. Lerotholi may have wanted to exert his authority over Masopha, but he did not want to go against the wishes of his people. Lerotholi finally received formal written, direct orders from Lagden:

> To Paramount Chief Lerothodi
>
> I, the Resident Commissioner, in answer to your request made personally at Maseru for a letter of authority, say you are, being the Paramount Chief and Chief Policeman of this Territory, to arrest and bring to Court Moeketsi the son of Masupha for having transgressed the law and for having since then fired upon and killed the Queen's subjects who were at the same time employed as policemen under you to uphold the law, and uphold the Queen's authority.[47]

The Resident Commissioner thus stood behind Paramount Chief Lerotholi at this critical moment. Letsie's son Maama was principal chief over the territory next to Masopha's stronghold at Thaba Bosiu and had married one of Masopha's daughters, which had more than once made him complicit in Masopha's subterfuges. He now contacted Lagden on behalf of Masopha, but Lagden would have none of Maama's arguments against Lerotholi's proposed use of force against Masopha. In a written response Lagden reminded Maama that his own man had said Maama was "going to fight for Masupha against the P.C. [Paramount Chief] and the law" in front of many witnesses, including Lagden and Lerotholi.[48]

Evidently, Masopha was finally trying to open negotiations with the Resident Commissioner through Maama and had apparently been engaged in a policy of brinkmanship, doubting that Lagden would ever sanction the use of military force given his long-standing opposition to violent conflicts.[49] Lagden, however, was unreceptive to Maama's overtures:

> As for your being sent by me to Masupha the moment for it and for words has passed. . . .
>
> You have had a long opportunity. I will not now interfere with Lerothodi's just and lawful demand that Masupha should surrender to him.[50]

On the same day that he had already sent Lerotholi his formal orders Lagden again wrote to him conveying the contents of a telegram from the High Commissioner that stated that the Imperial government had authorized the mobilization of troops across the border "so that *if necessary,* they should come to your aid and assert the authority of Government and of yourself in Basutoland which has been upset by the acts of Masupha and those who encouraged him." Before he could send the letter messengers arrived from Lerotholi indicating that he had given orders for the attack to begin the following day. Perhaps fearing Lerotholi might find further excuse for postponement, Lagden added a postscript to the letter he had already written:

> Now, I hear you say you are going to fetch Moeketsi at once. Very well. Do so. I do not wish to hinder you one moment. . . . Understand clearly that if you have given orders to attack tomorrow morning do not postpone it to meet me—It is best we meet afterwards. I am with you as I have always been. This matter is yours and mine if it is done well and quickly.[51]

Lagden thus stated his full support for Lerotholi and had reason to expect that Lerotholi's attack against Masopha and the arrest of Moeketsi were imminent. When nothing had happened after almost a week Lagden must have despaired of any action ever being taken, and he again wrote Lerotholi:

> Look sharp and remove Masupha from that stronghold and show me that you are his chief and let me hear his sorrow. Then you and your people may soon be weeding peacefully.[52]

It is not clear why Lerotholi's troops had not attacked on 17 January, as Lagden expected, nor why the delay was extended for a full week. But by 24 January heavy rains and swollen rivers inhibited troop movements. Lagden wrote to Lerotholi twice that day. In his first letter he provided confidential advice, couched in a familiar and casual tone: "Now a thought occurs to me and I give it to you," proposing that he could hold court near Masopha's village and after receiving Masupha's surrender in proper form . . . bring him without arms to the place I have named for him to express his sorrow for his transgressions against yourself, against the law and against the Government.

After this it would be for you & me to decide upon and announce the other terms we agree upon—The only other term I am bound to stick to is that I am not allowed to recognize Masupha again as principal chief of the Berea District.[53]

Lagden further told Lerotholi, "I say this is only confidential to you and is not meant to embarrass you or to turn you aside from any constitutional course you have determined upon," and "if you don't like it you can tear this letter up." In a second message that day Lagden asked Lerotholi, "if your brothers are not helping you, do you want me to ask for help for you?"[54]

Lerotholi's troops finally made their assault on Masopha's position two days later. They prevailed, and Masopha surrendered. Killed in the action were thirty-one of Lerotholi's men and twenty-four of Masopha's. Moeketsi was taken prisoner and handed over for trial. Masopha was forced to pay a heavy fine and abandon his village in Thaba Bosiu permanently, and he was deprived of the privileges of district chieftainship.[55]

Following a formal meeting in February 1898 that concluded the dispute between Lerotholi and Masopha, the public setting was used by the Paramount Chief and his sons to display silently their suppressed contempt for Lagden and the colonial rule he represented. Lagden wrote to Lerotholi to complain about his behavior at the end of the meeting:

I certainly was much annoyed and considered it an extraordinary thing that you should have left in the way you did carrying with you Seeiso, Nkoebe and your own sons and thus educating them to do the same and disrespect me—Not one of these persons greeted me—they all left like a lot of animals that had been fed and turned away from the feeder not having the intelligence to be respectful. It reminds me of the day your son Letsie galloped in front of us at Mafeteng scattering the mud in my face. Your footsteps are generally marked by your care of being polite and honouring my position as indeed I honour yours always. But you ended a matter, in which I befriended you & pulled you safely through, in an unseemly way that I can neither understand nor forget, and you may expect the example to be seen in your own children hereafter.

It was an insult to me.[56]

This message demonstrates a colonial discourse with the usual jargon of mutual loyalty and respect. But it also indicates that both sides, the British and the BaSotho, understood the importance of unspoken messages conveyed by public action, in this case insolence toward the Resident Commissioner on the part of the Paramount Chief and his sons and other chiefs. Both the colonizers and the colonized recognized that such publicly well-understood messages conveyed in a public arena—discursive acts—were significant tools in the contest of power. The British awareness of the significance of such discursive acts was such as to generate a written complaint from Lagden to the Paramount Chief and another from Lagden to his own superior, the High Commissioner. These acts of insolence even became points of reference in future communications between the British colonial officials and the chiefs through whom they exercised colonial rule. By citing the action of Lerotholi several days earlier and by citing the behavior of Lerotholi's son in a previous incident, Lagden demonstrated his own understanding that these acts were texts meant to be read by an audience of both BaSotho and British, and he further ensured that these silent discursive acts spoke louder than words, that they became part and parcel of the permanent record of colonial discourse, a public message about an unspoken but popular sentiment: continued discontent with colonial rule.

BaSotho chiefs were not powerless; they were not passive victims onto which colonial hegemony, either politically or culturally, was inscribed. The incident and its reporting by a colonial official raises significant issues about power and how it was exercised not only by rulers but also by the ruled. The public display of disrespect by Lerotholi and his sons and supporters on this occasion indicated to all present that British ability to rule was neither unrestrained nor uncontested.

After the war Lagden tacitly acknowledged that the war of 1898 was a colonial war. When one of Lerotholi's brothers, J. W. Moyela (Mojela) Letsie, requested in writing both compensation and a pension from the colonial government because he had been permanently injured in the fighting, Lagden asked Lerotholi to give him part of the fine collected from Moeketsi's conviction, saying, "[H]e worked for you and bled for you."[57] But when he had still not received his expected compensation, Mojela wrote to Lagden:

According to my knowledge, I know that the Queen's Government is right and straight. I have duly sworn to die for Lerothodi and for the Government.

At the end of his letter he added:

You should not be surprised to see this note, I am confidentially looking to you knowing that Masupha's war was the Government one, though there were not white men, but still it was so. Therefore I hoped that the people who are like me who received wounds would be helped by the Government. I think it ought to be like it was in Moorosi's war about the people wounded like me whose cases the Government looked into. Being therefore the Government property and as well the property of the Basuto chieftainship, I am confidentially looking to you my Resident Commissioner.[58]

Lagden subsequently approved a pension for Mojela, indicating that he agreed with him that the war had, indeed, been a "Government one."[59]

In this historic moment of crisis Lerotholi had nevertheless earned Lagden's trust and respect. Lerotholi won unqualified praise in Lagden's published retrospective, which contains not an inkling of the contentious correspondence between himself and the Paramount Chief. In spite of Lerotholi's role in spearheading anticolonial resistance during the Gun War and his sometimes insulting behavior, Lagden credited him for his later leadership. He remembered, as related in his history of this period, the moment when he had found himself surrounded by armed and mounted men, alarmed by the shot of a gun, and Lerotholi had remained calmly beside him with his hand on Lagden's shoulder. Lagden memorialized Lerotholi for posterity in unqualified terms, putting a gloss on the truth: "Lerotholi responded to the call and took up the burden."[60] Gone ten years later was the memory of the meeting of 3 February 1898, when Lagden, writing the following day, told Lerotholi, "I certainly was much annoyed and considered it an extraordinary thing that you should have left in the way you did carrying with you Seeiso, Nkoebe and your own sons and thus educating them to do the same and disrespect me."[61]

8

Of Laws, Courts, and Chiefs

The Twentieth Century

The assertion of central authority by Paramount Chief Lerotholi over Masopha in 1898 seemed to accomplish a major administration goal of the British colonial government, and Lagden later wrote, "Lerotholi, who behaved with gallantry and intelligence, enjoyed for the first time undisputed supremacy." But colonial authority and that of the paramountcy remained fragile and were challenged by regional events over the coming decades. War broke out across the border in 1899, and Sir Alfred Milner oversaw the British war effort to assume control over the Boer Republics of the Orange Free State and the South African Republic (i.e., the Transvaal) as part of a planned process of regional unification under the aegis of the British Empire that ultimately culminated in the formation of the Union of South Africa in 1910.[1] The Paramount Chiefs became preoccupied with the need to protect their people from incorporation into South Africa, while within the country various efforts surfaced to broaden political participation, and the words and actions of people from all levels of society came to influence the internal political dispensation of the country. The colonial records of politics in Lesotho, from 1898 through World War II, show a dynamic use of rhetoric, diplomacy, and discourse on the part of Paramount Chiefs defending the very existence of their country, Principal chiefs competing for authority and power, and commoners seeking a greater voice in directing the affairs of the country.

The BaSotho had honored Masopha for his strong efforts to resist European rule over many decades, but by the time of his final defeat the British presence in Lesotho, if unwelcome, had come to be seen as inevitable and preferable to an alternative fate in the hands of white settler communities across the border. After the brief war of January 1898 many of Masopha's followers deserted him and moved away from the Berea area, and Lagden wrote that Masopha's last months after his defeat and his death in July of the same year were humiliating, when there were "no chiefs of consequence being present, according to custom to witness his last moments."[2] Only his children attended the "unceremonious" burial, but Lagden gave Masopha a generous obituary:

> With all his faults, and in spite of the continuous trouble he caused by his contumacy, he [Masopha] had the merit of struggling gamely for independence of control, which for many years he succeeded in gaining.
>
> In addition to a winning and persuasive manner, he possessed considerable strength of character. So long as he directed his energies against Government, the other chiefs tolerated and allowed him to lead; but they declined to be led when they realised that his overpowering jealousy of the present Paramount Chief was tending towards tribal disruption calculated to wreck the whole nation.[3]

Lagden later described the results of the 1898 war in terms of typical colonial discourse:

> The Basuto, who with their usual sense rallied at the right moment, were made to realize that though their independence was respected it was the positive intention of Her Majesty's Government to insist upon law and order and to assert it with troops if the Chiefs failed to maintain it or failed to obey constitutional orders.[4]

Paramount Chief Lerotholi and the other chiefs lent themselves "loyally in the detection and punishment of offenders" and cooperated well "in matters where law and order were concerned," but land disputes recurred as a result of the practice of the Paramount Chief and Principal chiefs of "placing" their senior sons over the junior sons of the earlier generation of chiefs.[5] The allocation of land was a chief's prerogative and the primary tie between himself and his people, who thereby owed him loyalty and tributary labor in his fields. Many of the disputes occurred in mountainous districts, which had only been occupied permanently for a generation, and in the south, where Moorosi's BaPhuthi had come under the rule of the sons of the Paramount Chiefs. As a result, a major legal precedent was set through the courts with regard to the allocation of land and territorial political authority. The Assistant Commissioner of Quthing, S. Barrett, explained this principle:

By the enforced removal of a village belonging to one Raphera
from the vicinity of the chief Lefuyane's place in August, 1898, the
Resident Commissioner confirmed a judgement of the Paramount
Chief which had been evaded for several years, and affirmed the
useful principle that no one can be permitted to reside on the land
of a chief to whom he refuses allegiance.[6]

The disputes, often violent, over territorial authority and land allocation could be expected to continue. Lerotholi tried to send a letter
directly to the High Commissioner expressing his concern over disputes among the chiefs. No doubt offended by Lerotholi's attempt to
contact his own superior directly, Lagden intercepted the letter and told
Lerotholi:

I return you your letter to the H.C. which it is best you read over
and alter in your own words.
      You now speak again of lessening all other chiefs. Remember
they are already lessened by power you have lately gained.[7]

From the perspective of the Paramount Chieftaincy, Lerotholi had
good reason to be concerned. The correspondence files indicate challenges to the Paramount Chief's authority made by other Principal
chiefs.[8] This was partly the result of the 1898 war, after which the chiefs
who had failed to assist Lerotholi militarily were fined. The Paramount
Chief complained to Lagden:

I send you Jonathan's and Maama's letters [of apology] there they
are for you to see the mockery they are mocking me—It is as if they
wrote to come and laugh at me.[9]

Lerotholi took Maama to task in the strongest words, listing all his of-
fenses and writing, among other things:

There is nothing that has been paid for, you refuse to pay all my
judgements. What you do since the death of my father [Letsie, also
Maama's father] is to insult me Maama.
      Lately you advised Masupha to wage war against me, and truly
Masupha defied me and fought against me when I tried to support
[uphold] the law. . . . I have recently fined you and Jonathan, and I
fined you moderately, and not as I was told to, and it was by the approval of the governor and the Resident Commissioner, Jonathan
has paid the fine, you have not paid it although it is so moderate.
Now what am I to do? Shall I get into a scrape on your account, or
shall I take all this as a regular case to the court? Tell me.

> I am tired of you Maama. Your brothers do not deal with me in this way.[10]

When a dispute soon arose between Lerotholi and Jonathan, Lagden chided Lerotholi:

> This is more than stupid. It is childish. If you (plural) do not support each other you (plural) are teaching others to despise your (plural) chieftainship. Jonathan should be supported in his chieftainship and he should support and respect yours.[11]

Lerotholi replied that he was afraid to take a strong position against Jonathan, so Lagden also drafted a letter to the chiefs of Leribe, informing them that

> Lerothodi is the eye of Govt. In the whole Lesotho. Jonathan is the eye of Lerothodi. All matters in Leribe belong first to Jonathan and he is the door to Lerothodi in case of appeal being wanted.[12]

Following the continuing tensions between chiefs, including the Paramount Chief, in 1899 the country's Principal chiefs petitioned the Resident Commissioner collectively "for a National Council, which had been offered them in 1890 and would then have been established but for their rejection of it by lukewarmness and disagreement."[13] Through the council the Principal chiefs would have direct access to the Resident Commissioner and would be able to speak collectively and openly when they had grievances against or differences with the Paramount Chief. Action was delayed, presumably as a result of the outbreak of the war that year, but in 1903 the first Basutoland National Council was established, and in its first session the council encoded existing laws in use in the courts into a compendium that came to be called "The Laws of Lerotholi."[14]

Between 1899 and 1902 the war across the border challenged the unity of the nation. Those whom Lagden later identified as having committed treason in their dealings with the Orange Free State against the British government included most prominently Joel Molapo, but others took a more ambiguous position, not wishing to alienate whichever government was to emerge the winner.[15] For the first half of the war the prospects of the allied Boer Republics looked more promising than did those of the British, so Lagden, although he roundly condemned treasonous plans and acts coordinated with the Free State, was not surprised by them.[16]

But Lagden developed a deeper respect for Lerotholi because of his behavior during the Anglo-Boer War (1899–1902). Early in the war a British contingent of troops was surrounded by Free State troops at the Free State town of Wepener, across the Caledon River from Basutoland, and Lagden learned that the Boers were planning to enter Basutoland in order to cut off the British troops completely from the Lesotho side of the Caledon. The Paramount Chief responded instantly to Lagden's request for help by mustering within hours several thousand armed men at the threatened spot. Lagden wrote:

> Lerothodi, always gallant and at heart loyal, was unusually stirred at the sight of a few hundred Britishers penned up by the Republican forces several thousand strong in a hopeless position who, though standing their ground bravely, were short of food and ammunition and subject to perpetual bombardment from long-range guns to which they could not reply. He asked the simple question whether it was right to stand by and see the Queen's soldiers in such a predicament and whether he might be allowed to "cause a diversion." The Resident Commissioner answered that their united duties must be limited to protection of the border. In due course the garrison was relieved. This armed demonstration was legitimately made, was under control and served its purpose. The natives provided their own food during two weeks and did not commit a disorderly act.[17]

Lagden ultimately lavished praise on Lerotholi for his unquestionable loyalty to the British government throughout the war, even when it was an unpopular position because of the evident vulnerability of the British:

> In the Paramount Chief Lerothodi was found one who had the courage of his absolutely loyal convictions. He was threatened and cajoled by the Boers, taunted by many of his own people for being on the wrong side, and tempted by the situation to seek benefits for himself and the nation; but he suffered himself to be guided by the Resident Commissioner and never stirred from his allegiance.[18]

The Anglo-Boer War revealed the many links between Lesotho and the wider region. The country provided refuge to displaced persons from across the border, black and white, including Boer families from the Orange Free State, with their property. Basutoland was used by the British for supply lines, and BaSotho served in support capacities for the British troops. As the Assistant Commissioner of the Maseru District reported in the annual report for 1899–1900:

A very useful system of intelligence work was established, and the authorities were kept posted with what was going on in the enemy's lines. Natives were imployed on this dangerous work, and did splendidly. They got in, about, and out of the Boer laagers in a bold and daring manner, and many had thrilling adventures in making their escape upon being detected.[19]

The Paramount Chiefs and Resistance to Incorporation into South Africa

International politics continued to consume the attention of BaSotho political leadership because of the proposal to incorporate Basutoland, along with Bechuanaland and Swaziland, into the planned political union of the former British colonies, the Cape Colony and Natal, and the two defeated Boer Republics. Lerotholi took prompt and preemptive action to express unified BaSotho opposition to such a step. In October 1903 the Government Secretary, L. Wroughton, wrote to Lerotholi:

> I forwarded to the R.C. [Resident Commissioner] the letter which you wrote in which you said that you wished to remain under the King and not to be governed like the natives of Natal are governed. Mr. Sloley writes to me that I am to thank you for this letter, and to tell you that he understands it and that you need not be afraid of anything.[20]

The High Commissioner in Cape Town then replied directly to Lerotholi to reassure the Paramount Chief:

> I understand your wishes and at the proper time and place I will bring forward your words and will if necessary, give you advices to the best manner of letting the King's Government know what is in your heart. There is no word of any alteration in the affairs of Basutoland. I believe the welfare of yourself and your people is quite safe and I tell you now (as I have always told you) that the dangers I fear are among yourselves and will not appear from outside. There must be peace inside Basutoland. People like Moeketsi & Koadi will kill the Country if not rebuked.[21]

The issue remained unresolved for more than five years. Neither Queen Victoria nor Paramount Chief Lerotholi would live to see the provisions finally adopted in 1909 that culminated in the formation of the Union of South Africa in May 1910. But Lerotholi pressed the government to prevent incorporation to the last. On 30 June Lord Selborne wrote from the High Commissioner's office in Johannesburg to reassure him:

> I receive with satisfaction your assurance of the loyalty of yourself and the Basotho to His Majesty King Edward.
>
> I confirm the letters you have recently received assuring you of the intention of His Majesty to continue to protect and preserve the Basuto. . . . I hope to hear always that you and the Basuto are continuing to obey the law, that you are listening to the instructions of the Resident Commissioner and the officers of Government and that you are keeping peace in Basutoland.[22]

When Lerotholi died in 1905 his son and heir, Letsie II, known popularly as Letsienyana, assumed the office of Paramount Chief and led his country's efforts to prevent incorporation. In response to a letter he wrote to the High Commissioner, Resident Commissioner Herbert Sloley replied:

> He [the High Commissioner] directs me to inform you that no alteration in the position of Basutoland can be made except by the authority of King Edward VII and of the British Parliament and that you need not be apprehensive of any sudden alteration in the relations between Basutoland and the other South African Colonies.[23]

Letsienyana's fears were not assuaged. In mid-1908 he wrote to the Resident Commissioner:

> I see in newspapers a scheme for the unification of the South African governments. . . .
>
> The preservation and government of us Basuto differs from those of other colonies. Are we of Basutoland also thought of in this unification?[24]

The Paramount Chief and his advisers wanted to send a deputation to England to make their case directly against incorporation into the pending Union. Events then moved more quickly than even the High Commissioner had expected. In early October the Resident Commissioner told the Paramount Chief and other chiefs that the High Commissioner said it was too soon to send a deputation, as the process would take at least two more years.[25] Only two months later, however, Letsienyana was told by Wroughton, now Acting Resident Commissioner, that the time had arrived:

> I have returned from Johannesburg where I saw Lord Selborne, who gave me a message which he wished me to communicate to

yourself, your brother and uncles and the other chiefs of Basutoland for the information of the nation. One part of the message
was that he had promised to watch the course of affairs in South
Africa and would let you know when the time had arrived for you
to send a deputation to England to the King if you still wished to
do so. He has now directed me to say that the present is a good
time, and that the sooner the deputation leaves the better, if it is
going. He wishes me to see you and make all arrangements, and
wishes the deputation if possible to start within a week or two.[26]

In the end the deputation went, together with deputations from the
two other High Commission Territories, and all three countries (Basutoland, Swaziland, and Bechuanaland) successfully avoided being incorporated into the new Union of South Africa. The Basutoland National
Council had been active in voicing its opposition in addition to the Paramount Chief. And Letsienyana, in a gesture typical of precolonial Ba-
Sotho discursive acts, had sent a distinctive gift to the King of England
that ensured his message would at least be heard. In mid-July 1909 the
Resident Commissioner informed the Paramount Chief:

> I have received this pony which is being sent by you to the King,
> and I am making arrangements for it to be sent to England by the
> Steamer leaving Cape Town next Wednesday. I advise that you
> send me a message to go with the horse, through the High Com-
> missioner, to the King.[27]

Less than five years later, when war broke out in Europe, the King
needed help from the colony he had thereby retained, as from the rest of
the British Empire. A year before the outbreak of World War I, Letsienyana, whose health had finally deteriorated from the effects of alcohol,
died of natural causes. After some controversy his brother Griffith was
named as his successor, and he led BaSotho efforts to demonstrate their
loyalty to Great Britain. They raised money for relief funds, as they
were encouraged to do by the Resident Commissioner, who did not expect they would be used in any actual fighting.[28] They responded to recruitment for jobs as laborers in the region, such as the workforce sent
to build a railway in Southwest Africa, which the South Africans had
easily captured from the Germans in 1915. They were, however, deeply
afraid of the ocean and reluctant to volunteer for overseas service, which
caused controversy in Lesotho when active recruitment subsequently
began of Africans from South Africa and the colonies of the region. Colonial officials in Lesotho requested the chiefs to recruit men for military
service abroad, but the response was poor. Colonial officials seemed to

think that they would respond when they found out they would be employed in a variety of support jobs and did not understand why turnout was low, oblivious that fear of the ocean was the reason for the lack of response to recruitment.[29] They also tried to reassure the BaSotho that they would be serving under sympathetic officers who were familiar with the BaSotho. On 21 February 1917 the British ship *Mendi,* carrying military recruits from South Africa and Basutoland to the Mediterranean theater of war, was struck near the Isle of Wight, killing 615 African recruits, including more than two dozen BaSotho men.[30] When word reached Basutoland on 8 March the worst fears of the BaSotho were confirmed, dooming the chiefs' recruitment effort.

Paramount Chief Griffith met with the other Principal chiefs, the "sons of Moshesh," to consider recruitment for service abroad. After a series of letters caused a growing frustration on the part of the Resident Commissioner, Paramount Chief Griffith wrote him and indicated that the chiefs were able but reluctant to send men into military service, but those men would not be volunteers. The Resident Commissioner's use of language in his initial communications with the chiefs had allowed for ambiguity: he had asked them to raise men for the *letsema* of the King of England. The chiefs did have this prerogative of requiring men to work their fields in a work party, or *letsema,* for which the compensation was food for the workers. Such work, however, was obligatory, not voluntary. The Resident Commissioner had stressed the voluntary nature of recruitment, but the chiefs, facing a reluctant pool of possible recruits, wanted to be ordered to order their men to sign up for service.[31]

Alerted by a letter from them that Griffith and the chiefs were afraid they were being threatened with punishment if they failed to recruit the men, the Assistant Commissioner, James C. Macgregor, reassured them, but this reassurance did not improve recruiting.[32] Resident Commissioner R. T. Coryndon took the issue to the Basutoland National Council, which he called to meet him in March 1917.[33] Then Macgregor became Acting Resident Commissioner and pressed the issue directly with the Paramount Chief as well as other chiefs, but to little avail.[34] He did not believe the chiefs were unable to recruit their men for service in Europe, eventually prompting him to write a scathing letter, full of the tropes of colonial discourse, "To the Paramount Chief and Chiefs of the Basuto":

> You all know what the King's Government has done for you since it
> heard the cry of Moshesh and stood between him and his enemies

and has preserved his children up to this day. Now to-day the King calls on you Chief Griffith who are his servant to send him some men for his work. You [Griffith] gave your answer at the National Council and you chiefs gave yours. It was a good answer which the King had the right to expect from the children of the man whom his Grandmother, the Great Queen, saved from extinction. . . . Show the world that the Queen made no mistake when she took your father under her protection. . . . The chieftainship of the Ba-suto is on trial today. . . . Are you to be the only black people in South Africa to refuse the King's invitation [memo ea Morena]? . . . I now leave you to your deliberations with the earnest prayer that you may be guided aright in this crisis of your nation's welfare.[35]

The chiefs, however, were explicit in their reply that people were not unwilling to work, they were unwilling to take the ocean trip for overseas work.[36] Finally, the colonial officials took the recruitment out of the hands of the chiefs and allowed labor recruiters who touted for the mines to take over the job of recruitment.[37] For some reason their efforts were more successful, and after almost fourteen hundred men were recruited for overseas service by the labor touts, in December 1917 recruitment was ended.[38] At the end of the war a contingent of veterans came back to Lesotho with a new understanding of Europe, the British, and the rest of the world.

Political changes across the border in South Africa kept the Ba-Sotho wary of possible incorporation into the Union and abandonment by Great Britain, which was periodically proposed by South African governments for the next few decades. This was not an idle threat. The rapprochement between former and future Prime Minister Jan Smuts, head of the South Africa Party, and incumbent Prime Minister James Barry Hertzog, head of the National Party, led to the reunification of their political parties in 1933–34. Emboldened, Hertzog actively pursued the issue of the incorporation of the three High Commission Territories in 1934. In response, Westminster published the six-page *Memorandum Prepared by the Parliamentary Committee for Studying the Position of the South African Protectorates*. The Statute of Westminster of 1931 and the South African Status Act of 1934 repealed provisions of the 1909 South Africa Act that were reserved for consideration and approval or disapproval by the King in conjunction with the Privy Council and by implication the British Parliament. The memorandum concluded that with regard to the "transfer" issue, or incorporation of the three High Commission Territories, the prerogative of the King, Privy

Council, and Parliament to determine the issue had not been rescinded, and the South African government could not effect such a transfer without London's approval.[39] The committee itself was chaired by Lord Selborne, who had been High Commissioner at the time of the negotiations for and creation of the Union of South Africa, and its opinion was decisive.

The promise of Westminster and British MPs to take into consideration the opinions and wishes of the people of Basutoland, Swaziland, and Bechuanaland in any such decision prompted a public response in London and southern Africa. In Lesotho the issue was covered closely in the pages of the *Leselinyana,* and Tshekedi Khama, Chief and Regent of Bechuanaland, wrote the nineteen-page *Statement to the British Parliament and People,* published in London by the Anti-Slavery and Aborigines Protection Society, which had taken up the cause.[40] Even Lord Frederick Lugard, famous for leading military expeditions and establishing British colonial administrations in Uganda and Nigeria in the 1890s and early 1900s, published two articles in the *Manchester Guardian* in response. He both commended Khama's statement and asserted that although the time was not right for transfer and incorporation, the "British Government" should recognize "unequivocally" its intention of eventually transferring the three territories to South Africa.[41] The issue was explicitly raised toward the end of World War II, in 1944, and again in the mid-1950s.[42] By then, however, politics in South Africa had taken a dramatic turn, making incorporation more objectionable than ever to the peoples of Lesotho, Botswana, and Swaziland, who followed the path of independence of Britain's African colonies in the 1950s with the creation of legislative councils and adoption of a series of constitutions, culminating in full independence in 1966 and 1967. The fear of a worse fate under the rule of white-ruled South Africa that had kept the BaSotho obedient to British colonial rule in the nineteenth century continued to do so in the twentieth century.

Chiefs and Chieftaincy

The Paramount Chief was the most prominent symbol of the nation and of the survival of the nation, carrying with the office not only territorial and economic security but also the preservation of the core of SeSotho culture. Even as the abuses of individual chiefs brought complaints of oppression, the importance of the institution of chieftaincy overrode political differences as the BaSotho negotiated their status with their British colonial rulers.

The BaSotho were proud of Lerotholi. He was a war hero and had guided the nation through treacherous and dangerous times and events. When he died it was a foregone conclusion that his son Letsienyana, born in 1867, would succeed him. Lerotholi had no sons born in the first house of his first wife, so it was the first son of his second house who was his unquestioned heir throughout his life and who inherited his position when he died in 1905. Letsienyana, however, set up housekeeping with a woman ineligible to become his wife, and at the time of his death on 28 January 1913 his only legal male heir by a legally recognized wife, a boy named Tau, was less than three years old, necessitating a regency in the paramountcy until he came of age.[43] His uncle, Letsienyana's full brother Griffith Lerotholi, was approached to become regent but was reluctant because he was equally eligible to inherit his brother's position in his own right. The negotiations are well known in SeSotho lore, since Griffith used the metaphor of sitting on the stool of the paramountcy with "both buttocks," when he insisted that he himself be chosen as the new Paramount Chief. The young child died suddenly before the issue was decided, however, and the Principal chiefs known as the "Sons of Moshoeshoe" who had responsibility for the selection agreed that aside from Griffith there was no other possible choice for the paramountcy.[44]

It is not without reason that some BaSotho regarded the deaths of both Letsienyana and his small heir with suspicion. The British Resident Commissioner attended Letsienyana's funeral, which he described in a letter to the High Commissioner for South Africa. He had used the occasion to dispel any rumors that the death of the Paramount Chief might have been suspicious, since it had occurred while he was across the border on the farm "Runnymede" in the Orange Free State. Letsienyana was known to be in the habit of crossing the border to socialize and drink heavily, so his death at the young age of forty-five was not surprising to those who knew him. More surprising, however, was the information in this letter that at the time of his death he had been accompanied by his two uncles Chiefs Mojela and Maama, both of whom took primary roles in addressing the many thousands who attended the funeral at Thaba Bosiu. Both of these senior royal chiefs stated explicitly that the colonial government should support Griffith to become the next Paramount Chief:

> On conclusion of the service the Chief Moyela spoke, the Chief Griffith who sat beside me declining on the plea of illness—I think it would have been in any case unusual for him to have spoken in the circumstances. He related the facts of Letsie's illness as known by him, thanked the [colonial] Government for all that had been

done, and finally asked for Government support and encouragement for this "boy" indicating the Chief Griffith. The Chief
Maama followed in similar strain also commending the Chief
Griffith to the care of the Government. One other Chief only
spoke—Leshope from the Leribe District. He said very little
merely lamenting the death of Letsie and beseeching the Government to help and care for the Chief Griffith.[45]

The message was not lost on the Resident Commissioner, who also
reacted to the deferential tone of these speeches in the way that the discourse of the colonized chiefs was no doubt intended:

The fact that the only Chiefs who spoke all referred in this way to
Griffith shows that there must be a very large section of the Nation, even if it is not unanimous, in favour of his being chosen as
Paramount Chief. The other impressions the speeches left upon
me was the loyalty and trust felt for the Government and the feeling of dependence upon its help and guidance.[46]

Following formal protocols, the Resident Commissioner wrote to the
"Sons of Moshoeshoe" and asked about the plans were for the installation, or *peo*, of Chief Griffith and received a response from Maama on
17 March. By that time, then, the choice was already a foregone conclusion in the mind of the Resident Commissioner, even before this had
been confirmed formally by the Principal chiefs. Chief Maama told him
that they (presumably, he and Chief Mojela) had sent to the three senior
chiefs Masopha (a son of Joseph Molapo), Leshoboro (senior son of
Majara Moshoeshoe), and Peete (senior son of Moshoeshoe's favored
nephew Lesaoana Makhabane). Evidently they had not been previously
consulted, and "they say they know that there is no other besides Griffith," which merely left the date of installation to be decided.[47]

Accordingly, Griffith, born three years after his brother in 1871
and named after Basutoland's first Governor's Agent, Col. Charles D.
Griffith, was installed as Paramount Chief on 11 April 1913. Paramount
Chief Griffith's personality was indeed reflected in the metaphor and
circumstances of inheritance with which he is so closely associated:
strong willed, ambitious, and shady. There is no question that he had
been groomed for the position by the chiefs and that he would protect
the nation. He projected this to the BaSotho, winning him respect and
loyalty but also fear among other chiefs and the people. When he was
dealing with another crisis caused by Jonathan, late in Jonathan's life, in
the Leribe District, he wrote to the Resident Commissioner insisting

that he be consulted on all important matters affecting the welfare of the nation:

> Of all matters that may concern me here in Basutoland, there is
> nothing more serious than this of the land [mobu, or soil], which is
> my inheritance [lefa]; when a man thinks of taking and going his
> own way with the land and the people who live upon it—it is a
> matter of much more importance to me than his direct reference
> to me in his first letter. Let a man say anything direct [i.e., critical]
> of me, but if he does not touch [trouble] the land and the people
> who live upon it, he will still have respected me.[48]

The well-known and prolific Catholic missionary Father François Laydevant, O.M.I., who had known Chief Griffith since the time of Griffith's conversion and acceptance into the Catholic Church in 1912, was persuaded years later to write a biography of the Paramount Chief that appeared in 1953, after the chief's death.[49] The conversion of the brother of the Paramount Chief had been a momentous achievement for the Catholic missionaries in Lesotho, and they played important advisory roles to Griffith throughout the remainder of his long life. It is not surprising, then, that Father Laydevant's biography portrays Griffith in a favorable light. Griffith was sent by his father to be raised by his uncle Bereng Letsie in Masite, where he was first introduced to Christianity through the Anglican mission there. He was then sent to an Anglican mission school for a year but was unhappy and left before learning to read and write. Subsequently, Griffith was sent to the traditional *mophato*, the schooling for older boys in preparation for circumcision rites and acceptance into society as adult men. Years later, after his conversion to Catholicism, Griffith learned to read and write (in SeSotho), and Laydevant says that he loved to read.[50]

Griffith married his first wife in about 1895, and his father, Paramount Chief Lerotholi, arranged for the nation to pay the bridewealth for this wife, which indicated to the nation that her firstborn son would be considered his legitimate heir even if a wife married subsequently bore a son prior to the birth of the designated heir.[51] Griffith's older brother and Lerotholi's heir, Letsienyana, had been "placed" at Likhoele, so Griffith was sent with his new wife and his agemates to establish his authority and build a village at Phamong among the BaPhuthi in the Quthing District, where he encountered considerable resistance from the descendants of the old chief, Moorosi. He and his companions gained a reputation for wild and irresponsible behavior and for drinking too much alcohol. Rinderpest, the deadly cattle epizootic that swept across eastern and southern Africa in the 1890s, struck the herds of the BaSotho soon after Griffith's arrival in Quthing, and in this mountainous area BaSotho suspicions were raised on both sides of the border by the activities of colonial authorities, who built fences to prevent border crossings of cattle and the spread of the disease. Lerotholi was forced to intervene when Griffith and his friends were rumored to be talking of open rebellion against the colonial government, and his reputation for wild behavior followed Griffith for the next few years. However, he answered the call to military duty with his men in 1898, and he gained fame for his strong role in suppressing Masopha's rebellion against his father.

The proximity of Quthing to rebellious chiefs across the border in the Cape Colony had sporadically prompted coordinated plans for rebellions, most of which never materialized. The chief of the AmaMpondomise, Mhlontlo, then spelled Umhlohlo or (in SeSotho) Mohlohlo, had engaged in rebellion against the Cape Colony at the time of the Gun War in 1880 and had killed their colonial magistrate, Hamilton Hope, along with everyone else in the colonial office except a missionary.[52] Mhlontlo was forced to flee and seek protection from BaSotho chiefs in Quthing, where he remained in refuge for twenty years. Laydevant includes this information not merely because Griffith encountered him when he went to Quthing in 1895 but because ultimately, troubled by his past, Mhlontlo had sought out the Catholic missionaries who had converted him to Christianity. He was caught by Cape Colony authorities in 1903 and tried for his crimes in 1904, and he served two years in prison for ordering the murders of Hope and other colonial officials many years earlier. According to Laydevant, Mhlontlo's conversion to Christianity and to Catholicism in particular ultimately influenced Griffith to learn more about the Catholic Church, as his previous experience with Christianity had been with the Anglican Church and the French Protestant missionaries.[53]

During the Anglo-Boer War Griffith found himself suppressing a rebellion of Moorosi's grandson Mocheko, who was ultimately confined to the Maseru District and prohibited from ever returning to Quthing.[54] These events put Griffith into regular contact with both his father, the Paramount Chief, and the colonial authorities in Maseru, and he brought this experience with him when he became one of his elder brother's closest advisers upon the latter's accession to the paramountcy in 1905. It was his role in advising Letsienyana from 1905 to 1913 that made him the heir presumptive when Letsienyana died and was mourned by thousands at Thaba Bosiu.

Events, and BaSotho discourse regarding them, surrounding the inheritance of the paramountcy highlight the stratagems and mechanisms of power employed by BaSotho chiefs in the internal politics of twentieth-century colonial Lesotho. Long before his own death in 1905 Lerotholi had taken an intense interest in the inheritance of the paramountcy, which was essential for the preservation of the nation, and became concerned when his own first son and heir, Letsienyana, did not produce a male heir. Therefore, when Griffith's first wife, 'MaBatho, failed to produce a male child, Lerotholi arranged for the nation to pay bridewealth for a second wife, Sebueng, whom he hoped would bear a male heir for Griffith. Griffith's heir, born to the wife for whom the nation paid bridewealth, would inherit his status as a Principal chief and, if Letsieyana failed to produce a legitimate male heir, stood also to inherit the paramountcy. Although Lerotholi could not have known that Letsieyana's only legitimate male heir would be only three years old at the time of Letsieyana's death and would die immediately thereafter, leaving Griffith instead as the successor, his actions were prescient, and the circumstances of Griffith's marriages subsequently became central to the designation of his heir to the Paramount Chieftaincy.

Sebueng, the second wife for whom the nation paid bridewealth in designation of a presumed male heir, was Griffith's cousin, and the arranged marriage was a disaster, such that Sebueng deserted her husband and returned to the village of her father, Nkoebe. The latter, who did not want to return the bridewealth in any event, invited Griffith to take another daughter of his, Sebueng's sister Tsebo, as a wife. However, when he visited Nkoebe Griffith was attracted to yet another of his daughters, Thakane, and took her back with him, with Tsebo to follow as yet another, more junior, wife. It was Sebueng's sister, favored by Griffith, who bore Griffith his first son, Bereng, and who hence became known as 'MaBereng. Having deserted Griffith, Sebueng stayed at her father's for over two years and bore a daughter, given the unusual name Aa, by another man who wished to marry her.[55] However, Sebueng subsequently returned to her house in Griffith's village and bore him a male child, her first son, Seeiso, from which is derived the name by which she is known, 'MaSeeiso. Ultimately, according to Laydevant, Griffith married twenty-six or twenty-seven wives before these polygamous arrangements created a personal dilemma for him when he wanted to be baptized and confirmed in the Catholic Church. Decades later Griffith would try to obscure the circumstances surrounding his early marriages in an attempt to usurp from the "Sons of Moshoeshoe" and the nation the prerogative of designating and selecting his heir.

Laydevant was present when Chief Griffith was baptized and admitted into the Catholic Church in Phamong in October 1912. His sympathetic narrative of the crises of conscience experienced by Griffith leading up to this ceremony reflects the oral traditions surrounding Griffith's personal life. Griffith first consulted with three of his most important advisers and then told the priest at the church in Phamong, Father Foulonneau (Filone), that he wished to convert and asked him how he could do so. The Catholic priests told Griffith that in addition to the problem of his drinking alcohol excessively, his polygamous marriages were an obstacle to his conversion; at that time Griffith had twenty-eight wives. He told the priests he was willing to set aside and divorce all of his wives but his two favorites, his first wife, 'MaBatho, who had never borne a son, being one of them. 'MaBatho had converted to Christianity in the French Protestant Church and did not want to convert to Catholicism. The Catholic Church in Lesotho did not allow its Catholic parishioners to divorce their first wife, who was considered the only legitimate wife by the church. The priest advised Griffith to continue attending church services and to pray to God to show him the light, an answer to his dilemma. According to the story relayed by Laydevant, the devout 'MaBatho did not want to be an obstacle to her husband's conversion and told him, "If I should be an obstacle to your conversion, I beg that God will take me from this earth."[56] That same day, it is said, after her husband left her to return to his house, there was a downpour of rain that swelled the rivers. 'MaBatho left her house, and while she was walking she fell down and injured herself badly, breaking her arm severely. The European doctor was called from the government camp at Moyeni. When he began to set her broken arm she quickly weakened and died. Fearful, he rode away immediately, leaving others to enter her house and find she had passed away. Griffith is said to have sincerely mourned her death, but he pursued his conversion to the church with the approval of his priest. A huge celebration was held after the ceremony in October 1912 to which his brother, the Paramount Chief, sent an uncle as his representative.[57] Six months later, Nathaniel Griffith Lerotholi became Paramount Chief of Lesotho.

Griffith led the country through the tensions of World War I only to be confronted once again with the issue of the possible incorporation of the three High Commission Territories (Basutoland, Bechuanaland,

and Swaziland) into the Union of South Africa, which during the war had loyally assisted in providing troops in the British seizure of German Southwest Africa and German Tanganyika. Like colonized Africans elsewhere on the continent, the Basutoland National Council saw the European discussions following the end of the war at Versailles and in Britain as providing an opportunity to present African claims for self-determination and remedies for past wrongs. The Paramount Chief made plans to go to England with a contingent of representatives of the nation to present the case of the BaSotho against incorporation into South Africa, but the Basutoland National Council wanted him to do more. It passed a resolution that the Paramount Chief should ask the British to pursue the restoration of territory that had been lost to the Orange Free State in the wars of the 1860s. The High Commissioner got early word of this possible request and used the Resident Commissioner as a channel to the Paramount Chief to discourage him from taking this step, indicating that it might become grounds for the cancellation of the Paramount Chief's meetings in London. Griffith was determined to make the case for the preservation of Basutoland independent from the Union of South Africa and made the politically astute choice to ignore the petition of the Basutoland National Council and its insistence that he carry the council's territorial demands to London. When the party of fourteen men went to London in 1919, Griffith took along his priest, and the nation survived yet another political storm.[58]

Griffith created a new firestorm in the internal politics of the nation in the mid-1920s, one that exposes the dynamics of discourse and power in the inner circle of the Principal chiefs. In a politically provocative move the Paramount Chief called several of his top advisers and sent them with his two eldest sons, Seeiso and Bereng, to see the Resident Commissioner in Maseru. There, as explicitly instructed, Griffith's advisers informed the Resident Commissioner that Bereng was Griffith's senior son and heir and that Seeiso was junior to him. Suddenly, the significance of the events of Griffith's first marriages came into sharp focus. Seeiso was the son of Griffith's second wife; Bereng, although older than Seeiso, was the son of his third wife, 'MaSeeiso's younger sister. Because Griffith's first wife in his first and senior house, 'MaBatho, had failed to bear him a son, and because the nation had also paid the bridewealth for the second wife, Sebueng, now called 'MaSeeiso after her son's given name, customary law assigned the status of legal heir to the eldest son of the second house. Since Griffith tried to appoint Bereng as his heir on the basis of legal arguments, he did not explain any other reasons for his preference. Seeiso, as the son of Griffith's second wife, had every reason to assume he was the legal heir and would inherit the paramountcy, and he was stunned by the unexpected announcement at the meeting, its purpose not having been previously revealed to him. Although the heir presumptive was commonly known from the time of the marriage of the senior wife, long before his birth, it was not custom or tradition to recognize and proclaim the legal heir to the paramountcy prior to the death of the incumbent. The final decision lay with the "Sons of Moshoeshoe," who represented the nation as a whole and who could prevent a senior son, if he were deemed incompetent, from inheriting the position. However, such announcements had been made in other chiefdoms that had come under British colonial rule in southern Africa, and the colonial government did not find it unusual, nor did the Resident Commissioner pronounce against Griffith's action as being contrary to SeSotho custom and practice.

As a consequence, Seeiso decided to call the Principal chiefs of the nation together to hear witnesses regarding the evidence and arguments regarding his claim to being Griffith's senior son and heir, contrary to his father's announcement. It seems Griffith was playing a deep game, and it is doubtful he expected this reaction. The role of the British colonial government in the appointment of the Paramount Chief had been strengthened at the time of his own installation, and he evidently thought that if he chose a propitious moment to proclaim his heir, he would gain official colonial approval and create a new precedent while ensuring his personal choice for the succession.

The Principal chiefs of the nation came together in Maseru and heard the evidence from witnesses during hearings that lasted about three months in late 1926. As justification for the hearings Seeiso claimed that he was "seeking an explanation" from his father for the overturning of his seniority. The hearings, described in detail in a series of articles in *Leselinyana,* were filled with drama, and the seriousness of the implications of the case brought out occasional moments of humor and of intimidation. Sometimes the meetings coincided with those of the Basutoland National Council, so that participants and witnesses were delayed or absent. Several chiefs questioned the purpose of the hearings, since the issue was not a court case. Many participants questioned the value of spending so much time debating the question of the seniority of Griffith's sons, since the chiefs held firmly to SeSotho customs, which precluded any formal or official announcement of the heir to the paramountcy prior to the death of the current Paramount Chief. As they made explicit in their comments, the position that any opinion rendered by the collected chiefs would be moot anyway was widely held by the chiefs in the room. As a result, some voiced their objections to the process and advised Seeiso that he should listen to and obey his father, the Paramount Chief.

The inhibitions of some speakers, given their unwillingness to contest the position of their Paramount Chief, were often in evidence. Indeed, whenever a witness contested the Paramount Chief's position Griffith immediately and vociferously attacked his testimony, which created an obvious atmosphere of witness intimidation. At the first few meetings the moderator questioned why no one was coming forward to testify and frequently asked where witnesses were. In some cases they had not been called, in some they had not responded to the call, and in others vital witnesses were no longer living. This seems to have been an underlying factor in the timing of Griffith's announcement, since his deceased father (Lerotholi) and his father's advisers, most of whom were deceased by 1926, would have been able to provide the most serious evidence contesting the case he was trying to make. It was evident during the hearing that those elderly men of Lerotholi's court who were still alive and testified commanded great respect among the chiefs at hand, and they used polite and oblique statements to reinforce evidence and arguments that contested the position of Paramount Chief Griffith and supported that of Seeiso.

Reports on the hearings indicate an attempt was made to be thorough in the collection and consideration of all evidence and provide insights into various BaSotho perspectives about both the historical events under consideration and the proceedings themselves. Some written statements had been taken and were read to the hearing, allowing for complete and carefully considered responses to be submitted and responses from persons unable to attend. The appropriateness of allowing any of the women, whose testimony was vital, to attend in person was debated, but women were not permitted to testify, and their testimony was only referred to in passing, as customary, by others (men) in their absence. Most witnesses were chiefs or their counselors, but others played important roles in facilitating the proceedings, and occasionally a commoner who had played an important part in the marriages at issue testified about his actions and knowledge of events that had occurred more than twenty years earlier. A smattering of proverbs appear in the testimony: one person proffered the advice, in English, to "look before you leap." One witness, after presenting some testimony, declined to answer

further questions because he refused to be interrupted like a bunch of
fighting cats. Under the circumstances it is perhaps surprising that there
were sufficient witnesses willing to go on record to support Seeiso's position of seniority, and the preponderance of the evidence in the end
weighed against the position of Paramount Chief Griffith.

Griffith stated his legal position and sustained it consistently, claiming that because 'MaBereng had come as a replacement for 'MaSeeiso
she had taken her position and acquired her status as second wife and
that 'MaSeeiso had thereby fallen to the ranking of third wife. Several
key issues were raised with regard to the question of the ranking of the
two wives and of the seniority of the two sons as heir to Griffith. Considerable time and energy was devoted to the question of the payment
of the bridewealth, since it was a clear determinant of the ranking of
the wives. All were in agreement that 'MaBatho was Griffith's first wife
and that the second wife he took was Sebueng, that is, 'MaSeeiso. The
legal arguments hinged on whether or not Griffith and Sebueng had
been divorced legally when she deserted him and lived at her father's
village for two or three years, bearing the illegitimate daughter. Since
Griffith insisted that Sebueng's sister had assumed her place and rank, it
was necessary that he argue that they had been divorced and that the
bohali, or bridewealth, that had been paid originally by the nation on
behalf of Sebueng to her father was understood to have become the
payment for her younger sister. Griffith therefore tried to prove that no
bohali had been paid for 'MaBereng and that she had been a replacement, literally, for her older sister.

The evidence for Griffith's case was unconvincing. One witness insisted he knew that Sebueng was divorced when she lived at her father's
place because she began using the name of her father-in-law (Paramount
Chief Lerotholi), which was strictly forbidden to daughters-in-law, according to the rules of etiquette of respect, or *hlonepho.* This evidence of
Sebueng's behavior was not convincing, since Sebueng obviously had
wished to be divorced and had made every effort to bring about a legal
divorce. She had fallen in love with a man in her father's village who requested to marry her and who was the father of her daughter, but Griffith himself forbid it, insisting she was still his wife and could not be
married to another man. When the question had been raised with Paramount Chief Lerotholi he was adamant that the divorce was impossible,
that since he had collected and paid the bridewealth for the family and
the nation Sebueng was his wife, her children would be his, and no alter-
ation in the arrangements was possible. Her continued efforts to obtain

a divorce provides further convincing evidence that she never was divorced and was not considered to be by her own husband, Griffith, at the time.

As for the *bohali* for 'MaBereng, Griffith admitted that she had been taken in an elopement, or *chobeliso,* and he that he had paid four head of cattle for, as others said, having "stolen" her. This would not have been necessary had she been considered at the time to be replacing Sebueng as the wife for whom the nation had already provided bridewealth. Since her sister, the third daughter to marry Griffith, had also followed her to Phamong to be married, a dowry was indeed later paid for two daughters, as testimony showed. Griffith tried to argue that the double dowry was for the youngest of the three sisters and for a second dowry for Sebueng in a second marriage to him. Numerous witnesses who would have known about the arrangements, said by Griffith to have been made between himself and his wives' father, had never, in more than twenty years since, heard of the formal reversal in ranking of the two daughters. On the contrary, when Griffith's first wife, 'MaBatho, died, it was Sebueng who replaced her by moving into the house that had been built for the senior wife, signifying an understood replacement in ranking to that of first wife.

Other evidence did not weigh as heavily but was given consideration. Seeiso claimed that his father had given him Moshoeshoe's staff of office to signify his position as heir, but Griffith claimed it was a different staff. Several credible witnesses described how they had been called by Lerotholi to come to his court at the birth of his first male grandchild, Bereng, at which time Lerotholi declared that he now had an heir, and it was Bereng. This was discounted, since any such declaration had to be taken in context: at that time none of Letsienyana's wives had yet borne a legal heir for the paramountcy, which Letsienyana would inherit, and neither the first nor the second wife given by Lerotholi to his second son, Griffith, for whom the nation had paid *bohali* had yet borne a son. It was understood by the chiefs that Lerotholi had become desperate to see an heir born in his grandchildren's generation; the chiefs referred to the illicit relationship of Letsienyana as being with his *nkhono,* or grandmother, because Letsienyana had unfortunately fallen in love with a woman of his own generation but who was legally a very junior wife of his deceased grandfather Letsie I. The male child she had borne by Letsienyana could not be a legal heir of Letsienyana because legally he was considered to be a son of Letsie. The unspoken sentiment of the chiefs was that it was no wonder Lerotholi had celebrated the birth of his first grandson, Bereng, with a declaration that would become moot, however, with the birth of a younger but senior son of a senior wife. The chiefs did not accept Griffith's argument that he and 'MaSeeiso had been divorced and married a second time or that it was possible that 'MaBereng could have taken 'MaSeeiso's place as the second-ranked wife. But the hearings ended with the court telling Seeiso, you asked for an explanation to be made and evidence to be heard regarding your father's reasons for declaring you to have lost your seniority to your brother Bereng, and you have heard the explanations. Seeiso replied that he had heard the evidence that indicated there was no substance to the challenge of his seniority, but, as he was but a child, he could do nothing about it. The ambiguity with which the Principal chiefs worded their answer and with which Seeiso replied was in accord with BaSotho discourse surrounding serious political controversy. With that the hearings ended.[59]

Perhaps Seeiso was prescient after all. His father had wanted to create a record with the colonial government declaring Bereng as his heir to the paramountcy. Seeiso did not have grounds for a court case, but he could ask for explanations in a formal context and thereby involve all of the senior chiefs in the controversy. He was fortunate that his father had not delayed any later his unprecedented announcement of an heir, thus prompting the hearings; more than twenty years had passed since the marriages of the two wives, and already many witnesses were dead and could not testify. Griffith was to live thirteen more years, still insisting that Bereng was his heir, but it was the Principal chiefs, meeting in Maseru in 1939 with both Seeiso and Bereng making their claims to the paramountcy, who would have the final word after Griffith, as Laydevant says, fell into his final sleep on 23 June 1939.

Colonial Readjustment: The Paramountcy and Administrative Reforms

Not surprisingly, the succession to the Paramount Chieftaincy was contested after Griffith died in 1939. The two rival claimants, Seeiso and Bereng Griffith, whose cases had been heard in 1926, both now expected to inherit their father's position. Tradition ideally called for the nation to choose the Paramount Chief, and where there was no controversy, the Principal chiefs could be taken to speak for the nation. But this time people poured into Maseru for three days and waited without food to indicate both their opposition to Bereng and their support for Seeiso.[60]

The majority of the Principal chiefs also supported Seeiso, and only because the Government Secretary, Douglas W. How, accompanied Bereng was he allowed to speak at all; the chiefs tried to shout him down.

Seeiso was selected in August and installed as Paramount Chief
in September 1939. As World War II broke out in Europe he enthu-
siastically raised money to pay for a squadron of planes for the Royal
Air Force in Britain, and he was awarded the King's Medal for African
Chiefs. But the popular Paramount Chief died unexpectedly on 27 December 1940 at the young age of thirty-six after having held office for
just over a year. He had undergone emergency surgery, and the medical
evidence was that he died of gangrene, but it was widely believed that
he was poisoned. Rumor had it that both Bereng and Seeiso were in
love with one of their father's young widows and that Bereng had her
poison Seeiso. True or not, it is evidence that much of the nation did
not trust Bereng to the point of assuming he might have murdered his
half-brother.

The nation was swept up in the meantime by the imperatives of
World War II. BaSotho troops were recruited with other Africans into
the African Auxiliary Pioneer Corps, and many were stationed in the
Middle East, where they were led by some familiar officers, including
Lt. Col. Douglas W. How, their former District Commissioner, who lost
his life in service in the Middle East in 1942.

The succession to the paramountcy in 1940 was contested for the
second time in less than two years. There were two possibilities: Seeiso's brother Bereng in his own right or the senior son of Seeiso, also
confusingly named Bereng, who would require a regent to serve until he
reached his majority.[61] Once again the nation and chiefs objected to the
placing of Bereng and had Seeiso's senior son named as heir to the paramountcy. This led to a dispute over who would serve as regent, a cru-
cial question, since the heir was just two and a half years old; the regency would last for over fifteen years. In effect the regent would rule as
long as would a Paramount Chief in his own right. Over the next several years the claims of other potential heirs were raised, including that
of Leshoboro, Seeiso's son from his third wife, and, in what would have
set new legal and historical precedents, Seeiso's daughter Ntsebo by his
first wife, Amelia, who was therefore known as 'Mantsebo for the rest of
her public life.

Upon the declaration of the two-and-a-half-year-old son of Seeiso
as heir to the paramountcy, the two people considered for regent were
the late Paramount Chief's half-brother Bereng Griffith and the senior

wife and widow of the deceased Paramount Chief Seeiso, 'Mantsebo. Many assumed that the infant heir might die mysteriously, as had the infant son of Letsienyana in 1913. Since some people believed, rightly or wrongly, that Bereng's father, Griffith, had arranged for the death of his tiny nephew Tau in 1913 and that Bereng himself had poisoned his half-brother Seeiso, they were certainly able to believe that he might see to it that the two-and-a-half-year-old heir would lose his life in an "accident" before long, leaving the uncle Bereng as heir in his own right.

The alternative created something of a complication, however. Paramount Chief Seeiso's senior wife had never borne a son, only a daughter, Ntsebo, but the second and third wives had sons. It was the son of the second wife who was chosen as heir, although some people preferred Leshoboro, the son of the third wife, because she was of richer royal blood. In any event, the widow who was proposed to serve as regent was 'Mantsebo rather than the mother of the heir, and the mother of the heir, like the heir himself, was to be placed under the power of the regent. So it is possible to delineate the deeply divided and contradictory interests of the two major players in this contest: Bereng Griffith, who still aspired to the paramountcy himself, and 'Mantsebo, who harbored ambitions for her own daughter as heir. The claims of the son Leshoboro also continued to be voiced sporadically over the next two decades. The British colonial government did not consider 'Mantsebo to be qualified for the position, but they acquiesced, and they appeared to prefer her as a weak regent, which would allow them to push through their own reform agenda without strong opposition.

Bereng Griffith contested 'Mantsebo's appointment as regent in a case brought before the newly established High Court, and the British made a special appointment to ensure the legal decision carried the weight of an experienced judge. In the end Bereng's case was rejected, and 'Mantsebo was reconfirmed as Regent Paramount Chief in 1943.[62] The issues raised against her claim included that a woman could not in her own right serve as a chief, which she would be, de facto, because of the long duration of the regency; that a woman was subject to the control of her husband's male relatives and could not be given separate powers; and that, according to the *kenelo* custom, a widow was bound to accept, as a replacement for her husband, a male relative who would make legal decisions concerning her property, even if she refused that male relative access to her bed. But it was easy enough to find historical precedents for women serving as regents for their sons and even for women serving as chiefs in their own right, having been appointed by their fathers (less commonly) or having replaced their husbands even when there was no son to become heir someday. The court decision by Judge C. W. H. Lansdown further ruled that the *kenelo* custom was rarely followed anymore and that women were certainly not compelled to accept it.

But further arguments can be made that illustrate the complexities that were soon to arise. First, it is clear that Seeiso's brother did not have to take over Seeiso's wives, and the historical precedent was that this was done only if a chief lacked an heir. If there was a male heir, in fact, a chief's wife would never follow the *kenelo* custom, for it was assumed that a new male child would be produced who would have a living father to help him assert his claim to inheritance of the chieftainship over the first, legitimate heir. So according to historical precedent, the practice of *kenelo* in this instance would have been prevented. More important, however, is the fact that this case did set a new precedent, even though women had served as regents before (although never for the paramountcy, except in 1813, before the BaSotho nation came into existence). What was new was that the female regent was not the mother of the heir. This is the key point: the historical reason for appointing a woman as regent was to protect the line of inheritance for her son, and it was assumed that only she, together with her own brothers and male relatives by blood, would have an incentive to protect the heir. Further, it was assumed that the male relatives of her late husband would themselves have intentions to inherit, and the life of the male heir would be in danger. In this case the regent, 'Mantsebo, had no reason to want to protect the interests of the heir, her husband's son by another woman, or even his life. She actually indicated her belief that her own daughter should have been entitled to inherit, and she needed to protect the heir only as long as there was another claimant to the regency; once Bereng was out of the way, there was no reason why she should would want to see the heir, her temporary ticket to power, protected. According to custom, then, the heir should have been put into the protection and hands of his own blood relatives on his mother's side, and although 'Mantsebo was the senior wife, the heir's mother would have been just as legitimate as regent and would have protected his interests more fully.

Paramount Chief Griffith had passed away just as the nation was facing an era during which significant changes in the British colonial administration of Basutoland created political turmoil among the chiefs and the country at large. The Resident Commissioner and the Basutoland National Council had begun discussing the need for administrative changes in the 1920s, and the famine crisis of 1933 brought on by severe drought induced the colonial government to bring in A. W. Pim to survey the financial affairs of the colony and make recommendations. His 210-page study, *Financial and Economic Position of Basutoland,* commonly known as the Pim Report, appeared in January 1935 and provided the colonial government with justification to make reforms after little consultation locally.[63] Although the Resident Commissioner is said to have consulted with Paramount Chief Griffith, and the Basutoland National Council discussed possible provisions for three days in 1937, the latter was taken by surprise as, over the next few years, it came to understand the ramifications of two new government proclamations, the Native Administration Proclamation No. 61 and the Native Courts Proclamation No. 62, both of 1938. These reforms, which have been discussed widely elsewhere, dramatically reduced the number of recognized chiefs at all levels eligible to exercise chiefly prerogatives of allocating land, holding court and adjudicating cases, and collecting revenues as income for performing their duties as chiefs. As a result of new colonial policies the country experienced struggles over the installment or "placing" of chiefs and headmen.

The beginning of World War II distracted the attention of the council from the proclamations, which were not then discussed until it met in session in December 1941. Lord William Malcolm Hailey, author of the foremost survey of Britain's colonial territories in Africa (1938) and another of the High Commission Territories, explains:

> In the Native Administration Proclamation the chief point which attracted comment was the provision that a Chief who ceased to be "recognized" would lose the powers vested in him under the Proclamation, and some surprise was expressed at the suggestion that a Chief could ever cease to be a Chief. . . . Only one member raised the point that the Proclamations had not been placed in draft before the Council for discussion.[64]

The colonial government proceeded to issue warrants to recognized or "gazetted" chiefs, subchiefs, and (village) headmen, no doubt in imitation of the created warrant chiefs elsewhere in British colonial Africa. The process was plagued with inconsistencies, and the list of 1,340 chiefs in 1948–49 differed significantly from those listed in 1939, demonstrating the powers retained by district-level Ward chiefs in selecting which of their subordinates would retain official recognition and the perquisites of office.[65] Furthermore, over the next few years all chiefs were prohibited from collecting revenues for themselves in the form of court fines and labor tribute and were instead placed on salaries that were significantly lower than the incomes they had previously enjoyed. A National Treasury was created, the better to control centrally the expenditure of revenues from taxes, and tensions between the competing powers of the colonial government, the Paramount Chieftaincy, Principal and Ward chiefs, village-level chiefs or headmen, and their people intensified in the 1940s.

The legal status of the Basutoland National Council and the laws it had encoded in 1903 (revised in 1922) came under scrutiny just at the moment of the crisis in the succession to the Paramount Chieftaincy that arose with the death of Seeiso Griffith. The so-called Regency Case, which was heard in the Basutoland High Court in 1942, was significant well beyond its specific ruling on the inheritance of the paramountcy at that moment because the judgment handed down in the case also stated that the "Laws of Lerotholi" were not legally binding. In supporting the appointment of 'Mantsebo against Bereng's challenge, Lansdown noted that women could (and did) hold the office of chief in the country and further ruled that "by statutory law the High Commissioner chose whom he pleased to be Regent."[66]

The convenient fiction of BaSotho self-governance came to an end with the formal negation of the legal status of the "Laws of Lerotholi," which had been used in the nineteenth century long before they were codified in 1903. These laws were now deemed to be, like the National Council, an indication of custom and advisory only within the system of British colonial rule and law. For decades the British had delegated primary responsibility for the maintenance of the rule of law to the chiefs. Now they expected chiefs to continue to maintain law and order even though they had declared that the laws the chiefs had been upholding had no actual legal status in the country. Perhaps it is no surprise that the rule of law broke down in Lesotho in the 1940s and 1950s and that in contests for power at the highest levels some chiefs turned to murder and terror.

9

Of Paramente and Power

Terror in Basutoland

Paramente screamed. He didn't stop screaming until someone held something under his nose, sending him into a stupor that ended his awareness and resistance and allowed his attackers to guide him, stumbling on his own feet, to the hut where they would keep him, drugged, until the next night. He must have known when he first saw them that there was only one reason why a large portion of the adult male population of the village would sit waiting for him to return home in the early hours of the morning. He didn't know it, but this was their second try: the previous night they had also lain in wait, but he had never come. After fate offered him a day's reprieve he was finally caught, aware only at the last moment that he was destined to be a victim of *liretlo*, or "medicine murder."[1]

In the 1940s BaSotho chiefs threatened by a loss of privilege and power abandoned the use of rhetoric, discourse, law, and the courts to achieve their ends and found ways to use fear to accomplish their goal of retaining their positions of authority and control. It was during the High Court case over the succession to the Paramount Chieftaincy that the greatest crisis of the colonial period emerged in Basutoland. The connection was not evident at the time, but by the end of the decade a pattern of suspicious deaths caused the British to begin a formal investigation into the causes of what came to be called medicine murder. In 1949 two Principal chiefs, the contender for the paramountcy, Chief Bereng, and a close supporter, Chief Gabashane, were hanged after their conviction for medicine murder. During my research on the case in which they were involved I met in the archival court documents this man named Paramente Khothatso, and I became more intimately acquainted with the events surrounding his death than I ever wished to be.

I learned, to my surprise, that Bereng and Gabashane were not hanged for Paramente's murder, which they committed in December 1946. Although they were eventually indicted for Paramente's murder, in March 1948 they committed another medicine murder, the third of three related cases, that of a man named 'Meleke Ntai, for which they were hanged. The dates are significant, because witnesses to the first crime did not have to believe in the efficacy of the medicine derived from the murder in order to be intimidated by the threat that they might become the next victim if they spoke. And it took the police a long time to crack the Paramente case; I believe two more murders were committed as a warning to remind people not to break down and talk. One witness was held for nine months after the first murder, and he would certainly have understood that if he talked he would soon be dead after he was released. He was released in August and immediately rearrested, which is when he broke down and talked. It turns out, as I discovered in adding up the dates, that that is when a second murder associated with these chiefs took place, as if they made a last-ditch attempt to silence the witnesses as the story came out almost a year after Paramente's murder. Gabashane but not Bereng was indicted for the second of these murders. Both men were attempting to enhance their political positions, as senior Principal chiefs, by means understood in a SeSotho discourse on power that asserted that strength could be obtained from "medicine horns" containing, among other ingredients, human flesh and blood.

Paramente's Murder

After Paramente was captured he was taken to a hut, kept there drugged for a day, and then moved to another hut, where he was brutally murdered in front of a crowd of involuntary witnesses under the watchful eyes of the chiefs who had ordered them to be there. The record of Preparatory Examination, signed by the District Commissioner on 24 February 1949, contains the testimony of the witnesses and participants. Mapeshoane Masopha explained how he had become a participant in the murder of Paramente Khothatso on 12 December (Tsitoe) 1946:

> We answered the call of the chief and went to the court where the
> Chief was—that is the three of us, and we found chief Gabashane
> No. 2 accused at the Court.
>
> No. 2 Accused then said No. 4 should disperse us and he
> thanked us but said the matter should be kept as a Chief's secret.
>
> I know now that I took part in a Ritual Murder in 1946. I did
> not know then why the deceased was being killed. I was just carry-
> ing out an order of my chief.[2]

This was the recurring testimony: that the orders to participate and
the orders to keep quiet came from Chief Gabashane and Chief Bereng. The participants similarly indicated their ignorance of what was
to happen and why. The extent of their ignorance cannot be gauged,
but in his testimony Mapeshoane stated that he had also been a defend-
ant in another case for a later murder, and "in that Murder it had been
announced to us that we were going to kill a man. In that case I knew we
were going to kill a person and that it was to be a ritual murder." But he
professed ignorance of what was to happen in the case of Paramente's
death:

> I later saw deceased dead that night. I had never seen such a thing
> done before as was done to him that night. I did not get a reply to
> the question I asked myself, "what do these people want to do this
> for." I did not ask my Chiefs or brothers, why this was being done,
> or what they were going to do with human flesh and skin. I asked
> nobody else about this and I did not discuss this with Bale (No. 19)
> or anybody else, although they were my friends. When this hap-
> pened in 1946, I had heard whispers about Ritual Murders but this
> was quite public in Basutoland. I had heard about Ritual Murders
> but I did not know what was done with the flesh etc. I know that
> people were arrested, charged and convicted and sentenced for
> Ritual Murder. I have heard it said that human flesh is used for
> filling Medicine horns. When I saw flesh being taken from the de-
> ceased I found that I had been taking part in a Ritual Murder.

There was consistency in the evidence presented at trial by many
witnesses whose testimony was corroborative in content and details that
implicated the senior chiefs. Malefane Sebatso reported that, "On that
Tuesday a man called Lazarus (No. 8 Accused) came to me after dark
and said that Chief Gabashane was calling me to the Court. I went with
Lazarus to the Court." Sebatso testified that when Paramente was kidnapped he had screamed repeatedly and shouted at his friend Lazarus
by name and that the group had sung a war song to cover up the sound

of the screams. Daniel Kome testified he had been ordered to participate in the capture and that when Paramente was surrounded

> [the] deceased screamed very loudly indeed and said "Lazarus my
> friend, why do you want to kill me" and said "J-o- here are people
> killing me cruelly"—we then sang a War song, which was sufficient
> to drown the screams. "Where does he go, 'Saule,'" was the song
> we sang. When we sing War songs ordinarily, it is not a sign for
> other people to come and join us, especially at night time.

Khabo Khomakatso reiterated what others had said about the capture.
Paramente cried out,

> "Is that you Lazarus, my friend, who is killing me?" Lazarus swore
> at him and said he was carrying out orders. Deceased cried out
> loudly and then a War song was sung to conceal the cries of the
> deceased.

Sotho Chela had also gone both evenings to capture Paramente, having
been called to the Chief's courtyard by Makiane Mpiko. Again, the tale
of the capture was heartrending:

> We caught him, myself included—I recognized him as Paramente.
> He did not submit quickly—he tried to escape but there were many
> of us. He cried loudly and said "Lazarus, my brother, why do you
> want to kill me." He said a lot and a War Song was started. Lazarus
> replied saying "I have caught you I am carrying out orders."

Like other witnesses, Chela testified that Majautu had made Paramente
smell a medicine, after which the screaming stopped; he added that
Paramente was forced to sniff it again at the hut of Letsatsi Piiti, where
he was taken and held for the day. Some witnesses who had not been
participants in the murder itself also testified to Paramente's terrible
screams at the time of his kidnapping.

A crowd of people was later ordered to appear at the hut where the
murder was to take place. Kome testified that he was coerced into
watching the murder against his will:

> When we entered the Hut No. 4 Accused [Makiane Mpiko] specif-
> ically told me and the others I have mentioned to remain in the
> hut. He just picked us out amongst all that were there. I and Mape-
> shoane were told not to go out of the hut, by No. 4 Accused. I do
> not know why we were picked upon. No. 4 is not my friend but my
> chief. I wanted to go out but No. 4 stopped me. I was tired and

frightened. When I went out the operation was finished. I did not
know why they put the skin and flesh into a Billy-can—that was the
first time I had seen, or heard, of this sort of thing being done.

Kome then provided details of the murder:

> At this time [in the hut] deceased was still alive but he was breathing
> slowly and appeared to be in a dream. No. 6 then started to cut. . . .
> I do not know when the deceased died. I went outside to pass water
> [urinate] after the fat had been taken out of the deceased. When the
> fat was removed deceased was still alive but he was speaking very
> feebly—he spoke like a person in a dream. This was after his tongue
> had been removed. I did not catch any of the words that he said.
>
> I noticed when some fat was cut from the side of the deceased
> that he then died as he did not move after that.

Like other witnesses, Sepalami Mothibe testified that he had been ordered to participate by Chief Gabashane and that he saw part of the
murder: "I saw No. 6 cutting the neck of my [wife's] Uncle—I cried."

Paramente's fate was graphically revealed by the report of the Medical Officer at Teyateyaneng, Robert Cuthbert:

> I formed the opinion that the skin had been removed from the
> head by a sharp instrument—I looked carefully for teeth marks of
> animals, but could find none. . . . The scalp was completely re-
> moved except for the narrow band of skin attached to the back of
> the head. . . . The tongue and everything from the top of the head
> to the neck had been completely removed—I presume with a sharp
> instrument—there were no teeth marks. The eyes were removed
> from their sockets. I found no wound consistent with the removal of
> some fat in the region of the kidneys. Haemorrhage must have
> been great if these wounds had been inflicted before death. There
> was no blood in the large blood vessels which means that the de-
> ceased died from haemorrhage.

Witnesses testified that the "operation," cutting flesh from the victim, had been performed by Michael Tseki, Accused No. 6. Cuthbert
confirmed that Tseki had, until his recent retirement on account of ill
health, served as the Medical Officer's Senior Dispenser, assisted at
postmortems, and retained access to all knives and chloroform from the
mortuary because he, along with the rest of the staff, had access to the
key that was kept in the Medical Officer's kitchen.

Kome spoke about both the terms under which witnesses were
bound and the threat that they faced if they broke their silence. The

threat was explicit: anyone who talked about the murder would suffer the same fate as Paramente:

> No. 4 [Mpiko] called No. 2 Accused from his house and the Chief [Gabashane] said, "You who are here, dare not speak about this: Those who speak about this will be treated in the same way as this young man."
>
> The Chiefs said we must not talk about this Murder. I obeyed my Chiefs in that respect. Since this Murder I have not told anybody about it, until I spoke to the Police I am sure I have not mentioned it to anybody since then. I have not even spoken to any of the others who took part in the Murder. I have never spoken to either of my wives about this.

Malefane Sebatso further testified that after the murder "we carried it [the body] to the Cannibals' place" and that Gabashane told them: "Whoever makes any report about this will be like the deceased." Confirming the previous testimony about the orders of the chiefs, the murder itself, and Gabashane's threat to kill anyone who talked, Beaumont Morese expressed clear reluctance and regret but said he would not have disobeyed his chief: "I was only obeying an order of my Chief in what I did—actually I did not approve of what was being done to the deceased and when I saw what was being done I was frightened."

Sepalami Mothibe confirmed that he helped carry the body out under orders and that afterward Gabashane told them that "there should be nobody who can mention this thing—whoever speaks about this will be like the deceased." Like others, Mothibe said he had no prior knowledge of what was going to happen, and his response to questioning suggests that he viewed his ultimate confession as a liberating experience:

> I was arrested on the 9th month of last year and I made a statement to the Police on the same day as I was arrested—I did not know then that I would be free if I made a statement but I thought that if I told the truth I would be free and even if it killed me I still wanted to tell the truth and so I made a statement to the Police and signed it the same day.

In response to questions Sotho Chela stated that he had participated against his will, and he directly implicated Chief Bereng:

> I knew the deceased very well, he was a friend of mine, a good friend. The name of the man we had to catch was not mentioned on the Tuesday night when we got our orders. I did not know then what was going to happen to that man and if I had known that he

was going to be caught and killed I would not have gone, even if I had been ordered to do so. I was afraid to run away after I saw what was being done to deceased because I was afraid of my chief. . . . At that particular time No. 1 Accused [Bereng Griffith Lerotholi] was staying at Mamathe's with No. 2 Accused [Gabashane]—I saw him there—I do not know how long he stayed there and I do not know when he left.

Khabo Khomakatso said he had been told that a man was to be killed, and he also placed Bereng Griffith, Gabashane Masopha, and Jonathan Masopha, in the courtyard as the original orders for the kidnapping were being given. This witness was also important in then placing each of the primary defendants—Bereng, Gabashane, Jonathan, and Mpiko—at the actual scene of the murder as it took place, saying the three chiefs "entered the hut and the work was started." He continued to indicate that each time the chiefs gave the orders

I stood at the door as the hut was full—there were many others outside. I heard an order given inside the hut—Nos. 1 and 2 held torches and then No. 1 [Bereng] said to No. 6 [Tseki] "cut him." I saw No. 6 start cutting the deceased. I became frightened and walked away. No. 6 started to cut him from the neck and I saw him cutting the skin from the face. . . . Deceased was dead when the cutting was being done.

Khomakatso's actions just after the murder also indicated that he had well understood the jeopardy in which he stood as a participant; he stated that he had "left for the Mines the day after deceased was killed." The prosecutor questioned why he had not left sooner, as his pass had been issued three days before the murder, and his words do not betray the remorse that was evident in other participants. He stated he was willing to follow any orders from his chief, even killing a man, but he was cognizant of the threat to his own life if he failed to follow orders.

Ralefika Kheme testified that "the deceased did not submit easily—he was fighting and struggling—he screamed when he saw he had been overpowered," and he corroborated previous statements that placed the three chiefs and Mpiko at the court both evenings when orders for the kidnapping and murder were given. He stayed through the entire killing and was able to provide a detailed description of the "operation" on the victim without indicating any unwillingness on his part to be a witness to the entire proceedings:

> Deceased had his eyes open and was placed on the skin—he screamed when he was placed on the skin [where the killing would take place]. No. 6 Accused [Tseki] then took up some medicine and made him smell it—thereupon the deceased seemed to become tired and he slept: the medicine had a smell, not a strong smell. . . . The deceased was still alive when this operation was over [the cutting of his head]. I did not hear deceased make any noise while this was going on, but he was kicking.

Two witnesses testified that they had helped to tan the hide on which the murder had been committed, destroying the evidence. Paramente's wife, Malino Khothatso, explained that he had gone out early that morning to look for his horse, which had broken loose, and she never saw him again. When she reported his disappearance to Mpiko he did not help search, and she had to pay Fusi Rakakola to search for him. The body was not found until Monday; there was no blood at the scene where it was recovered, and the flesh was peeling off badly in many parts. The belt and trousers disappeared from the evidence room at Teyateyaneng after they had been recovered with the body.

As a result of the Preparatory Examination four of the accused were discharged, and thirty-three were committed for trial. The testimony of the full trial took up 693 pages. Some were acquitted, while others were discharged, and a few were convicted of assault and accessory after the fact to a murder. The judge explained that he imposed these lesser convictions because chiefs had been known to order kidnappings that had not resulted in murder, and "I will not presume that when the deceased was kidnapped everyone there knew that it was preparatory to murder."

Jonathan Masopha, Gabashane's brother, was among those acquitted. The High Court concluded that Jonathan had not acted with guilty intent but rather under his brother's coercive influence:

> However, in the case of Jonathan, that is No. 3, we do know that he was in fear of his brother Gabashane, and anyone who knows anything about this country and who has had anything to do with this type of case knows that the first thing a man does when he is contemplating a murder of this kind is to endeavor to implicate those who might give evidence against him. . . . Whatever one may say with regard to his moral responsibility, in my opinion—and I may say in this judgement that I am giving the judgement of the whole Court—Jonathan was not there with any guilty intent; he was not

interested in his brother's medicine horn, or whatever it was, and
he is therefore acquitted.

By the time the judgment was handed down Gabashane and Bereng
had already been hanged for their conviction in the March 1948 murder
of 'Meleke Ntai. However, their coconspirator, Michael Tseki, who had
actually committed the murder, was convicted and then hanged. The
court condemned Tseki in no uncertain terms:

> He is an educated—or semi-educated—man; he has learned and
> practised his trade as a dispenser over a number of years. He is not
> living in Gabashane's village. If he had wished, his rheumatism of
> which we heard so much could easily have excused his presence
> that night. He preferred to attend. And having got there, to play
> the major part in the cruel, wicked and atrocious murder of this
> unfortunate man Paramente. The court is allowed only one pun-
> ishment. I have no discretion in this matter. . . . The sentence of the
> Court upon you is that you be taken from this place and returned
> to Custody and at a time and place appointed by His Excellency
> the High Commissioner you will be hanged by the neck until you
> are dead, and may the Lord have mercy on your soul.

I did not have a hard time believing, after reading hundreds of pages
of repetitive evidence from dozens of witnesses, that Bereng and Gabashane were guilty of the planning and execution of Paramente's murder
and that their methods of intimidation were deliberate and effective, although they maintained their innocence to the end.

The execution of two prominent chiefs, close relatives of the late
Paramount Chief and second and fourth in line to inherit the paramountcy, failed to serve as a deterrent, and the rash of medicine murders continued, afflicting the country for more than a decade afterward.
Why? What purpose did these murders serve, and who benefited from
them? What do the medicine murders reveal about the social dynamics
of power at the height of colonial rule in Basutoland? Fear generated
compliance and served the ends of those in power.

The Invention of Tradition

Traditional beliefs in the efficacy of human flesh obtained from an
enemy killed in battle and then burned to ashes, which were then mixed
with other substances into a paste that was kept in a so-called medicine
horn and applied to warriors about to go into battle in order to

strengthen them, had prevailed in southern Africa since at least the early nineteenth century. These beliefs, which predisposed Basotho seeking power to use medicine horns as a means of enhancing fear and ensuring compliance, persisted regionally into the mid-twentieth century. However, medicine murders were also called "ritual murders" because of the presence of witnesses and the procedures used in the murder. This was new in the twentieth century, as was the use of murder victims instead of heroic enemies slain in war. There were no early historical precedents for the committing of ritualized medicine murder in Lesotho or elsewhere in southern Africa. No form of murder was acceptable in precolonial southern African societies, nor was mutilation of a living person. In 1823 or 1824 the king of Matola near Delagoa Bay sent a messenger to the Portuguese governor at the bay to sue for peace and propose terms, but "the governor cut off his ears, nose, and lips, and returned him [the mutilated messenger] to the king with a message that he would destroy them."[3] It is not inconceivable that the mutilation of a living person in this way came to be associated by African witnesses with supernatural powers attributed to Europeans, setting in motion a copycat effect with the additional presumption that the human body parts themselves were a source of power. Early stories about the wars between the AmaNgwane chief Matiwane and the BaSotho chief Moshoeshoe in the 1820s also refer to the mutilation of the body of a warrior killed in battle, only to be recovered and buried later, but the victim was already dead at the time of mutilation.

There does not seem to be any question that in the region of southern Africa, including among BaSotho and their Nguni-speaking neighbors to the south and east, human flesh was used in concoctions called "medicines" used to prepare men for battle and for initiation ceremonies, at least as early as the nineteenth century. Describing a journey among the AmaXhosa in 1839, James Backhouse wrote about a specific occasion on which the missionary Richard Tainton had dissuaded Chief Faku from performing "the diabolical custom of killing a near relative, in order to wash himself with a decoction of the viscera, out of the skull of the victim, with a view of rendering himself invulnerable."[4] Contrary to Tainton's assumption, there is no evidence to confirm that Faku's ancestors had engaged in any such practices, but there is evidence that similar uses of human body parts continued in the area subsequent to this incident. Writing in 1896, Charles Brownlee, who had been skeptical of reports of medicine murder, revealed the facts of a case in Griqualand East, the first that for him "dispelled all doubts on the subject."[5] After the disappearance of several children, an old woman was finally arrested in the disappearance of a little girl whose body was then found with "two or three places where small portions of flesh had been cut out." On her testimony they arrested and convicted her husband, the child's grandfather, who confessed to the crime and said he had been promised payment for the murder by an "accomplice" who "was making a potent charm." In 1859 Eugene Casalis Sr. described the use of human body parts by BaSotho in the making of ointments that were used for healing and to prevent harm to warriors about to enter battle. The substances, including various other mineral, vegetable, and animal substances as well as human flesh, were turned to ash and pulverized into ointments kept in a medicine horn, and a tiny amount was smeared on the body or head of every man on his way to war. Hence the contents of a single horn would suffice for the "doctoring" of hundreds or even thousands of men, and the actual ingredients of the concoction were kept secret by "doctors" who specialized in performing these wartime rites.

> This belief in the inoculation of the virtues of certain substances, is the principal cause of the mutilations which the natives sometimes inflict on the corpses of their enemies. The bleeding pieces which they bring from the battle-field are used in the composition of a powder, which is supposed to communicate to them the courage, skill, and good fortune of their adversaries.[6]

The use of body parts taken from warriors killed in battle was well known in Lesotho during the wars of the 1850s, which is why precautions were taken by British and Orange Free State troops to retrieve the bodies of their fallen soldiers. When the Free State troops swept through the area of the mission station at Morija during the 1858 war, they found the bodies of Free State soldiers that had been mutilated in the young chief Letsie's village nearby; the burning of the mission station in retaliation must be viewed in this context, even though the missionaries themselves were not aware of these circumstances.

Early BaSotho drew a sharp distinction, however, between the use of human body parts taken from a brave warrior who had already been killed in battle and the murder of a person, no matter who, to obtain body parts for use in medicine horns. The first evidence suggestive of murders to obtain body parts from noncombatants for use in medicine horns comes from references to the civil strife in Leribe between the chiefs Jonathan and Joel in their struggle for control of their father's chieftaincy and lands. Several sources noted the discovery of mutilated bodies, including villagers not involved in fighting, during the period of the Leribe civil wars.[7] In an 1895 case six accused were found guilty of obstruction of justice and sentenced to seven years in prison, but the "Zulu doctor" who instigated the crime died in jail awaiting trial.[8]

In 1913 there was a medicine murder case that appeared to implicate Chief Griffith at the time he was pursuing his ambitions, with the aid of other senior chiefs, to become Paramount Chief.[9] If "medicine" derived from this murder was used on the Paramount Chief, he may have died of inadvertent blood poisoning, as the intention would have been to strengthen him rather than to kill him. Griffith was a close adviser to his brother, but he might have wanted strengthening concoctions for himself, and neither the actual events nor his intentions can be definitively construed from the evidence. However, if Griffith Bereng was involved in this medicine murder case or was believed to have been, it would explain his reputation for being feared, as was evident in the 1926 meetings to decide the succession.

There was also a medicine murder scare in Swaziland in the 1920s, when the Swazi king Sobhuza reached the age of twenty-five and was about to put on his headring; people believed that he needed a human sinew to bind it to his head. In Lesotho there were four other cases in the 1910s and five cases in the 1930s. Of these, a murder in April 1928 in the Mokhotlong District was vigorously pursued and prosecuted, with two persons hanged for the murder; another person served fifteen years, and an accused headman died in prison while awaiting trial.[10]

Resorting to murder to fill the medicine horn for initiation purposes was reported by the Reverend Paul Ramseyer as early as 1926. In an article on circumcision among the BaSotho he described how the "indigenous sorcerer-doctors" acquired human flesh to "renew" their medicines and noted that the discovery of mutilated bodies in ravines and on mountains had long been mentioned by missionaries in Lesotho. He stated that crimes of this nature had been committed in 1924 and 1925 in Griqualand East, in the Berea District of Lesotho, and elsewhere connected with rites at circumcision lodges. Ramseyer stated that the sorcerer-doctor, who needed to make a black powder from charred human flesh, would choose a victim for his virtuous qualities and arrange to have pure alcohol added to his drink at festivities where others were consuming the weak locally brewed beer, *joala*. Once he was drunk, the victim would be lured to a secluded spot on a pretense by several people ordered to assist the "doctor," at which point the victim would be held down, tied, and rendered immobile, while the "sorcerer" cut off the parts of the body considered most effective for use in medicines: the eyes, genitals, feet, and internal organs. Ramseyer noted that the corpse was then generally thrown into a ravine and abandoned.[11]

Ramseyer believed the BaSotho who told him that the atrocious "custom" did not originate among themselves but had been imported from sorcerers and "Cafres," a term used to signify the people of the neighboring areas of Natal and Transkei. Other evidence supports Ramseyer's assertion that victims were sometimes murdered for the purpose of obtaining "medicines" used at circumcision lodges. In 1963 an anonymous report on initiation appeared with the title "Buka Ena e Matsohong a Batho Ba Baholo Feela" (This Book That Is in the Hands of Old People Only). The paper scandalized both BaSotho and Europeans, as it revealed secrets of initiation, including practices and songs. The author was clearly a Christian, dismayed at the changes that he asserted had taken place in initiation ceremonies recently. He noted that initiation required the use of meat from cattle that had been captured in battle, but these were no longer available. He further stated that human flesh had been used in the past in medicines prepared for initiates but noted that this had to be taken from a dead foreign enemy killed in a legitimate battle; flesh taken from other BaSotho in the civil conflicts of the 1880s and 1898 would not suffice. He pointed out that human flesh that met these requirements had not been available to refill the medicine horns since the Gun War of 1880–81 and asserted that this was why the lamentable changes, including the increase in medicine murders, had come about in recent times.[12] This anonymous MoSotho attributed the practice of using human flesh in medicines to the AmaZulu, from whom the BaSotho had copied it.

How and why did the use of witnesses and rituals then emerge in association with murders to obtain body parts for filling medicine horns? These appalling ritual murders were probably started by Edward Tau, also known as Edward Lion or Lyon, and Ignatius Lekgagane. A connection has been made between the rising incidence of medicine murders after their arrival at Kolonyama in the Leribe District and later in the Quthing District and their mission as so-called Zionist leaders. Lekgagane founded the Zionist mission in the Transvaal, and Lion was already active in the Maloti Mountains as early as July 1912, when he was visited by two missionaries of the Apostolic Faith Mission based in Johannesburg. By 1919 Lion was carrying an identity card issued by the Johannesburg mission, but he was dumped by the Apostolic Faith Mission in 1923 for misconduct and from then on acted as a free agent, leader of his own congregation in Lesotho. Based in Kolonyama, he accumulated a following that was described by the local British administrative officer as including "all the blackguards in the country, and his village appears to be a general refuge for runaway wives." His followers caused trouble for the local chiefs, using land without permission and ignoring grazing controls, and eventually he was brought to trial on a charge of adultery. Evidence of scandalous sexual practices associated with the church emerged, and Lion was found guilty, jailed, and then expelled from the country. Paramount Chief Griffith tried to have his followers completely disbanded, issuing orders to that effect in 1927 and 1929, but it was not until 1935 that the District chief, Chief Motsoene, confiscated their property. Gordon H. Halliburton notes that the trigger for this precipitous action remains a mystery, but if Lion was involved in using medicine murder to strengthen his power against the chiefs, the chiefs would certainly have acted immediately in response.[13]

Rumor, innuendo, and circumstantial evidence link the two Zionist leaders to medicine murder during this earlier period. However, when Lion's son Solomon Lion returned to Lesotho in the 1940s, he was given a site in Matsieng, the Paramount Chief's village, which had hitherto been the exclusive preserve and terrain of the Catholic Church since Griffith's conversion; even the Protestants had never managed to get a mission site there. By 1949 Solomon Lion had been charged in Pretoria, South Africa, with a medicine murder that had been committed there in 1943, and he was said to have committed a ritual medicine murder, as a demonstration, at Matsieng in the 1940s. Lekgagane, an associate of the younger Lion, paid at least one visit to Matsieng, reputedly in the 1950s, and rumor attributed to his Transvaal mission the practice of fertility rites that included ritual murders similar to those committed in Lesotho in the 1940s and 1950s. The inclusion of pseudoceremonial procedures in front of many witnesses was new in Lesotho in the 1940s, setting them apart from earlier medicine murders, which were done secretly, and the evidence strongly suggests they were copied from rituals among the followers of Lion and Lekgagane, which they resembled. There was an obvious disproportion of cases in the areas of Leribe and Teyateyaneng, in the mountain area of Mokhotlong, in areas around Matatiele and Griqualand East, and in Qacha's Nek, where a secret society emerged and Edward (Tau) Lion had connections.

Murder and Power

Medicine murder was a tool of power. It would not have been as effective if it had not been so horrifying to the BaSotho. Ritualized medicine murders induced compliance not only if the witnesses believed in the potency of medicines containing human flesh but also because of the fear they induced. Thirty-seven people were originally indicted for Paramente's death, all but one of whom were men between the ages of twenty-eight and sixty. The one woman indicted had been asked to serve as a decoy, and she was among those discharged after the preliminary hearing. Eight were taken from jail, where they were on trial for another murder, in order to attend the preliminary examination; they included Bereng, Gabashane, and Gabashane's secretary, Accused No. 4 in Paramente's case, Makiane Mpiko. The tale of Paramente stands out from the stories of the many other victims of medicine murder in that the murder was particularly gruesome and an unusually large number of witnesses were forced to observe and participate. Over sixty people were involved. The murder was committed by two of the most prominent chiefs in the country; Paramente had been murdered to increase the powers of Bereng and Gabashane. Even among BaSotho who did not believe in the powers of the medicine, these chiefs gained leverage from the terror the murders induced. That they got away with it for so long confirmed for some BaSotho that the medicine as well as the terror were effective means of gaining or increasing power.

Gathering the evidence in Paramente's death took so long that the trial for the second murder the chiefs committed together ended before the first trial. On 3 August 1948 they were committed for trial in the death of Meleke Ntai at the village of Mamathe's in Teyateyaneng District, a murder that had occurred on 4 March 1948. In that case there were twelve accused, including both chiefs. The victim's lips were cut off while he was alive, but according to testimony he did not bleed as expected, so he was beaten and suffocated and thrown into a ditch full of water. The medical report showed death by drowning.[14] Both chiefs and two others were hanged for this death, and seven more served jail terms, while the last was discharged. Bereng and Gabashane remained defiant to the end. From the prison yard where they were held pending their execution the two chiefs, knowing their voices could be heard over the yard walls as well as throughout the prison, were heard to protest as loudly as possible that the entire business was a plot of the British government to get rid of the chieftainship and that they were innocent.[15] Bereng Griffith continued to generate fear among those around him until the day he was hanged on 15 November 1949.

Sir Walter Harragin, CMG, QC, who served as High Court judge in some of the "medicine murder" cases, delivered a paper that was subsequently published in which he asserted that BaSotho "recreations are beer drinks, cattle and sheep-stealing, and ritual murders." But Harragin also pointed out that participation in medicine murder was fear driven rather than voluntary:

> The practice is indulged in almost exclusively by what might be called the upper classes, the Chiefs and Headmen, when for some reason they think they require to be built up. While it is true that they are assisted by the ordinary man-in-the-street, I can assure you that this person is far from enthusiastic about it, as he is never sure when his turn may come. But the feudal system is so strong, and the fear of the witch-doctor so great, that these people never dare refuse to help, and once he has helped, naturally he will endeavour to hide his crime.[16]

The British were ineffective in curbing the wave of murders, and even the execution of Bereng and Griffith failed to act as a deterrent. Medicine murder was intricately connected to the struggle for power in colonial Lesotho in the 1940s, in which British colonial rule was by definition implicated. The first victim murdered by two of the highest chiefs in the land, Bereng and Gabashane, may not have been chosen at random, for he carried a highly symbolic name: Paramente, or "Parliament."

10

Discourse and Subterfuge

Responses to Medicine Murder

The struggle over "medicine murder" in the 1940s and 1950s highlights that there was no one local position, "the African perspective," posed against a single colonial perspective in the discussion of *liretlo*. In the conversation that ensued, European colonial discourse, embracing discordant voices and views of the problems, revealed common ground and common assumptions in the language of the "primitive"; of "illness," "psychosis," and "treatment"; of racism and the teleology of development, Westernization, and the achievement of "civilization." On the other hand, the recoverable discourse produced by BaSotho voices was driven by a divide between those who were the victims and those who were the perpetrators of the crime. The British system of indirect rule was predicated on the assumption that chiefs represented their people and could be used both to transmit and enforce colonial policies from the top down and transmit and support popular interests from the bottom up. Over generations the chiefs had become adept at turning colonial jargon back toward the colonizer, as it was a discourse that legitimized their own authoritative voice as "the voice" of their people, but now common people were the victims of medicine murder.

The British colonial government only gradually became aware of the rising incidence of medicine murders. At the time of the January 1941 recognition of 'Mantsebo as Regent Paramount Chief there were no known, outstanding, unsolved, recent medicine murders.[1] Four murders suspected to be medicine murders were committed between the time 'Mantsebo took office in late January 1941 and the time Resident Commissioner Charles Arden Clarke arrived at the end of 1942, but none of these murders had any apparent connection with BaSotho politics or the chieftaincy; hence there was no obvious reason for alarm when Arden Clarke first arrived.

The situation changed during Arden Clarke's tenure as Resident Commissioner, during which time the regency dispute was brought to the High Court for consideration in 1943, pitting 'Mantsebo against her deceased husband's brother, Bereng. Between 1943 and 1945 twenty-four medicine murders were eventually reported, of which the authorities knew of seventeen. Arden Clarke must have been alarmed at the high incidence of these murders by the time he left the country in 1946.

The first official response came in the form of circulars issued from the Office of the Paramount Chief beginning in January 1946. 'Mantsebo's first message, presumably dictated by the Resident Commissioner perhaps after consultation with other chiefs, ordered all Ward chiefs to call a *pitso* and read the message from 'Mantsebo to their people. With the bold caption "RITUAL MURDERS," the circular opened by quoting Moshoeshoe's 1855 proclamation outlawing witchcraft, with the implication that participation in medicine murder was a form of witchcraft. The most striking feature of the message was that it explicitly controverted the defensive strategy typically adopted by many chiefs and laid the blame, at this early date, precisely at their door:

> These ritual murders which are committed for the sole purpose of obtaining chieftainship medicine horns etc. I feel I cannot tolerate them and the [British colonial] Government will also not tolerate them.[2]

The remainder of this circular ordered full cooperation with the police and placed restrictions on "witch doctors," who were explicitly blamed for the problem. The message was certainly composed and sanctioned by the colonial officials, but it went out over 'Mantsebo's signature. On 31 July of the same year a second circular was issued and signed by the Regent Paramount Chief. Although she had previously identified chiefs as the cause of the murders, they were now ordered to report the murders and assist in investigations, but a warning was issued to them as well:

> I cannot pass this matter without saying a strong word of warning to you Chiefs. In these murders your names are being mentioned and the people say they have been ordered by you. . . . You should know that whoever will be found involved in such matters will lose his rights.[3]

Chiefs were thus put on notice that they would lose their rights if they were involved in these murders, but they were not reminded that murder was a capital crime. All persons who withheld information would be punished, and they were instructed to bypass their own chief if necessary to report what they knew:

> I order, therefore, that any person hearing of a suspicion in such a matter, and being unable to do anything, will be held responsible in the same way as the perpetrator of the crime himself. I conclude by directing these words to every person in Basutoland who will obtain an order from his Chief to kill a person that *he should come direct to me to report so that I can take measures to punish such a chief.* This is my order to you and it remains for you to choose whether you choose to report to me or to carry out the order of your Headman to murder a person, which is the excuse most people give in such cases that they were ordered by their chiefs.[4]

Chiefs were thus expected to tell their people to disobey the chiefs' own orders to commit medicine murders, an absurd expectation of any chief who was indeed guilty of such a deed. In closing the people were told: "Follow my order as head of the nation and leave these orders which you get from your chiefs which are dangerous to you." Yet since failure to follow the orders of a murderous chief would certainly carry immediate dangers, the efficacy of the circular was doubtful from the first.

It must have almost seemed as if the circulars were effective at first. Only two new cases came to the attention of the authorities in 1946, one from the previous year, and there were no reported murders for a period of almost twelve months, from December 1945 to November 1946. The murder of Paramente on 12 December 1946 would eventually make it impossible for the colonial government to turn a blind eye to the complicity of the chiefs in the rising tide of medicine murders, but it was two years before the case was cracked. The 1946 cases, and three more in early 1947, prompted another message from 'Mantsebo to the country's chiefs on 4 July 1947. Four months later, after eight more murders, another circular was sent from 'Mantsebo asserting the right of the police to conduct their investigations without a representative of the headman present and noting that persons should report murders first to the police and then to the headman. In addition to subverting the authority of the chiefs once again, these orders were also intended to protect witnesses, who had good reason to fear they would be killed if they talked.[5] The failure of these circulars to curtail the murders is hardly surprising.

Nine new murders prompted the next circular in April 1948, which was contradictory. This one, signed by David Theko Makhaola, prohibited the "smelling out," or identification, of witches.[6] Previous orders had defined the perpetration of ritual murder as witchcraft and called for persons to reveal their suspicions, but now anyone voicing suspicions was put on notice that they might be accused of smelling out and face punishment for fulfilling the previous orders to report the crime.

In September 1948 the High Commissioner, Sir Evelyn Baring, came for the opening of the Basutoland National Council, where he made a strong public statement against medicine murder. After ten more medicine murders a new circular dated 18 December 1948 went out over 'Mantsebo's signature, with a notice from the Resident Commissioner, Aubrey Denzil Forsyth Thompson, to all Ward chiefs.[7] By adding a threat, Forsyth Thompson put teeth in the message. If the chiefs did not act to end the murders, direct force would be brought to bear on the people:

> His Excellency warned Council that if these murders did not cease forthwith, without hesitation he would give effect to the new law which had recently been promulgated. The new legislation would empower the High Commissioner to impose collective fines on people residing in an area where a medicine murder occurred, or quarter Police of Representatives in the area and charge the local inhabitants with their maintenance until such time as the people would come forward and furnish information as to who the instigators to the commission of the crime were.[8]

The law, if enacted, would usurp the chiefs' policing powers, providing protection to witnesses but punishing those who remained silent. The notice was also the first to notify commoners directly that their chiefs did not have the legal right to require them to commit murder:

> If there are any Basuto who think that Chiefs have a legitimate right of ordering the killing of a person, they should understand full well that this is an erroneous notion. NO CHIEF HAS SUCH RIGHT. For this reason any person who will be ordered by another, whether the person giving him the order is a Chief, Subchief or Headman, or a commoner, to contravene or to assist in the contravention of the law by committing a medicine murder, should refuse to carry out such an order, and should immediately come to government. Should such a person help in the murder, he would be guilty of a very serious offence, and might be sentenced and hanged together with the person who has committed the murder.[9]

The notice reiterated that it was everyone's "duty" both to prevent such crimes and to protect witnesses. As an official colonial document, it ended with typical colonial jargon of colonial rule and responsibility, stamping the words with all levels of authority:

> This is a call to arms by Government and the Paramount Chief of you, Basuto, to whom this country belongs, that you should assist the [colonial] Government to save Basutoland from rotting away and from the widespread disgrace in which it is. Your co-operation is necessary and it is your duty as Basuto to give it.[10]

Nevertheless, a spate of new murders followed, and although some did not come to light immediately, by 1949 forty-one known murders had been committed since 'Mantsebo's original installation in January 1941, and thirty more were still under investigation.

Colonial Officials and the Chiefs

It is not exactly clear when British colonial officials first knew that the chiefs through whom they ruled were the primary culprits in the spread of the medicine murders. Arden Clarke was first posted to Basutoland as Resident Commissioner in 1942, having served previously in several capacities in Nigeria from 1920 to 1936 and as Assistant Resident Commissioner and Resident Commissioner in Bechuanaland in the intervening years. He arrived just as the appointment of 'Mantsebo as regent was being upheld by the High Court and at a time when the chiefs in the Basutoland National Council were actively pursuing the interests of their constituents by seeking to make their council more representative and making some of the seats elective. These changes began to be implemented in 1944, even before they became law in 1948, with the creation of a District Council in each of the nine districts, each of which was allowed to elect from its members a representative to the one hundred–seat National Council. When the changes finally became law in 1948, each district was given two seats at the national level. Although the remaining seats were held by hereditary chiefs and appointees of the Paramount Chief, the principle of moving toward an elective representative body had been established, implicitly challenging the powers of the paramountcy. The powers of the regent were further restricted by the Basutoland National Council in 1948, when she was forced to accept three advisers chosen by her from a panel of eighteen of the national councilors.[11] Further changes were to follow.

During his tenure in office Arden Clarke must have become aware of the rash of medicine murders, as yet mostly unsolved, that had occurred in recent years, and he may well have already known that prominent chiefs were involved. He complained about the recalcitrance of Queen Regent 'Mantsebo, and he ultimately issued her a threatening ultimatum:

> I have just told the Paramount Chief that I am no longer prepared to tolerate her conduct and that if she will not mend her ways and cooperate with the Government, I shall have to recommend her dismissal from office, a serious ultimatum that may cause a local crisis or, as I hope, effect some serious improvement.[12]

Arden Clarke issued this warning to 'Mantsebo in late 1944, just before the new High Commissioner, Sir Evelyn Baring, came to Lesotho in November. The interplay of these three important actors cannot be judged through the public record, as Arden Clarke wrote his own speech as well as Baring's speech and told the regent what to say in hers.[13] In 1944 and 1945 Baring reported that the administrative reforms that had reduced the number of recognized and gazetted chiefs, placed them on salaries, streamlined the court system, and created a national treasury had been effective, even though 'Mantsebo had reacted by becoming "silent, sulky and noncooperative." Baring stated a strong British intent to reform but preserve chieftainship in order to prevent the danger of a tyrannical oligarchy and noted that the regent appeared to have become more cooperative.[14] Arden Clarke left in 1946, the same year that the first circular against medicine murder was distributed under 'Mantsebo's name.

It was into this emerging turmoil that Aubrey Denzil Forsyth Thompson was plunged upon his appointment to the position of Resident Commissioner in 1946, following his work as Resident Commissioner in Bechuanaland. He may not have been informed about the medicine murder problem at first. In a private memo entitled "First Impressions of Basutoland," dated January 1947, he surveyed the issues of importance in administration, from the public works department and medical department to education, the police, the treasury, and native administration, but made no mention whatsoever of the medicine murders and referred to the Paramount Chief in neutral terms.[15] In 1947 the Resident Commissioner was preoccupied by the royal visit of King George, Queen Elizabeth, and Princesses Elizabeth and Margaret; Chiefs Bereng and Gabashane were among those who greeted and were honored by the King, and there was no mention yet, in the annual report for 1947, of any medicine murder problem.[16] By 1948 domestic politics involving the affairs of the Basutoland National Council and Josiel Lefela's organization, Lekhotla la Bafo, were heating up, and Forsyth Thompson responded energetically to the serious problems at hand, including that of medicine murder. His diary entry of 13 July reads simply, "Cfs. [chiefs] Bereng and Gabashane arrested on charges of ritual murder."[17] On 15 July he referred in his diary to a well-known political incident: "Members of the Lekhotla la Bafo executive arrested in connexion with the Roma fire." His diary entry of 22 July reads:

> All quiet here—No upset by Gabashane's and Bereng's followers. Josiel Lefela & others of the Lekhotla la Bafo in Jail on charge of burning a boy at Roma

On 15 September, the day when a Mr. and Mrs. Mohapeloa came to tea, he noted:

> P.C. [Paramount Chief 'Mantsebo] asked if she cd see Bereng & Gabashane [in jail]. I agreed & had it arranged, but learn that when she saw them she just screamed & went away.

By that time, however, 'Mantsebo herself was under suspicion for involvement in medicine murders. High Commissioner Baring had certainly become aware of what was going on with the Paramount Chief over time. The lack of an active British response to 'Mantsebo's involvement in the rising incidence of medicine murders was truly disturbing, for Baring's correspondence shows that the British knew long before they hired expert outside help exactly what the problem was. In a letter Baring wrote to his wife, Molly, he noted that he had gone to Lesotho in September 1948 to give an explicit warning to 'Mantsebo. The passage reveals the certainty of his belief in her complicity at that time:

> It was clear that the chiefs were organising these crimes and that the old girl is deeply involved. So I put on my smart blue uniform and went down to the first day of the Basutoland national council's session and I made them a terrific speech praising the work of the chiefs in every other respect but speaking frankly on ritual murder. Later I gave a further long lecture to the old girl and about fifteen of the leading chiefs. They presented a petition complaining that the police did not consult the chief of a district before they started their investigations—naturally since in 18 out of 19 cases chiefs of one grade or another have been involved. I replied by a very vigorous

counterattack saying that the continuance of the murders proved that the chiefs were either guilty or ineffective. Their eyes really popped out of their heads. I thought the old girl was going to cry. This would have been awkward as I wanted to give her a further lecture more or less alone [which he did] . . . saying that if the murders did not cease the results to her personally would be very painful indeed, and remarking "I have spoken" [I] dismissed them on the spot—very proud and haughty like.[18]

The language of this passage and phrases such as "their eyes really popped out of their heads" indicate the colonial mentality that governed Baring's thoughts and actions along with his belief, as of September 1948, that 'Mantsebo was implicated in medicine murder. It also demonstrates the conscious colonial mentality of staging events with attention to detail such as dress, bearing, word choices, and dramatic gestures to convey silent but strong messages on a public stage.

Forsyth Thompson kept track of the trial proceedings against Bereng and Gabashane, and his diary commentaries are brief but revealing. On 4 November 1948, he wrote:

Trial proceeding. Apparently the witnesses, contrary to expectation, are sticking to their evidence. C/P told me that frequently powder (medicine) scattered surreptitiously in the court, on judges seat, in doorway etc. etc. It is just swept up ea. day.

Forsyth Thompson struggled to exercise control in a daunting political situation. He noted that the Paramount Chieftainess was avoiding meeting with him for the purpose of appointing new advisers. By 1949 he was beginning to understand the thorny complications of political actors with divergent agendas who were nevertheless jointly engaged in perpetuating the problem of medicine murders. In January 1949 he noted that he had met with "a deputation from a meeting of the Sons of Moshesh and others called by the P.C." The delegation had come "to ask that Bereng & Gabashane might be allowed to appeal to Bloemfontein instead of the Privy Council; & that the UNO [United Nations Organization] might be requested to persuade Gt. Britain to be merciful." Forsyth Thompson wrote in exasperation: "Obviously the whole thing was Lefela inspired." The following day he went to Matsieng to encounter the Paramount Chieftainess and the Sons of Moshoeshoe directly to chastise them for "now relying on Lefela," but the meeting had broken up, and most chiefs had already left before he arrived. He had reason to worry, and the worries were in part caused by the scrupulous

examination of evidence by the Privy Council, per British legal tradition, before its admission to trial or in consideration of verdicts. On 28
February he wrote:

> Privy Council inquiries in Tumabole Bereng case recd. Many don't
> like evidence of accomplices. This will affect our ritual murder
> cases.

The implications were indeed chilling. Bereng and Gabashane had
systematically ensured, with overt and explicit death threats to anyone
who failed to follow their orders, that all witnesses to their crimes had
become de facto if unwilling "accomplices." Their strategy of implicating and thereby discrediting all witnesses appeared to be working. But
Forsyth Thompson found other ways to undermine 'Mantsebo, and he
was willing to talk to anyone in the hope that moral suasion would end
the murders. This meant confronting Josiel Lefela, the Lekhotla la Bafo
leader who was using false complaints about police actions in medicine
murder cases to stir up anti-British sentiment. Forsyth Thompson confronted him directly, which had the desired effect of disabusing Lefela of
his naive support for guilty chiefs:

> 2 March. Wed. Read [contempt of court] case of [Josiel's brother]
> Maputsang Lefela. There seems little doubt that evidence of
> Lefela's crowd abt. maltreatment by Police of witnesses fabricated.
> Saw Josiel. He told me that he had never heard, before I told him,
> that people were so afraid of ritual murder that they wd. not go out
> at night.

Over the next few months the energetic and determined Forsyth
Thompson met with 'Mantsebo and senior chiefs Griffith Monaheng,
Kelebone Nkuebe, and Bophila Griffith to discuss the problem of ritual
murder, and he flew to Cape Town in a "Piper Super-Cruiser chartered
for the purpose" to discuss with the High Commissioner issues related
to police handling of witnesses. Pursuant to these conversations, the following week he received a "long letter fr. Baring expressing his concern
abt. ritual murder." Finally, nine months after Baring had told the Paramount Chieftainess and the Basutoland National Council that he knew
they were involved in the murders, Forsyth Thompson set in motion the
official public inquiry into medicine murder:

> 8 June [1949]. Gold of CRO rang up to say G. A. [*sic*] Jones wd do
> the anthropological enquiry into Ritual Murder. Spoke to him at
> Cambridge.

Forsyth Thompson was thus active in trying to end the medicine murders before the Jones investigation. By October 1949 he must have been hopeful of making progress in suppressing medicine murders, but he was evidently still somewhat in the dark about which chiefs were guilty of complicity. He smoothed over a tiff between 'Mantsebo and Chief David Theko Makhaola after the Paramount Chieftainess requested he punish Theko "because of his absence from Matsieng during Bereng's & Gabashane's execution." He then threw a dinner party for G. I. Jones, the Cambridge anthropologist who had been hired as a consultant; held several meetings with the Paramount Chieftainess or her advisers; and flew to Mokhotlong, where he "saw Cf. Matlere in meeting & chatted abt the affairs of the district."

High Commissioner Baring hoped that the execution of Bereng and Gabashane would be sufficient to act as a deterrent to medicine murders, even though 'Mantsebo was escaping unpunished. In November 1949 he wrote to Forsyth Thompson, saying that he thought they had made progress with her, without acknowledging a connection between 'Mantsebo and the ongoing problem of medicine murder. He asked what Forsyth Thompson thought was the real key to stopping witchcraft murder and commented:

> I had particularly wanted to talk with you again about witchcraft murders since you told me that one has occurred subsequently to the execution of Bereng and Gabashane. Do you think that this is the only case that has occurred after the executions or alternatively do you think that there have been several and this is the only one in which the body has been discovered? I think we shall have to consider what is to be done if in spite of the executions the number of ritual murders does not greatly decrease. I fully realise that there is no hope of sudden and complete cessation. What do you think I should say in this connection to the Secretary of State if I am questioned as I think I shall be? In any case he is sure to ask me about Jones' enquiry and perhaps it might be a good plan for Jones to come to Pretoria for a day before I leave on Thursday, the 8th December, since I think I should have seen him before I reach London.[19]

On 1 December Forsyth Thompson went "through to Pretoria w/ G. I. Jones" and returned with him two days later, followed by trips to Mohale's Hoek, Quthing, Qacha's Nek, Kokstad, and Pietermaritzburg. Forsyth Thompson was not complacent about the problem of medicine murders. On 12 January 1950 he went with Chief David Theko Makhaola, who was "representing the P.C.," to the district where

the murders of Bereng and Gabashane had occurred and met privately
with the chiefs following the public meeting:

> After the meeting I spoke to the sons of Masupha & said if the
> murders didn't stop we should have to consider whether the house
> of Masupha was competent to consider ruling. They now had col-
> lective responsibility.

This was the atmosphere in which Jones was to conduct his investigation.

The Anthropologist and the Missionary's Granddaughter

Circular announcements to chiefs, efforts to prosecute offenders, and
even the execution of Bereng and Gabashane did not stop the murders.
The futility of these efforts to curb the epidemic of murder finally generated a response from a high-profile public official, and an expert
anthropologist was brought in to explain the phenomenon and offer
advice. Baring insisted they not bring in a South African, so the Cambridge anthropologist G. I. Jones arrived in 1949 to study the problem.[20]
He spent over six months in the country, touring districts and consulting
with both chiefs and commoners, and another anthropologist, Hugh
Ashton, provided him with the notes he had made on a visit to the country at the invitation of the Resident Commissioner earlier in the year.

Jones dated his official published report July 1950. His opening chapter presents the problem in typical colonial terms. Referring to the difficulties the BaSotho faced in an impoverished country with a large "ruling class" to support, he identified the fundamental problem as being
one of insecurity:

> This feeling of insecurity finds its most obvious expression in the
> intensification of the Basuto belief in magical supernatural aids
> usually referred to as "medicines" and it is with one of these "med-
> icines" that has recently become fashionable with the ruling class
> that this report is concerned.[21]

It is significant that Jones immediately identified the problem with
"the ruling class," or chiefs. Jones correctly clarified the issue when he
explained his use of the term "medicine murder" rather than "ritual
murder":

> This term "ritual," which implies the taking of a human life for reli-
> gious purposes or in accordance with a religious or magic rite, is not
> a particularly happy [appropriate] one for there is no such element

of human sacrifice in these Basutoland murders. They are not committed from any religious motives but for the purely material objective of cutting from the body of the victim strips of flesh or portions of particular organs, called by the general term *diretlo* and used in the making of certain magical compounds usually called "protective medicines." In this report, therefore, such murders are referred to by the Sesuto term *diretlo,* or the nearest English equivalent "medicine."[22]

Jones further observed that the object of the murders was to obtain medicine, that the murders were prearranged, and that they were committed by a group of people. While the flesh and blood were taken while the victim was alive, the victim also had to be killed and the body had to be subsequently discovered in order to give the concoction its power, hence the need to disguise the murder as an accident. Of ninety-six victims identified in Jones's report, fifty-six were male and forty were female. Ten were children: eight boys and two girls. Some victims may have been selected on the basis of virility and fertility, while the elderly might have been favored for their proximity to deceased ancestors. People from every *seboko* (clan totem or symbol) had been killed, but no chiefs or members of the ruling family had been victims. The chiefs could successfully stage these murders as accidents, making it appear as if the victim had fallen off a cliff, because of

the Basuto conventions regarding what may be termed official and private statements. An incident may have happened, people may have seen it happen, but if the official version is that it has not happened, then it has not happened. People may talk about it privately amongst themselves, but that is off the record. In public there is only one correct version which may be given—the official one.[23]

The Jones report provides a useful summary of the various suggested causes for the outbreak of the murders, which were blamed alternately on "native doctors"; initiation schools; the Roman Catholic mission; contamination by European civilization and criminal whites from Johannesburg; the chieftainship and the personal ambitions of chiefs, lesser chiefs, and headmen; the administrative changes of 1938 and 1945; and, finally, the colonial government, which was allegedly conspiring to break the chiefs before selling out the country to South Africa.

Jones was not the only European to provide extended commentary and analysis of the medicine murder scourge in Lesotho. Marion How was appalled by portions of the Jones report. A granddaughter of the famous missionary D. F. Ellenberger, author of *History of the Basuto An-cient and Modern,* and daughter of J. C. Macgregor, a District Commis-sioner who had married Ellenberger's daughter, translated his book, and written his own on the history of the BaSotho, Marion How had grown up steeped in the history of the BaSotho and loyal to both the Protestant missionaries and the British colonial administration. She had married a colonial official, Douglas How, herself, and her observations suggest she understood BaSotho culture, society, and politics as well as any European of the time. She was not a totally objective observer, as she regretted that her husband, who had died while with the BaSotho troops in the Middle East during World War II, had not been appointed Resident Commissioner himself. She had her own reasons for disliking the Roman Catholics, since her grandfather had been a prominent Prot-estant missionary, and for disliking Charles Arden Clarke, who had re-ceived the appointment she believed her husband deserved. The bitter-ness of disappointment comes out in the margins of her report. But she had grown up in Lesotho, was fluent in the language, and was counted by many BaSotho as a sympathetic and understanding European at a time when few were to be found.

How's comments shed important light on the Jones report. Although she had left Lesotho fourteen years earlier, eventually she put all of her ideas together in a thirty-four-page typed report, which she sent in a let-ter marked "Private and Confidential" to the Government Secretary in the Resident Commissioner's office in Maseru on 20 March 1957. How's reaction to Jones's report, best represented in the margin comments she made in her copy of the report, provides great insight into the social and political dynamics surrounding medicine murder. Further, How wrote that the murders were *not* "Sesuto" or part of the culture, and she re-jected Jones's conclusion that belief in "medicines" was the fundamen-tal cause of the murders, concluding succinctly: "It is power."[24]

How looked to recent historical changes as the source of the crisis and argued that medicine murder was a recent perversion of old prac-tices using medicine to "place" and protect new chiefs and villages. Cit-ing the observations of her husband, Douglas, twenty-five years earlier, she concluded that the proximate cause of the crisis was overcrowding, which intensified the struggles over placing chiefs. She argued that an historical prohibition of medicine murders in SeSotho culture dated to the famous meeting between Moshoeshoe and the elder chief Mohlomi, when Mohlomi offered the youthful Moshoeshoe advice before he be-came a chief:

Mohlomi refused "placing" medicine for power. Modern diretlo murders are for power. Mohlomi refused "power" medicine to Moshesh. . . . If Mohlomi's words are examined they refer exactly to this placing medicine—& Moshesh followed Mohlomi's teaching—he told Dr. Andrew Smith so. . . . His [Mohlomi's] words are still preserved[:] *"Motse ha o na sehlare"* [A village does not have protective medicine].

Both Jones and How suspected that new practices involving the use of human flesh might have been recently introduced into old rituals of initiation. Jones convincingly dismissed suggestions that medicine murders were imported either by BaSotho soldiers returning from service in World War II or from the criminal world of Johannesburg, and he debunked theories about Catholicism having played a role by reinforcing existing beliefs in relics, fetishes, and sacrifices. Jones also believed that Solomon Lion was implicated:

It has been suggested that she ['Mantsebo] was first induced to believe in the value of Ritual Murder by Solomon Lion who demonstrated such a murder before her at Matsieng in order to regain the position his father had lost in Basutoland. Whether this is true or false, I am unable to say, but consistent with this suggestion are the facts (a) that Solomon has been granted a building site at Matsieng, which indicates that he has successfully overcome the antipathies that previously existed between the paramountcy and his sect, and (b) that at the moment in Pretoria he faces a charge of ritual murder alleged to have been committed in 1943.[25]

How questioned Jones's conclusion that the reforms introduced by Arden Clarke had been sufficient to spark the crisis, and she attributed the problems to his personality and poor communication with the BaSotho:

It wasn't so much the reforms that Arden Clark tried to bring in but his ruthless way of doing things that frightened the chiefs. Also the natives realized very quickly that he never really liked the Basuto.

She wrote at greater length:

This new RC [Resident Commissioner, meaning Arden Clarke] did not take much trouble to hide the fact that he didn't like these obstinate mountain people the Basuto & that he much preferred the Bechuana. The Basuto set great store by a chief or official of whom they can say *"O rata Batho"* "he Likes the People." . . . This

stranger, who they feared to trust & who didn't like them, brought
in changes arbitrarily & in a ruthless manner.[26]

There is no question that most BaSotho did not condone these murders and found them completely incompatible with all their religious
and moral beliefs, Christian and indigenous. Those who committed the
murders underwent purification afterward, indicating that they knew
they had done something morally wrong that would have serious consequences for them in this life or the next if they failed to undergo purification. Jones revealed his Western colonial mentality when he argued
that only Christian-educated, Westernized BaSotho regarded medicine
murder as a horrible crime. In fact, the rejection of medicine murder
and the chiefs who committed them was the popular perspective of men
and women, both those with formal educations and those without. His
misleading interpretation of the behavior of terrorized participants led
Jones to the false conclusion that "neither the community nor its head
feels the same sense of guilt in attacking one of its innocent members,
or the same obligation to find him should he disappear, or to bring his
murderers to justice when his body is found."[27] In response to Jones's
comment that the average person adopted "a very tolerant attitude" toward the medicine murders, How wrote in bold letters, "???!!! Not those
I spoke to!" She further wrote that "commoners" were "helpless" in
bringing the murderers of their family members to justice. And yet the
victims always were commoners, and the murderers always were chiefs.
It simply would not have been possible for a commoner to commit or
order a medicine murder and get away with it in the community. Commoners could never mobilize participants and sustain secrecy; their attempts to increase their power would have so threatened a chief that a
chief would indeed have stopped and punished them.
    Although Jones failed to identify fear as the primary motive for invol-
untary participation and silence in these murders, he finally identified it
as the reason for the end to popular acquiescence:

> When the chief is no longer content with one killing, then feeling
> swings away from loyalty to the chief, and from fear of the results
> of careless talk towards the fear that it may be one's own turn next,
> and towards the feeling that these killings are wrong and must be
> stopped even if it means the arrest and prosecution of the chief.

Jones wrote that "the only complaint was that they had not hanged
those accomplices who by their own admission had participated in the

crime."[28] The problem, of course, was that someone who had once served as an accomplice might well do so again; hence people's fears did not abate, and the rule of terror continued.[29]

The Problem of the Regent

Jones correctly cited the dispute over the succession from 1940 to 1942 as a trigger for the *liretlo* crisis. The succession dispute involved Bereng and 'Mantsebo, both of whom became implicated in medicine murder. In the official published report Jones only indirectly indicated that the outbreak was begun by the highest chiefs in the land and subsequently became a crisis because of the precedent they set. However, he finally pointed the finger directly at 'Mantsebo. Jones wrote that some BaSotho "merely blame the Regent for her incompetence" rather than for direct complicity, but

> others take a more serious view. *The Regency has failed to take a stronger line about these murders because, directly or indirectly, it was involved in them itself.*[30]

Further, Jones concluded more explicitly:

> The murders in the Regent's own ward of Mokhotlong, in Chief Bereng's ward of Phamong and in Chief Gabashane's ward of Ma-mathe's are thus attributed to a kind of battle of medicine horns between the regent and Chief Bereng. The other *diretlo* killings in Basutoland are attributed to lesser chiefs copying the fashion set by their superiors.

Significantly, Marion How wrote five checkmarks next to that comment in her copy of the Jones report, indicating her strong concurrence with him regarding the evidence of 'Mantsebo's direct involvement in medicine murders in the ward of Mokhotlong. In addition, people recognized that the Paramount Chieftainess had not taken disciplinary action against other implicated chiefs. As long as higher chiefs, lesser chiefs, and headmen were still in positions to commit new murders with impunity, people would not talk.[31] Jones pointed out that new constraints on the police actually made it more difficult for the police to complete successful investigations leading to arrest, prosecution, and conviction. The police were no longer allowed to detain witnesses for questioning, which had actually protected such witnesses, and several witnesses who had given evidence had been murdered. In one case the

murderers of a witness were convicted but then received sentences of
only either a ten-pound fine or a six-month prison sentence.[32] Appalled,
How was moved to write in the margin: "The Gov. are positively *helping*
medicine murder," noting with irony that the high record of success in
committing murder without punishment "must give them great confidence in the powers of their medicines."

During his investigation Jones had indeed uncovered consider-
ably more information implicating 'Mantsebo and Mokhotlong chief
Matlere Lerotholi that was withheld from his published report. This evidence was included in two unpublished typed reports, marked "Secret," leading to the inevitable conclusion that at some stage of the process and at some level of colonial authority Jones was asked to exclude
important information from the formal report that, when published,
would become public. In their recent study of the medicine murders
from a primarily anthropological perspective Colin Murray and Peter
Sanders sharply contest my conclusion that British colonial officials suppressed evidence uncovered by Jones on the basis that only one para-
graph was deleted from Jones's submitted report prior to publication.
They attribute the two unpublished documents on medicine murder,
labeled "Secret," to Hugh Ashton, while I have concluded they were
written by Jones.[33]

From my inquiries I learned that when asked directly Ashton indicated that everything he knew about medicine murder had been
published. Moreover, the BaSotho indicated they had confided in Jones
himself. My assessment of the typescripts and their contents indicates
the probability that Jones was the writer, although he and Ashton shared
information, and Ashton certainly had input into what Jones learned
and wrote. I am not aware of any definitive evidence to the contrary,
and no author is indicated on the documents themselves.[34] Murray and
Sanders are evidently mistaken to credit Ashton for these two reports.

However, Ashton certainly assisted Jones when he began the investigation. Ashton had conducted two months of fieldwork among the
BaTlokoa in the mountain region of British Basutoland in 1934 and then
another six or seven months from October 1935 to April 1936. At the invitation of the Resident Commissioner he returned to Lesotho for three
and a half weeks in March and April 1949, when he spent his time "examining all the relevant official documents dealing with 'ritual' murders
and inquiring into the various factors that may have contributed to
them." At that time he returned to revisit the BaTlokoa "for a few days."
Murray and Sanders confirm that the resulting report by Ashton,

"Ritual Murder in Basutoland," was sent by Forsyth Thompson to Baring in April 1949, not long before the Resident Commissioner requested the lengthier inquiry subsequently made by Jones, who was given access to Ashton's notes when he arrived later in the year.

Ashton had included the results of his original fieldwork in a small 1943 publication entitled "Medicine, Magic, and Sorcery among the Southern Sotho."[35] Chapter 16, "Medicine, Magic and Sorcery," in his book *The Basuto* repeats the earlier publication, with an extension of about ten pages in which he discussed the new issue that had subsequently emerged: ritual murder. Ashton's book ends with this extension from his original work in which he uses the evidence of thirty-four of the earlier ritual murder cases to explain common patterns in the murders, their causes, and their connections with older customs related to medicine and its uses among the BaSotho.[36] The evidence in the unpublished secret reports was more specific and more recent, and it is not likely that Ashton would have withheld more recent information in his book, which was published later, if it had been in his possession in time for publication, also suggesting that Jones was the author of the secret reports. No matter which anthropologist was the author, however, I do not find it credible that either Ashton or Jones would have failed to report to the colonial officials the information that is included in the two secret reports. The evidence that British officials knew the information in these reports but prevented it from being made public is conclusive.

The unpublished reports reveal that the writer believed in the culpability of 'Mantsebo and her close confidant, Chief Matlere, in Mokhotlong. Matlere had used the investigation to profess his own innocence in spite of evidence to the contrary. He gave contradictory statements, both denying the effectiveness of medicines made from human flesh and blood and yet attributing just such powers to "the Zulu."[37] Matlere was 'Mantsebo's representative in the Mokhotlong District, and

> at Mokhotlong, no attempt is made to deny that these murders exist. Matlere frankly asserts that Mokhotlong is a bad area. . . . Matlere further says that the people assert that it is the chiefs who are committing these crimes and that they (the people) even accuse him of being behind the murders. He says he can't think what is causing them, and that he is really uneasy and baffled by them.[38]

Referring to the chiefs Lerato Rafolatsane, Bereng, and Gabashane, Matlere "did not doubt that the murders of which these people had been accused had actually been committed by them," but, as the target of allegations himself, he then tried to cast doubt that any chiefs were involved in such murders with an accusation against "ordinary people" and an allegation that the police were telling witnesses what to say in order to implicate chiefs with false testimony. Matlere asserted:

> Ordinary people who believe in murders are committing them for their own personal ends but in order to escape the consequences of their action they place the corpse near some Chief's village, accuse that Chief of having committed the murder himself and then turn King's evidence in order to save themselves and substantiate their accusation.[39]

Some BaSotho were courageous enough to accuse chiefs of being the culprits in the medicine murder crisis in public settings with the accused chiefs present. Two witnesses, a European and a MoSotho chief, reported that at a public meeting, after Chief Matlere "rebuked the Rafolatsane people for having committed the murder" (for which Lerato Rafolatsane was tried and acquitted), one of the coaccused "had angrily asked Matlere who he was to rebuke others for what he was doing himself."[40] Using his peremptory authority to suppress accusations against himself, Matlere fined him in his court for defamation.

Jones considered allegations against 'Mantsebo and her henchmen, including Matlere, to be true. According to one of the secret reports,

> the attitude of other people [besides Matlere] at Mokhotlong was that these murders were being committed and that the Chiefs were involved and that the Paramount Chief ['Mantsebo] and Matlere together were behind most of them. All these Chiefs had resorted to the use of human flesh and blood in order to increase their personality *(seriti)* and to enhance their position and authority.[41]

This secret report builds an indictment against 'Mantsebo through a careful study of the district of Mokhotlong, detecting the correlations between specific murders and political events, including the placing of chiefs locally and in the paramountcy. The situation in Mokhotlong was complicated: Seeiso had been placed there over Chiefs Rafolatsane and Lelingoana, the hereditary BaTlokoa chief, in 1925. Seeiso succeeded in subduing local resistance to his placement as District chief at Mokhotlong, bringing with him and placing many of his followers in the area. The struggle there over landholdings reemerged in the 1940s, prompting several court cases.[42] By 1939 Seeiso had placed fourteen of his own followers as headmen, displacing existing headmen under the new system of gazetting. Among those he placed was his key supporter, Chief Matlere Lerotholi, who was his *rangoane* (father's brother) as well as his uncle by marriage and his brother-in-law, Matlere's second wife being the half-sister of 'Mantsebo, Seeiso's first wife. The report details the relatives who were placed at Mokhotlong and notes that a number, including Matlere, Mahlomola Lerotholi, Mabina Lerotholi, and Absalome Letsie, had been implicated in medicine murders.[43]

The struggle for power in the Mokhotlong District, then, revolved around the placing of Seeiso and his followers, which became a crisis after his death, when their positions would only be guaranteed if his widow, 'Mantsebo, retained the power to ensure their own. The interdependence of 'Mantsebo and Matlere, along with Matlere's other kinsmen, and their vulnerability from 1941 to residual resistance to their earlier placing thus fuelled the contest over land and the medicine murders.

There were a variety of influences operating on 'Mantsebo, but the most compelling evidence against her comes from the correlation between the challenges she faced and the specific murders that occurred in the mountain district of Mokhotlong, the only district under her direct control. She left Matlere (with whom she was rumored to be on very intimate terms) there to act for her. A ritual murder occurred at Matlere's village on 25 January, just as the regency case was being discussed and when 'Mantsebo "needed" medicine to win the case over Bereng. A subsequent murder committed in Mokhotlong in February 1945 occurred at the same time it was said that she needed medicine in connection with the proposed placing of her daughter, Ntsebo, as chief at Makhaleng. Another murder ordered, reputedly, by Matlere (and carried out by his brother-in-law, who was convicted and implicated Matlere) occurred in Mokhotlong in April 1948 and was possibly connected with the need for 'Mantsebo to counter the new medicine that Bereng had acquired from his second medicine murder. And on 25 December 1948 another murder was committed in Mokhotlong just after Matlere had flown to Mokhotlong and stayed there for a few days before returning to Matsieng. Mabina Lerotholi and Sejakhosi Rafolatsane were subsequently accused of this murder, but Jones reported that "rumour has it that this ritual murder was committed for medicine to help the Paramount Chief's daughter, Ntsebo, who was facing a charge of murder at the January 1949 High Court session." If so, the medicine acquired from the murder must have seemed to have been effective, as "Ntsebo, the Paramount Chief's daughter, was acquitted of a charge of murdering her uncle although there was well based suspicion against her."[44]

Alternatively, 'Mantsebo might have wanted to boost her power to win a court case brought against her by the young Bereng's mother, 'MaBereng, that was also heard in January 1949 at Matsieng. 'MaBereng was seeking greater oversight over her deceased husband's property, fearful that it was being used for 'Mantsebo's daughter, Ntsebo, rather than for her son, the heir to the paramountcy. The case lasted through several hearings. The real (biological) mother of the young heir to the paramountcy had initiated a court case against 'Mantsebo, asking to be allowed to oversee how her son's estate was being used. She won initially, but 'Mantsebo defeated her on appeal.

'Mantsebo's rivals, Bereng and Gabashane, were also found to have been responsible for four medicine murders and were believed to have been involved in five more. No less damaging is the evidence against Matlere in at least seven additional medicine murders in Mokhotlong that were directly tied to Matlere and his relatives, all of whom owed their positions to 'Mantsebo.[45]

Yet the details of the case against 'Mantsebo was only reported in the secret reports:

> It is widely held in Mokhotlong that she is involved in the murders that occur there, and personally, I have little doubt that such is the case. The correlation of ritual murders in Mokhotlong with crises in her career is too close to be simply coincidence;—the accused in those cases that appear to concern her are all closely connected with and dependent on her or her henchman, Matlere, and the rewards that have been given to or proposed for those concerned with such murders are not consistent with her expressed desires to eradicate the evil and punish its perpetrators.[46]

Evidently, according to the secret report, 'Mantsebo "had Matlere commit the Masaleng murder," and

> when this step appeared to be so clearly vindicated by her success in the Regency case, she was doubtless tempted to resort to it again when beset by difficulties and dangers. As she was personally successful every time even though some of her pawns were caught, so the murders grew. This may sound fantastic, but I believe we are dealing with a morbid person, unsure of herself, who has had astonishing luck in overcoming various difficulties (such as the Regency case and her daughter's acquittal of murder) and who attributes her good fortune to the use of human parts in her lenaka [medicine horn]. Even if I am wrong, the fact remains that some Basuto believe that she does indulge in Ritual Murder and *they* attribute

her successes to her lenaka derived therefrom. While this belief is current, whether it be true or not, the Paramount Chiefship is bound to be ineffective against Ritual Murder and in repressing belief in the value of human flesh.[47]

Popular belief in the involvement of the Paramount Chieftainess gave the ultimate sanction to the practice of medicine murder. Since she could not only get away with it but also actually consolidate her power under the British each time she committed a murder, the crime was mistakenly perceived to be both effective and acceptable to the colonial government. The ramifications of her participation did not escape her people. They knew that as long as she did it and got away with it, other chiefs would as well. They were right.

BaSotho Responses: Public and Private Discourses

The public response of chiefs to the problem of medicine murder was fairly uniform, that the crisis was an invention, a conspiracy against the chiefs and chieftaincy as an institution. From their statements one would indeed take these chiefs as colonial resisters, protectors of the older, better, "traditional" order against the European, Western, colonial order and even against the threat of South Africa. These arguments and their voices sound convincing even today. But other chiefs acknowledged that the murders occurred, and they deplored them. In a newspaper interview Chief David Theko Makhaola, MBE, said that the murders were "from beliefs foreign to the Basuto" and that "the murders are being instigated by 'certain political bodies' who are using witchdoctors (Maquega) as instruments to further their aims." Makhaola defended the colonial government, saying it was doing all it could to end the practice, and he insisted that "it is an entirely new belief, that when a chief is to be installed there must first be human sacrifice to give him superiority and authority. This has never been a Basuto custom."[48]

Marion How received a poignant five-page handwritten letter about medicine murder signed only "Basuto." Referring to "the black cloud of medicine murders," the anonymous letter said:

> We the common people have today changed into sheep for the chiefs under the reign of the Chieftainess Mantsebo Seeiso, ever since she took the reins of Basuto Government there appeared this defilement and bestiality; these medicine murders appeared with her government. I believe that they will end with it. While she is

> governing there is no way in which medicine murders can end; we
> being Basuto we have cried greatly for the Government of Her
> Majesty to rescue us, we have found no help to this day, and for
> those who have not yet been cut up alive this governing is upon
> their necks like the yoke of King Pharaoh the cruel.[49]

The writer believed that 'Mantsebo was without doubt behind the murders. The text of the letter, which was full of images, language, proverbs, and metaphors common in SeSotho culture and references to Christianity and biblical texts, is heartrending:

> Being basuto we have no way in which we can end this cutting up
> alive of us, not even a way to avoid or escape this heavy governing,
> we have no way to do anything for ourselves; our anxieties and our
> cries which go to the Government of her Majesty we have to send
> them by this very one who is holding us wickedly, we have no other
> way. (a sheep asking help from a jackal is it a thing that can be
> done.)

The writer was explicit:

> Ever since medicine murders began there is no one of a house of
> the chiefs of Basutoland that have been cut up alive; it is the chiefs
> who are conducting and commanding medicine murders with
> their orders and their wishes and with rewards; there is no common person who can refuse to carry out the order of a chief under
> this civil government; many common people agree to commit
> medicine murders under orders.

The writer again made clear the condemnation of 'Mantsebo:

> People are astonished [*Batho ba maketse*] when they see that people
> who have dabbled in medicine murders are treated with great respect and are in the forefront of the work for the nation. Even if
> one looks back there has been no chief that governed with blood
> like this one.[50]

The MoSotho historian Mosebi Damane directly linked the rise of medicine murder in the 1940s to the need not only to replenish medicine for initiation ceremonies but also to strengthen the powers of chiefs who felt increasingly threatened by the British. According to Damane,

> most Basotho felt that the Administration had purposely manoeuvred the appointment of the regent in order to weaken the authority of traditional bodies so as to prepare the people for eventual incorporation in the Union of South Africa. Although at this time

there was much public talk about the diminution of the power of the chiefs by the representatives of the movement of popular opinion, all the people feared incorporation into the Union of South Africa more than they feared the chiefs.

Unscrupulous herbalists and doctors took advantage of this state of affairs and began to sell "horns" for personality, for success in court cases and disputes, for luck etc. When the contents were exhausted, the "horns" had to be replenished. Those who claimed to replenish horns used *maime*, a kind of Sotho "chloroform" a sip of which is sufficient to deprive the victim of all conscious volition. They also claimed to possess charms which would prevent the police from interfering. These charms had the general name *velabahleke* (come so that they may smile).[51]

A prominent MoSotho politician, A. C. Manyeli, raised the subject of medicine murders spontaneously when I asked him about popular attitudes toward the institution of the chieftaincy, saying that the BaSotho supported the institution because chiefs were viewed as their protectors. When I asked if this had been true under colonial rule, he responded:

> No, under the colonial rule . . . chieftainship began to lose its popularity because the chiefs themselves regarded themselves as being nothing but servants of the colonial rule, unlike what pertained before the colonial rule, so they thought their power had been usurped by the British and then resorted to ritual murders, and that made them very unpopular because in the ritual murders, um, it was only the commoners who were murdered but never never *never* one of the royal blood—never. So people began to realize bit by bit that the chiefs were no longer their protectors, so that's how the chiefs lost their popularity.[52]

Stimela Jason Jingoes wrote about medicine murder cases that involved people he knew well, and he believed they had resulted from the attempts of chiefs to ensure they were gazetted after the reforms. He wrote:

> That there was a correlation between the Proclamations and reforms and the outbreak of ritual murder was clear to the people, who coined the phrase, *"Marena a ts'aba ho faoloa"*— "the Chiefs are afraid of being castrated." During those black years the saying was often on people's lips. Parents would warn their children when they were going to the fields to walk in groups and not to stay out until after dark because *"marena a ts'aba ho faoloa."* When the commoners of Lesotho began to realize that their Chiefs were finishing them

off like sheep with these murders, they started to lose confidence in their Chiefs.[53]

The BaSotho used several channels to inform the British that the problem and the solution to the medicine murders lay at the level of the Paramount Chief. When the British hired Jones they got more than they had bargained for; they got the people's version of what was going on as well as the people's recommendation of a solution, which was to depose 'Mantsebo. The secret report on Mokhotlong, with the evidence Jones had collected from his own investigation and from Ashton, reads:

> The most outspoken of my informants considered that the murders would not cease until the Government had shown its determination and strength by taking action against the very highest in the land, i.e., against 'Mantsebo and Matlere themselves.[54]

Jones had done a good job. He had indeed uncovered the deepest secrets of the nation. He had earned the trust of many people, and they had confided in him. That his report reflects the colonial discourse of its time does not detract from his ultimate success in uncovering the causes of the outbreak of medicine murder and recommending administrative action to address the problem.

Medicine Murder and Colonial Rule

The British may not have gotten what they wanted, but they did get what they asked for. Forsyth Thompson commented at length on the Jones report in the draft of a private letter to Lord Hailey:

> I have this morning answered the telegram about the Jones report. On thinking it over I came to the conclusion that, as I have already given my views on it and as the S/S. does not seem disposed to listen to any further criticisms on it from me, the best thing I cd. do wd. be to appeal to him to hold his hand until there had been an opportunity of ascertaining your views on future policy since your views seem to be at variance with those of Jones.
> I find on looking up the files that, when we hoped to get a higher-powered chap than Jones (whose abilities even when he was apptd. later we were ignorant) we laid down the terms of reference.[55]

Noting that their third stipulation had been that he make recommendations, he added, "So I am afraid in view of (iii), we asked for what we got!"

Jones produced for the official published report a highly censored version of what he had discovered, but he had raised the awareness of colonial officials to the seriousness of the problems with the secret reports, copies of which were sent to Cape Town and to England to ensure their preservation. Given the evidence Jones and Ashton had uncovered and to which British officials had access and without a consideration of volatile regional politics at the time, it is hard to believe that culpable chiefs were allowed to stay in office.

But in the context of southern African politics after 1948 it is not difficult to understand why colonial officials would have wanted to prevent this evidence from becoming public knowledge in a published colonial report. They needed as much accurate information as possible in order to counteract the problem, but publication of the information would have caused a scandal in Britain and in South Africa as well as in Lesotho. There is no evidence that the British retained 'Mantsebo in her position and withheld from publication incriminating evidence against her with the intention of exacerbating the medicine murder crisis, but this may have been an unintended effect of their actions.

The imperatives of regional politics governed the British colonial government's decisions regarding the High Commission Territories of Basutoland, Bechuanaland (Botswana), and Swaziland. The colonial situation in southern Africa was complicated in 1948 by the victory of the National Party, upsetting British relations with South Africa. Over the next few years the High Commissioner was confronted with threats from the South African government to break away from the Commonwealth and to assume control over colonial Basutoland and the Swaziland and Bechuanaland Protectorates. Baring's priorities were to retain the Commonwealth link and access to South African sources of uranium needed for atomic development in Britain as well as suppress scandals in the High Commission Territories that might provoke South Africa to seize control over them.[56] The 1949 executions of Bereng and Gabashane were expected to suffice as a strong deterrent, even to the highest chiefs, in the prevention of further medicine murders, and removal from office of 'Mantsebo on the grounds of her own complicity in similar murders would have perpetuated publicity about the medicine murders just as Baring was trying to contain the scandal associated with the marriage of Seretse Khama to a white British woman prior to assuming his position as a senior chief in Bechuanaland. With these troubles brewing and extreme pressures being exerted from the South African government regarding affairs in the High Commission Territories, it would not have been difficult for Baring to persuade Jones to refrain from including anything scandalous regarding 'Mantsebo in the published version of his report.

Jones was a highly experienced former colonial officer with experience in conducting such investigations, eliciting confidential information, and reporting about it. He had access to the information and written documents of Ashton as he conducted his work, and it is inconceivable that Ashton withheld information of this nature from Jones or that Jones withheld this kind of information from the Resident Commissioner, who had hired him, or from Baring, with whom he met. As a former colonial official Jones had every reason to put every shred of information he gathered into the hands of the man who held the position and faced circumstances similar to those he had previously faced as a colonial official. The correspondence of Forsyth Thompson indicates he was frustrated with the response and attitude of the High Commissioner, and his energetic attempts to end medicine murder indicate he was supportive of Jones in the carrying out of the work.

As he had been asked to do, Jones suggested a series of "political remedies" to resolve the medicine murder crisis. He suggested that the "greater chiefs" be given greater responsibility "in the councils of the nation" as an outlet for their ambitions. More radically, he suggested that the Basutoland National Council be given a legal administrative role, in place of its current advisory capacity, so that the recognized Native Authority would be the Paramount Chief with the National Council, or a smaller council, rather than the Paramount Chief alone. In the end, his core recommendation was to reverse the process of centralization, which had been the primary means of achieving indirect rule, and, via councils at the district, ward, ward section, and village group, decentralize administrative and financial powers.[57] One way or another, the power of the Paramount Chief was to be severely restricted, so that even if 'Mantsebo remained in power as regent, the damage she could inflict would be minimized. In the end, this is largely what happened.

Administrative Reforms in the 1950s

The British were not as complacent as they seemed. They supported administrative reforms that were in line with Jones's recommendations and curbed the power of the Paramount Chief's office. Forsyth Thompson's strategy of strengthening the hands of advisers in order to control 'Mantsebo appeared to have results. He believed that after many all-day meetings with Chiefs David Theko Makhaola and Griffith Monaheng he had achieved "complete frankness, trust & accord between us." He was discrete in what he wrote, but eventually Forsyth Thompson, like Baring, came to believe that 'Mantsebo had a direct role in the medicine murder problem. In 1950, writing to Baring in hopes of a transfer, he reflected:

> You will remember that when I came to Basutoland in November 1946 the people were seething with discontent because of the maladministration of the Paramount Chief and as a result of the recent reforms which, they felt, had been pressed forward too quickly, and which discontent found expression next year and in 1948 in a number of ritual murders; there was open conflict between the Paramount Chief and large sections of her people; there was a movement amongst the senior chiefs to depose her; and there was passive resistance to many of the functions of government.[58]

In a confidential report of March 1950 to the High Commissioner, Forsyth Thompson wrote:

> The Paramount Chief's realisation of the growing clamour of the *vox populi* [against her] was demonstrated by the surprising tameness with which the year before last she agreed to have advisers chosen for her. The people were thoroughly tired of her selfishness, weakness, vindictiveness, partiality, ignorance, and above all her choice of bad self-seeking advisers, and the Basutoland Council of September 1948 demanded that it should be allowed to choose advisers for her. Finally a panel of 18 was presented to her from which she was asked to choose three which ultimately she did, and precautions were then taken to see that she did not continue covertly to follow the counsel of her old advisers. The new advisers assumed office in the first quarter of 1949, and the tone of her administration and the temper of the people has since undergone a striking change for the better. This too is a big constitutional advance: never has a Paramount Chief had hs [*sic*] advisers chosen by the people before.[59]

The report included an explanation of the creation of elected District Councils in nine districts in 1946 and the plans to identify young chiefs who, following their formal educations at the secondary school level, would receive on-the-job administrative training with District Commissioners and at the Resident Commissioner's office in Maseru over two-year periods before being placed back in their districts. Like all colonial reports seem to be, this one was hopeful:

> There is generally an air of great activity, co-operation and even
> friendliness in the Territory today. The shadow cast by medicine
> murders seems to be passing; the Paramount Chief, sensibly, is tak-
> ing a back seat and leaving much of the work to her Advisers with-
> out interference, and the people seem happier about the way things
> are now going.[60]

The confidential report revealed some of the behind-the-scenes activities at the Paramount Chief's offices in Matsieng, showing a surprising knowledge of the dynamics of those chiefs who were indeed trying
to rein in the criminality of 'Mantsebo and Matlere:

> The Paramount Chief's recent attitude may be partly due to the
> fact that she is very unwell. She is drinking heavily (gin is her pref-
> erence), has recently got much thinner and looks wretchedly ill. It
> seems likely that she is diabetic. She has quarrelled violently with
> Chief Theko Makhaola the Senior Adviser for no other reason,
> it would seem, than that he had refused "to share her pillow," and
> she has recently slighted and insulted him on every possible occa-
> sion. He has borne this with commendable restraint, though his
> position must be very uncomfortable. She fortunately pays great
> attention to the advice given her by Griffith Monaheng (who for
> nearly thirty years was in Government employment, ending up as
> the Senior Interpreter). He is a wise and good councillor but on oc-
> casion is inclined to be jealous of Theko and is not above having a
> sly dig at him. The third Adviser is Bofihla Griffith Lerotholi a
> member of the "Royal" house but a person of no outstanding
> character.[61]

Under Resident Commissioner E. P. Arrowsmith the Basutoland
National Council finally achieved effective control over the Paramount
Chief in national affairs. 'Mantsebo was convinced to accept the formal
appointment of an additional adviser, making four altogether, and each
was given a portfolio, putting responsibility for administration, judicial
matters, finance, and agriculture into the hands of prominent members
from the Basutoland National Council and effectively depriving the office of the Paramount Chief of any real power.[62]

The reported number of *liretlo* cases dropped somewhat in the mid-
fifties but then rose alarmingly in the last years of the decade. As the ultimate political dispensation of Basutoland was being debated, the sense
of insecurity in the country, which feared incorporation into South Africa, continued. Once the British decided against incorporation, however, the stage was set for an intensification over the struggle for power

in what would soon be an independent country. The heir was reaching adulthood, and the days of the regency were numbered. As 'Mantsebo faced the prospect of losing one position, she needed to secure her hold over another. In 1959 sixteen new medicine murders were reported, the highest since 1948, when 'Mantsebo's principal competitor, Bereng, had been eliminated from the contest for power. The era of the old political scene closed with the accession to the throne of King Moshoeshoe II in 1960, ushering in a new era of political parties, a new parliament, and new players in the political arena.

The British were not ignorant of the belief among the BaSotho that the murders would not cease as long as 'Mantsebo was in office, but to the victims of the murders it appeared that the British turned a blind eye to the evidence. No one believed that the British wanted the medicine murders to occur or that they caused them, nor did they believe the defense of the culpable chiefs taken up by Lefela that the murders did not occur and were an invention of the British as a way to attack the chieftaincy. Rather, people believed that the removal from office of 'Mantsebo herself would undermine any remaining belief in the efficacy of the medicine in protecting the murderers from punishment and in enhancing their power. But the vocal backlash of the perpetrators, assisted by Lefela, had a powerful silencing effect, leaving the British caught between two bad options. To the victims of the crimes and those who lived with the terror of a murderous chief, the British seemed culpable for failing to remove 'Mantsebo from office. Their voices were barely heard, however, while the chiefs and politicians, pressing an anticolonial agenda, loudly denounced the British when they upheld the rule of law and tried to bring chiefs to justice.

'Mantsebo was left in power until 1960, when she was only removed at the urgent insistence of the Principal chiefs of the country so that the new Paramount Chief, Moshoeshoe II, who had been two and a half years old when his father died, could be finally installed. Not surprisingly, the incidence of reported medicine murders rose in 1959, just as she became aware that she was about to lose her position as regent, when 'Mantsebo again had reason to resort to whatever means she considered effective to ensure her stay in power, this time as Ward chief in Mokhotlong.

It seems surprising that the heir, young Constantine Bereng Seeiso, survived, because he stood in the way of many aspirants to power. The difficult life of the young Constantine Seeiso has been called a "bitter childhood."[63] First he was sent to live with Chief Khethisa Tau in

Pitseng; then he was placed under the care of Chief Gabashane for as long as the latter remained a staunch ally of 'Mantsebo, which was a couple of years; and then he was put under the care of Chief Matlere in Mokhotlong. As soon as Bereng was hanged, 'Mantsebo decided Constantine Seeiso should come back to Matsieng so he could "go to school with other children," but, at this tender age of ten, he continued to be tutored individually for a few more years instead of starting school right away. His life was often at risk:

> During this period tensions between the rival cliques of the royal lineage were at their fever pitch and the future King of Lesotho absorbed the full effects of the horror stories and political intrigues surrounding his right to high office. These included one acute episode, on an occasion when it had seemed propitious for him to be in Matsieng, when it was put into circulation that he was going to be garrotted. He and his elder sister, Princess 'Mampoi, had to be hidden in a cave for some two days.[64]

There is another rumor that once as a boy or young teenager he was found and rescued after having been beaten up and abandoned on the verge of death. But the young heir completed his Junior Certificate level of secondary school in Lesotho in 1953, and he must have been safer once he was sent off to Britain for the rest of his education. After completing secondary school in Britain, Constantine Bereng Seeiso was admitted to Oxford University, where he completed a degree in politics and law. After a dramatic meeting of the Principal chiefs the month before, the young heir was installed as Paramount Chief, King Moshoeshoe II, on 12 March 1960.[65]

11

Seeking Sovereignty and the Rule of Law

Contests over authority, policy, and the political dispensation in government were waged in colonial Lesotho by means of force and persuasion, involving guns, rhetoric, and a more encompassing discourse of colonialism that defined the parameters of the possible and the preferable. Within that colonial discourse about politics and authority colonial officials and BaSotho chiefs deployed their rhetorical skills to achieve their goals and, when that failed, resorted to forms of coercion and force. During the nineteenth century the BaSotho, under their chiefs, had used guns and military force as well as diplomacy in their efforts to ward off rule by white settlers, and they decided collectively in 1868 and again in 1884 to compromise their sovereignty to British overrule in order to retain their land and their culture. The effective use of military force, rhetoric, and manipulation of competing discourses by BaSotho chiefs and their people over the previous century finally won them in 1966 the recognition, by the British and the world, of their independent sovereignty and right to self-determination.

The political dispensation meted out to Basutoland by the British came to follow the pattern they had established elsewhere, with the creation of a legislative council and the introduction of constitutional changes from the late 1950s, leading to full independence in 1966. A Resident Commissioner from South Africa, A. G. T. Chaplin, oversaw the initial process. Following the publication in 1954 of a report recommending administrative reforms, a commission headed by Sir Henry Moore was formed in 1956 to chart out the future of Basutoland. Since the British were still toying with the idea of transferring control of the country to South Africa, the issues were urgent for the BaSotho. The Constitutional Reform Committee's recommendations were accepted in 1958, and under the new 1959 constitution the former Basutoland

National Council, keeping the same name, became a legislative body, and a small executive council, which included colonial officials, was established. Half of the new eighty-member Basutoland National Council were elected from the nine District Councils, twenty-two were Principal chiefs, fourteen were nominated by the Paramount Chief, and four were official British representatives.[1]

Party politics were born as the country imagined independence even before the British conceded it was possible. Ntsu Mokhehle founded the Basutoland African Congress (BAC) in 1952, which changed its name to the Basutoland Congress Party (BCP) in 1960 just prior to the 1960 elections. The party had strong leadership with important international ties and support, but these included Communist Party links and participation and led it in a more radical direction than might otherwise have been the case. Although the BAC/BCP supported the position of the Paramount Chief, it did not take a similar stand for other chiefs at lower levels and wanted to restrict the role of the paramountcy to largely ceremonial functions. There was also a reaction against it prompted by fears, realistic if exaggerated, of the known communist influences in the BAC/BCP. As a result other parties emerged. In 1957 Chief Samuel Seepheephe Matete formed the Marema-Tlou Party, which strongly supported the future king, Moshoeshoe II, and in 1959 Chief Leabua Jonathan founded the Basutoland National Party in order to run more conservative candidates for office. In April 1961 Bennet M. Khaketla founded the Basutoland Freedom Party after leaving his position as Deputy President of the BCP, and this party merged with the Marema-Tlou Party at the end of 1962. Although both party leaders involved in the merger, Matete and Khaketla, soon left the new party, the Marema-Tlou Freedom Party survived under new leadership to win seats in future elections.[2]

The elections of 1960 under the new constitution revealed the political divides among parties and leaders that had been festering in the 1950s. Perhaps not surprisingly, it was the party that had been in existence the longest, the BCP, that won the most seats in the elections of 1960, giving it control over six of nine District Councils and therefore a majority of the indirectly elected seats in the National Council, but its lopsided victory masked weak organization and internal dissension, falsely conveying an image of mass popular support.[3] Saddled with the problems of governance in the waning years of colonial rule, the BCP revealed a lack of preparation for the challenges of administration and rule that would be remembered by the electorate in the next elections.

Holding the balance of power, the BCP oversaw the period in which a Constitutional Commission formed by the National Council collected popular input for the drafting of a new constitution and produced a report in 1963 that was debated by the National Council and then used to negotiate terms for independence with the British government. With independence scheduled for October 1966, new elections under a new constitution were held in 1965, and an overly confident BCP suffered a reversal of fortune with the victory of the BNP, which had energetically mustered electoral support in the countryside, gaining a predominance of support from women voters in the process. The BNP victory also reflected weaknesses in the BCP caused by ideological divisiveness and local fears of the radical and well-known affiliations, including communist, of the BCP abroad. It was thus Chief Leabua Jonathan, one-time adviser to Regent 'Mantsebo, who claimed victory and led the country to formal independence as the Kingdom of Lesotho on 4 October 1966.

The rights, privileges, responsibilities, and expectations of self-governance are neither a Western invention nor exclusive to the European world in history. In August 1879 Émile Rolland, missionary for the Paris Evangelical Missionary Society in Lesotho who had been born and raised in the region, testified to the Select Committee on Basutoland Hostilities that when national meetings were called for the Paramount Chief to consult with the adult men of the nation,

> no matter what speeches might be made at the pitso, it is the national custom to ventilate grievances, and they sometimes even insult their own chiefs at the pitso. There is no political importance in it.

Pressed on the issue, that of expressing open dissent, Rolland replied in more detail, supplying significant insight into SeSotho political culture:

> No, it is not considered at all treasonable. They have a proverb to the effect that statements made at the pitso are privileged communications. When a man wants to make a very strong attack against the Government or against a chief at the pitso, he begins by quoting that proverb to the effect that "I speak as a privileged person."[4]

The elements considered most central to democracy, rule by the people, were thus present in Lesotho prior to the advent of British colonial rule. The use of rhetoric and persuasion as tools to be deployed in the pursuit of power was deeply ingrained in SeSotho culture from long before the colonial era, and the British parliamentary system adopted at

the time of independence conformed to SeSotho principles of governance. Through their system of governance the BaSotho of the precolonial era had enjoyed popular consultation by the chiefs in legislation, in
policy decisions, including those of war and peace, and in the administration of justice. Commoners retained the right of free speech in public
political consultations without fear of repercussions, and chiefs were held
to the rule of law. The codification of precolonial laws is not evidence
that colonial officials in Africa "invented tradition," nor is it evidence
that African elites privileged by the colonial manipulation of power and
authority did so. The study of laws and the administration of laws and
justice in Lesotho reveals, on the contrary, that central to the preexisting,
precolonial social systems and value systems of colonized Africans were
the recognition, application, and enforcement of laws intended to provide justice and a fair dispensation of power between ruler and ruled. As
remarkable as it may seem that one hundred prominent BaSotho men
could meet for only three days in 1903 and come to consensus about the
prevailing laws of the land, it was a reflection not of their manipulation
of power and authority but of the common knowledge and acceptance
of SeSotho laws that had long been applied every day in SeSotho courts
based on principles and practices that had been applied and handed
down for generations. The "Laws of Lerotholi" were indeed a tradition,
not a colonial invention or perversion of the past.

    Because British colonial officials responsible for Basutoland were
motivated by a desire to maintain law and order at minimum expense
to Great Britain, the systems of courts and laws were of central concern
to them. These officials allowed a dual system of courts and laws to
emerge that they employed to control the chiefs and that they expected
the chiefs to use to control their people. Not surprisingly, the record of
written letters to and from British colonial officials in colonial Basutoland reflects the central legal concerns of the ruled as well as the rulers
and contains the jargon of the discourse of colonialism that all sides attempted to deploy in the service of their own interests.

    The BaSotho had been pressing for self-representation in govern-
ment since at least the time of Émile Rolland's testimony in 1879, as
evidenced in their delegation and petition to the Cape Parliament the
following year in which this specific request was explicitly made. The
eventual formation of the Basutoland National Council in 1903 was
the result of years of sporadic discussions on the subject between the
BaSotho and colonial officials, and if its formal designation and structure were a product of colonial intervention, nevertheless it served to

help protect the interests of the BaSotho as a nation. Its importance as a bulwark of protection of the limited sovereignty enjoyed by the BaSotho under the British was almost immediately made evident during the negotiations over the creation of the Union of South Africa. The promise of the British before the final dispensation was reached that, no matter what, the BaSotho would be able to retain what was referred to in the documents as their "National Council" underscored the importance of the mere existence of this national institution from its very inception. Josiel Lefela, who eventually founded the Lekhotla la Bafo, or Council of Commoners, in 1919, never renounced the institution of the chieftaincy in BaSotho politics, only the corruption of specific chiefs and the inadequacy of the Basutoland National Council to address the needs of the people so long as it was controlled solely by chiefs.

The British were aware that they were enabling abuses by chiefs toward their own end of implementing colonial rule. The political strategy of the British to convert or subvert the popular assembly of the *pitso* to implement colonial rule had remained unchanged from 1880, and the Basutoland National Council was seen by the British as an extension of this process. They used both to announce government policies and decisions that they expected the chiefs to implement. Similarly, the British hoped to maintain British rule via the chiefs through the existing court system, a goal they pursued in part through the codification of the "Laws of Lerotholi" and their periodic revision and publication.

Conflicts between subordinate chiefs periodically escalated into open hostilities in colonial Basutoland, but the British were reluctant to interfere as long as internal conflicts did not actually destabilize British rule, and they preferred to leave such problems to be dealt with by the Paramount Chiefs. That the Paramount Chiefs did not or could not always maintain order and peace between their subordinates indicates either their unwillingness to play the role of policemen and enforcement for their British rulers or their inability to be effective in implementing settlements that they might have adjudicated. But the fact that the various litigants frequently appealed to British colonial officials, annoying as this was to the British, reveals the BaSotho insistence on the principle of the rule of law. They were told to obey British and SeSotho law, and they insisted that the British enforce these same laws and enforce judicial judgments. Litigants resisting the judgments of the Paramount Chief or of District Magistrates had no choice but to appeal to a higher level. When BaSotho chiefs felt they were being required by colonial officials to take actions that would run counter to popular sentiment or to accepted customary law or practice, to which they were accountable in the internal dispensation of power, they insisted that they be given direct orders to absolve them from culpability in the eyes of their constituency. It is no wonder that the dramatic changes in the courts introduced by the reforms of the 1930s and 1940s, the increased distance between commoners and the chiefs who had judicial powers over them, and the intensified competition between chiefs over officially gazetted positions that afforded them salaries and rights to hold court undermined confidence in justice and the rule of law in colonial Basutoland.

The so-called medicine murders inspired a horrified fascination on the part of Europeans, and European reactions at the time took on the tone of a Conradian story of a depraved non-Western society, the type of colonial discourse so rightly condemned by Edward Said as serving the purposes of creating the "other."[5] The 1953 novel *Blanket Boy*—by Peter Lanham, a South African, and A. S. Mopeli-Paulus, based on a short story written by the latter, who was a chief in the Witsieshoek Reserve in South Africa—follows the travels of an antihero who was a participant in the medicine murder of his best friend on the orders of his chief, a murder that resembles that of the real victim Paramente. The novel reinforced the negative impressions of Africans commonly held among Westerners just as African colonies were pressing for their independence. What European observers failed to observe, however, was that it also conveyed a BaSotho perspective, that medicine murder was no more a part of BaSotho culture or acceptable to the BaSotho than it was a part of European culture. The BaSotho were as horrified as were Western observers—even more so, as they were its double victims, victims of the murders and victims of the increasing repression that accompanied the growing terror-based power of certain chiefs. The ritual-like atmosphere of the medicine murders, involving proceedings observed by involuntary witnesses, had no precedent in any societies whose peoples and cultures had been blended into the BaSotho nation and SeSotho culture. As we react with justifiable revulsion, we need to remember that it is revulsion against specific ambitious individuals who represented neither their people nor their culture when they committed or ordered acts of murder and that it is a revulsion that was shared by the BaSotho themselves. That these murders caught the attention of the West and fuelled Western stereotypes of primitive Africa only makes it more imperative that the forces and influences at work be deconstructed and the events and acts demystified.

Medicine murder became a "pattern" not because it was compatible with past or contemporaneous ideologies or accepted norms of behavior but because British failure to act against the regent, 'Mantsebo, had the effect of making medicine murders appear to be effective in achieving the objectives of those who planned and ordered them. Their power increased through terror, and when they were not called to account it was perceived as a clear sign that their new powers made them untouchable even by British colonial rulers.

Medicine murders did not remain secret in the local arenas where they occurred; they were powerful discursive acts, and local secrecy would have defeated the perpetrator's purpose of increasing his or her known power among his or her constituency. The power of those guilty of committing the murders was extraordinarily effective in ensuring silence toward police and colonial officials. The means of ensuring silence is not difficult to discern. What the involuntary witnesses to Paramente's murder saw appalled and terrified them. Some were brought into the hut (one found an excuse to leave), and some watched from the door. All of the witnesses indicated that they knew this was a deliberate strategy to implicate them—if they talked, they incriminated themselves. But worse yet was the more immediate threat to themselves. In Paramente's case they saw his eyes plucked out, his nose, ears, and tongue cut out, his head skinned, all while he was still alive, drugged, and mumbling; he didn't die until he was cut in the abdomen. All witnesses indicated that after the body was disposed of they were told collectively that anyone who talked would be the next victim. The witnesses to this murder were silenced by their fear that they too could fall victim to a horrendous form of murder.

After experiencing a backlash in public opinion, voiced by politicians such as Lefela, following the hanging of Bereng and Gabashane, the British did not take serious steps that they knew they might have taken to rein in other guilty chiefs, including 'Mantsebo, and in their inaction and silence became unwillingly complicit in two decades of rule through fear. This is therefore not a story á la Conrad, in which we gaze in horror at an inexplicable "other" culture; rather, it is a story of a multitiered struggle for power between the British, who were responding to regional and international constraints, the Regent Paramount Chief, Principal and lower-level chiefs, and their BaSotho constituents. It is a human story, a tale that has been told in many contexts in human history, of power and greed, and it is as much a story of British colonial dilemmas as of BaSotho participation and misery.

But not all chiefs were corrupt, much less criminals and murderers. As across the continent of Africa, the emergence of Ghana as a free and sovereign nation inspired the nationalist drive for independence in Basutoland and the emergence of political parties trying to shape the future of Lesotho according to their own ideological dreams. Some prominent leaders cavorted with and sometimes became formal members of the Communist Party and pursued an agenda of trying to discredit the roles of kings and chiefs in ideal systems of governance. But the BaSotho people did not agree. Well into independence most BaSotho strongly respected the roles their chiefs could and did play in resolving conflicts peacefully, bringing criminals to justice, and maintaining the rule of law through the respect they commanded by virtue of their status as chiefs. The political history of the late colonial period was one in which chiefs and commoners alike strove to achieve representative governance and the dispersal of power from the center to the periphery and to the people at large. The composition of the Basutoland National Council was changed several times to include more commoners and fewer chiefs, becoming partly elective in composition, and the council moved steadily between 1944 and 1958 to bring the regent under its control.[6] The ensuing political debates revolved around whether the role of the Paramount Chief, who after independence and full separation from Great Britain would be designated "King," should be strictly ceremonial or include control over police and military functions as in the model of a constitutional monarchy.[7] The separation of powers was a vital consideration in the prevention of future abuses by elected governments, but the communist-influenced parties and leaders were more motivated by their desire to limit as much as possible the authority of the future king and gave the powers of police and military force into the hands of the Prime Minister.[8] The conservative elements of the rural population and influential Catholics were not mistaken when they emphasized fears of communist influences that had been in evidence since the time of Paramount Chief Griffith, which helps to explain the popular acquiescence to the postindependence seizure of power by Leabua Jonathan in the 1970 coup after the BNP lost the national elections. He was able to do this because Left-leaning politicians had given too much power into the hands of a single office, and the dream of the rule of law through democratically elected leaders was lost to new generations of BaSotho in the now independent kingdom of Lesotho.

Throughout the era of British rule colonial Basutoland remained the nation of Lesotho, struggling for its sovereignty and cultural traditions in the eyes and hearts of the BaSotho. This collectively shared sentiment justifies a generalization about "the" BaSotho, the descendents of those who had originally given their allegiance to the first *Morena e Moholo*, Moshoeshoe. The missions, schools, hospitals, and other social works of the Catholic, Anglican, and French Protestant religious communities working in the country promised to fulfill the British Western colonial vision of "civilization," which was, culturally, Westernization in its intent. The end of overt violent rebellions had ushered in a new century of apparent quiescence and consent on the part of the BaSotho chiefs and people. Had their consciousness been colonized? Had Western cultural beliefs and practices been imprinted on the minds of chiefs and "commoners" such that resistance, both political and cultural, was unthinkable? Of course not. Life went on: life cycles of birth, education, marriage, family, service to community, old age, death, and remembrance of the newly dead and ancestors. SeSotho rituals and ceremonies marking these social milestones persisted, reflecting a strong cultural resilience even as Christian and Western practices were grafted on to daily life practices and major ceremonies. BaSotho acceptance of the value of many of the practices and beliefs of their ancestors persisted throughout the colonial era alongside genuine Christian beliefs and in spite of colonial pressures and political and social crises. From their earliest interaction with Westerners via traders and missionaries, the BaSotho had accepted the accoutrements of the West only selectively, from prayers to clothing, and had openly symbolically rejected them on occasion as a means to convey a message of political resistance to colonial encroachment and the expropriation of their land and sovereignty.[9] As the generations passed this self-conscious selective acceptance and rejection of things Western remained in evidence.

Throughout the era of British colonial rule in the twentieth century the BaSotho were confronted with the prospect of something they were certain would be worse than British colonial rule: annexation and incorporation into the Union of South Africa. This fear, and the abiding desire for sovereignty, underlay the actions of BaSotho of all ilk with otherwise very divergent self-interests. The discourse of colonialism expressed by both the colonizers and the colonized reveals both unity and division among the BaSotho. Not all BaSotho responded alike to life under colonialism or to their colonial rulers; the differences of status evident in inequalities of wealth, access to resources, and access to office that had been present through the nineteenth century persisted into the twentieth century and influenced individual and group responses to colonialism.[10]

The British attempted to reinforce the power and authority of the chiefs over their people even as they tried to disempower the chiefs relative to colonial authority and power. There were hierarchies of authority among the chiefs, resulting in power struggles within and between family lines of descent in the inheritance of chieftaincies and the allocation of attendant resources, most particularly, land and people. The correspondence that came and went from the offices of British colonial officials, between themselves but, more important, with BaSotho correspondents—chiefs and their constituents—provides glimpses into the dangerous political terrain navigated by BaSotho individually and collectively in the era of colonial rule and into the strategies employed by the British officials, the Paramount Chiefs, the subordinate chiefs, and the BaSotho at large.

In the twentieth century the struggle for power was waged with words, and the people of Lesotho were motivated by deeper principles, just as they had been in the wars with guns during the nineteenth century. They were concerned with defending their country and their culture, with enforcing the rule of law, and with preserving customs that conferred on them rights of participation in governance. They sought political and social equality between chiefs and their people and to maintain SeSotho and Christian values of faith and religion as well as customs of respect for marriage and family. For well over a century, through the conflicts and struggles of the colonial era and since, these values have persisted as part of an enduring but evolving discourse of culture and politics, still today shaping the lives of the BaSotho people.

NOTES

BIBLIOGRAPHY

INDEX

NOTES

Chapter 1. Power in Theory and Practice

1. Hoy, "Power, Repression, Progress."

2. A sample of important works include Lyotard, *The Postmodern Condition;* the articles in Hoy, *Foucault;* Bhabha, *The Location of Culture;* and others listed in the bibliography.

3. See, for example, Said, *Representations.*

4. Engels and Marks, "Introduction."

5. Sarkar, "Hegemony and Historical Practice."

6. Foucault, "Two Lectures," 83, 87, 88–90, 92.

7. Foucault, "Truth and Power," interview with Alessandro Fontana and Pasquale Pasquino, in *Power/Knowledge,* 109–33, 122.

8. Foucault, "Powers and Strategies," interview with the editorial collective of *Les révoltes logiques,* ibid., 134–45, 141, emphasis in original.

9. Foucault, "Truth and Power," 119.

10. Foucault, *The History of Sexuality: An Introduction,* 94.

11. Foucault, "The Subject and Power," afterword in Dreyfus and Rabinow, *Michel Foucault,* 208–26, 219.

12. Foucault, "Two Lectures," 102; Foucault, "Truth and Power," 118.

13. Foucault, *History of Sexuality: An Introduction,* 100.

14. Ibid., 100–102.

15. Terdiman, *Discourse/Counter-Discourse,* 12.

16. Ibid., 38–39.

17. Terdiman, *Discourse/Counter-Discourse,* 39, emphasis in original.

18. Ibid., 57, 62, 18, 39, 56.

19. Scott, *Domination,* 18–19.

20. Roberts, *The Colonial Moment.*

21. Spear, "Neo-Traditionalism."

22. Cooper, "Conflict and Connection." See also the essays in Engels and Marks, *Contesting Colonial Hegemony,* and my review of it in *African Economic History.*

23. The study of colonial India inspired the school of Subaltern studies two decades later, with a similar agenda defined in terms of a postcolonial mindset. The blend of theory and empirical research produced by these scholars has been impressive and demonstrates the ways in which biased documents produced by colonial rulers can nevertheless be used to uncover Subaltern perspectives. Scholars of the Subaltern school have tried to reconcile the fundamentally incompatible theories of Marxism and Foucault, largely with reference to the Marxist work of Antonio Gramsci. See Prakash, "Subaltern Studies"; Mallon, "The Promise and Dilemma." For a sample of studies from the Subaltern school see Guha and Spivak, *Selected Subaltern Studies;* and Landry and Maclean, *The Spivak Reader.*

24. Lonsdale, "The Moral Economy of Mau Mau."

25. Feierman, *Peasant Intellectuals.*

26. Comaroff and Comaroff, *Of Revelation and Revolution: Christianity, Colonialism, and Consciousness,* 5, 22–24, 25.

27. Ibid., 26, 29.

28. Moffat, *Missionary Labours,* 348, 246.

29. Ibid., 228–39; and Eldredge, "Slave-Raiding."

30. Comaroff and Comaroff, *Of Revelation and Revolution: Christianity, Colonialism, and Consciousness,* 17–18.

31. Larson, "Capacities." For similar studies see the essays collected in Spear and Kimambo, *East African Expressions.*

32. Setiloane, *The Image of God.*

33. Landau, *The Realm of the Word.*

34. Penvenne, *African Workers.*

35. Ibid., 4. See my review of Penvenne, *African Workers,* in *African Economic History.*

36. Vail and White, *Power and the Praise Poem.*

37. Crais, *The Culture of Power.*

38. Keegan, *Colonial South Africa.*

39. Crais, *White Supremacy.*

40. Shillington, *Colonisation.*

41. McClendon, "Coercion and Conversation."

42. Atkins, *The Moon Is Dead!*

43. Eldredge, *A South African Kingdom.*

44. Scott, *Domination,* 203.

45. The classic works are Thompson, *Survival in Two Worlds;* and Sanders, *Moshoeshoe.* For a discussion of sources in the precolonial history of Lesotho see Eldredge, "Land, Politics, and Censorship."

46. Machobane, *Government and Change;* Burman, *Chiefdom Politics;* Burman, *The Justice of the Queen's Government;* Kimble, *Migrant Labour;* Edgar, *Prophets with Honour;* Weisfelder, *Political Contention.* Earlier secondary works dealing with the colonial history and culture of the BaSotho include Lagden, *The Basutos;* Dutton, *The Basuto of Basutoland;* Tylden, *The Rise of the Basuto;* Ashton, *The Basuto.*

Chapter 2. Transcripts of the Past

1. Damane and Sanders, *Lithoko*, 59.

2. Ibid., 60.

3. For details on the early history of the BaSotho see Thompson, *Survival;* and Sanders, *Moshoeshoe.*

4. Lagden served as the Assistant Resident Commissioner and Resident Commissioner of Basutoland from 1884 to 1901, except for a brief stint in Swaziland in 1892–93. Published in 1909, his two-volume, 690-page work, *The Basutos: The Mountaineers and Their Country,* was begun after fifteen years in Basutoland while he was still Resident Commissioner, delayed while he was assigned to duty in the Transvaal in 1901, and completed upon his retirement from active service in 1907.

5. Ibid., 2:464, 465.

6. John Burnet, 29 July 1861, quoted in Dutton, *The Basuto of Basutoland,* 45 n.2. As Dutton points out, Burnet had long experience of negotiations with Moshoeshoe on behalf of the British.

7. Ibid., 45.

8. Lagden, *The Basutos,* 2:464–65.

9. Ibid., 2:469.

10. Eldredge, *A South African Kingdom,* 60, 62–63.

11. Ibid., 80–81.

12. The British, however, denied at the time that their action created a precedent for future policy and practice. Machobane, *Government and Change,* 73, 100–101.

13. Eldredge, *A South African Kingdom,* 81, 161, 175–76, 188–92.

14. The most complete analysis of the Basutoland National Council is provided by Machobane, *Government and Change,* 76–125 and passim.

15. Eldredge, "Women in Production."

16. Machobane, "The Political Dilemma." Letsienyana sired a biological son who was fourteen at the time of Letsienyana's death, but the mother had been a very junior wife of Letsienyana's grandfather Letsie I, and law dictated that the bridewealth originally paid on her behalf by Letsie I made this child legally a child of Letsie I, not of the biological father, Letsie II. Machobane, *Government and Change,* 106.

17. Edgar, *Prophets with Honour.*

Chapter 3. Prelude to Rebellion

1. Rolland, Acting Governor's Agent, to Secretary for Native Affairs (SNA), 17 September 1878, no. 47 of 1878, S9/1/2/1, Lesotho National Archives (LNA). A younger son of Moshoeshoe, Nehemiah Sekhonyana had taken followers into the Matatiele (Griqualand East) area in the late 1850s prior to the arrival of immigrant Griqua. In 1877 he was acquitted on charges stemming

from an attempted rebellion in April by some of his associates there in his absence. See Orpen, *Principles of Native Government*, 30–36.

2. Rolland to SNA, 17 September 1878.

3. Ibid.

4. "Statement of the chief Morosi," Quthing, 16 July 1877, in Cape of Good Hope, *Copies of Correspondence*, A. 49–1879, 3.

5. Hope to the Governor's Agent, 23 June 1877, ibid., 113, 114, 115.

6. Ibid.

7. "Statement of the chief Morosi," 6.

8. Hope to the Governor's Agent, 26 June 1879, in A. 49–1879, 116.

9. Brownlee to the Governor's Agent, 7 September 1877, ibid., 6–7.

10. C. D. Griffith to Hope, 4 July 1877, ibid., 118.

11. Telegram from Hope to SNA, 25 November 1877, ibid., 8.

12. Hope to SNA, 29 November 1877, ibid., 7–8.

13. "Translation of the Chief Morosi's Reply to Mr. Hope, taken down in Sesuto by Chief Constable Segata, at Morosi's Dictation," ibid., 11.

14. Hope to Rolland, 24 November 1877, forwarded to SNA, 5 December 1877, ibid., 9–10; Rolland to Chief Morosi, Qhobosheaneng, 28 November 1877, ibid., 12.

15. Rolland to the Resident Magistrate of Quthing, 28 November 1877, ibid., 13–14.

16. Deposition of Monaheng before Charles J. Maitin, Justice of the Peace, witnessed by Hope and Segata Abraham, 26 November 1877, ibid., 15–16.

17. Deposition of Makhoa before Maitin, witnessed by Hope and Abraham, 27 November 1877, ibid., 14–15.

18. Rolland to the Resident Magistrate of Quthing, 30 November 1877, ibid., 16.

19. Rolland to the Resident Magistrate of Cornetspruit, 30 November, 1877, ibid., 17.

20. Brownlee, Office of the SNA, to Rolland, 20 December 1877, ibid., 18; Rolland to SNA, 25 January 1878, ibid., 19.

21. Rolland to the Resident Magistrate of Quthing, 30 November 1877, ibid., 16.

22. Rolland to SNA, 25 January 1878, ibid., 19, 17.

23. Ayliff, SNA, to Rolland, 9 February 1878, ibid., 19–20.

24. Hope to Rolland, 16 February 1878, ibid., 21–22.

25. Ibid., 23. The context makes it clear that he was not referring to the person Makhoa in this statement.

26. Hope to Rolland, 18 February 1878, ibid., 23.

27. Rolland to SNA, 6 March 1878, ibid., 20–21.

28. Ayliff to Rolland, 16 March 1878, ibid., 25.

29. Hope to SNA, 14 March 1878, ibid., 26.

30. Bowker, Governor's Agent, to Ayliff, SNA, 18 April 1878, ibid., 29–30.

31. Ibid., 30.

32. Bowker, 7 August 1879, in Cape of Good Hope, *Copies of Correspondence,* A. 6–1879, 59, 30. Chief Langalibalele of the AmaHlubi in Natal was captured with armed followers in Basutoland after fleeing from arrest in Natal in 1873.

33. Ayliff to Bowker, 25 April 1878, in A. 49–1879, 31.

34. Bowker to Ayliff, 18 April 1878, ibid., 30–31.

35. Austen, Resident Magistrate, Quthing, to the Acting Governor's Agent, Maseru, 28 September 1878, and Griffith, Governor's Agent, Maseru, to SNA, 20 November 1878, ibid., 32–33.

36. Austen to the Acting Governor's Agent, Maseru, 28 September 1878, and Austen to the Chief Magistrate, Maseru, 23 November 1878, ibid., 33–34.

37. Joseph M. Orpen, 15 July 1879, A. 6–1879, 15–16.

Chapter 4. The White Horse and the Jailhouse Key

1. Anthony Atmore presents a strong narrative and analysis of events in his essay "The Moorosi Rebellion." An excellent survey with critical details is found in Tylden, *The Rise of the Basuto,* 111–37.

2. C. D. Griffith to SNA, 3 January 1879, S9/1/2/1, LNA.

3. C. D. Griffith to SNA, 29 January 1879, ibid.

4. C. D. Griffith to SNA, 5 February 1879, ibid.

5. C. D. Griffith to SNA, 19 February 1879, ibid.

6. C. D. Griffith to SNA, 18 February 1879, and C. D. Griffith, telegram no. 20, to SNA, n.d., ibid.

7. Maitin, Quthing, to Griffith, 10 February 1879, in Cape of Good Hope, *Copies of Correspondence,* A. 49–1879, 20 (misplaced in sequence of documents).

8. C. D. Griffith to Austen, Resident Magistrate of Quthing, 26 January 1879 and 29 January 1879, in S9/1/3/3, LNA.

9. Memo of message sent to the Chief Morosi by Sgt. Isaak Masin from Austen, Resident Magistrate, 13 January 1879, in A. 49–1879, 41.

10. C. D. Griffith to Austen, 5 February 1879, S9/1/3/3, LNA.

11. C. D. Griffith to Austen, 17 February 1879, S9/13/3/3, LNA.

12. C. D. Griffith to Austen, 22 February 1879, S9/1/3/3, LNA.

13. C. D. Griffith to Austen, Palmeitfontein, 26 February 1879, S9/1/3/3, and Griffith to SNA, telegram no. 20, n.d. (ca. 27 February 1879), S9/1/2/1, LNA.

14. C. D. Griffith to Resident Magistrate of Leribe, 27 February 1879, S9/1/3/3, LNA.

15. Ibid.

16. C. D. Griffith to Letsie, Ha Bakhuirw, 27 February 1879, ibid.

17. Rolland, 27 August 1879, in Cape of Good Hope, *Copies of Correspondence,* A. 6–1879, 87.

18. Ayliff, SNA, to Griffith, 13 February 1879, in A. 49–1879, 50–51.

19. C. D. Griffith to SNA, 26 February 1879, ibid., 56.

20. Ayliff, Alwyn's Kop, to Colonel Brabant, Morosi's Mountain Camp, 9 June 1879, ibid., 102.

21. "Statement of Japhta, who resides at the Village of Ncazela, son of Morosi, in the late ward of Doda," 29 January 1879, signed before Austen, Resident Magistrate, Quthing, ibid., 58.

22. "Voluntary Statement of Mapara" in the court of the Resident Magistrate for Quthing, 24 January 1879, ibid., 46.

23. "Statement of Jonas Morguanga," 24 February 1879, ibid.

24. "Statement of Henry Benson" before A. J. Knowell, Justice of the Peace, captain, Second Regiment, Morosi's Mountain, 3 June 1879, and "Statement of Alfred Darrall Robinson" before Knowell, 3 June 1879, ibid., 107.

25. "Statement of Maso" before Austen, Resident Magistrate, Quthing, 17 June 1879, ibid., 105.

26. Ibid., 106.

27. Ellenberger, *Some Notes,* 9.

28. Crais describes a similar incident that occurred the following year in October 1880, but on that occasion Hamilton Hope was gruesomely murdered by the uMpondomise chief Mhlontlo ("Conquest, State Formation, and the Subaltern Imagination"). See also the description of the murder of Hope and his men in Brownlee, *Reminiscences,* 213–15.

29. Ellenberger, *Some Notes,* 10.

30. Austen to C. D. Griffith, 7 June 1879, in A. 49–1879, 108.

31. "Statement of Uhlowoa, alias Marman Lunko," signed "Mhlowoa, his X mark," before M. S. Liefeldt, Matatiele, 19 January 1879, ibid., 45.

32. "Voluntary Statement of Mapara" in the court of the Resident Magistrate for Quthing, 24 January 1879, ibid., 45–46.

33. Orpen, in A. 6–1879, 16.

34. Bowker ibid., 51, 56, 61.

35. Rolland ibid., 76.

36. See correspondence of colonial officials in A. 6–1879, A. 49–1879.

37. Ayliff, 17 July 1879, in A. 6–1879, 25, 27.

38. Griffith to SNA [8 March], received 9 March 1879, in A. 49–1879, 86.

39. Memo, Colonial Secretary's Office, Cape Town, 14 March 1879, ibid., 86.

40. Griffith to Ayliff, camp near Paladis Village, 20 March 1879, ibid., 87.

41. J.G.S., Office of the Chief Magistrate, Kokstadt, 1 April 1879, ibid., 88.

42. Stevens quoted in a letter of Emma Ellenberger in *Journal des Missions Évangéliques* (1879): 218–22.

43. Ayliff, in A. 6–1879, 28.

44. Mr. J. Wood, MLA, 23 July 1879, ibid., 33–34.

45. "The Taking of 'Quitini' or Moirosi's Mountain, Basutoland, Nov. 21st 1879," handwritten ms., signature illegible, D. F. Ellenberger Papers, Lesotho Evangelical Church/Paris Evangelical Missionary Society (LEC/PEMS) Archives.

46. "Memorandum of Statement made by Moeletsi, who was sent by the Magistrate of Quthing District to accompany Makhube at Makhube's own request, this 18th February 1879," in A. 49–1879, 65.

47. Message from Letsie to the Governor's Agent, 24 February 1879, ibid., 75.

48. Telegram from SNA to C. D. Griffith, CMG, 1 March 1879, ibid., 83.

49. Letsie to Ayliff, SNA, by A. Mabille, Bethesda, 27 April 1879, ibid., 96.

50. Austen, Alwyn's Kop, to SNA, 19 June 1879, ibid., 103.

51. Bowker, 7 August 1879, in A. 6–1879, 53.

52. "Statement of Litsila" before Austen, Resident Magistrate, Quthing, 31 July 1879, in A. 49–1879, 135.

53. Austen to C. D. Griffith, 18 January 1879, ibid., 37, 40.

54. "Voluntary Statement of Mapara" in the court of the Resident Magistrate, Quthing, January 1879, ibid., 47.

55. "Isaak Masin, sworn statement" before Maitin, Justice of the Peace, Quthing, 15 January 1879, ibid., 42.

56. Austen to C. D. Griffith, 18 January 1879, ibid., 40.

57. C. D. Griffith to SNA, 22 January 1879, ibid., 39.

58. "Statement of Nepha" and "Statement of Supone" in the court of the Resident Magistrate for Quthing, 17 February 1879, ibid., 61–64.

59. "Reminiscences of M. Stevens, Resident of Herschel District of 36 Years Standing; the Baputi Chief Morosi," copy of a document prepared for Orpen, handwritten by Ellenberger, Ellenberger Papers, LEC/PEMS Archives.

60. Ibid.

61. Ibid.

62. Atmore, "The Moorosi Rebellion," 32.

63. "The Taking of 'Quitini.'"

Chapter 5. Guns, Diplomacy, and Discourse

1. Rolland, 27 August 1879, in Cape of Good Hope, *Copies of Correspondence,* A. 6–1879, 93.

2. C. D. Griffith to SNA, 6 January 1880, S9/1/4/1, LNA.

3. C. D. Griffith to SNA, 26 January 1880, ibid.

4. C. D. Griffith to Mabille, 25 February 1880, S9/1/3/4, LNA.

5. C. D. Griffith to SNA, 21 May 1880, S9/1/2/2, LNA.

6. C. D. Griffith to SNA, 19 March 1880, S9/1/4/1, LNA.

7. C. D. Griffith to Mabille, Morija, 17 March 1880, no. 114, S9/1/3/4, LNA.

8. C. D. Griffith to SNA, 19 April 1880, S9/1/4/1, LNA.

9. C. D. Griffith to SNA, 27 April 1880, ibid.

10. Ibid.

11. C. D. Griffith to H. Elliot, Kolonyama, 6 July 1880, S9/1/3/4, LNA.

12. C. D. Griffith to Rev. L. Duvoisin, 19 July 1880, ibid.

13. C. D. Griffith to J. H. Windall, J. Breen, and Humphries, n.d. (ca. 20 July 1880), ibid.

14. C. D. Griffith to SNA, S9/1/2/2, LNA.

15. C. D. Griffith to the Resident Magistrate of Cornet Spruit, 28 July 1880, S9/1/3/4, LNA.

16. C. D. Griffith to "Chief Letsie and the Other Chiefs and People of Basutoland," 22 December 1879, no. 87A, ibid.

17. Ibid.

18. C. D. Griffith to Chief Magistrate, Griqualand, 24 December 1879, no. 90A, and C. D. Griffith to Resident Magistrate of Quthing and Resident Magistrate of Cornet Spruit, 3 March 1880, no. 93A, ibid.

19. C. D. Griffith to Chief Masopha, Berea District, 10 February 1880, no. 48, ibid.

20. C. D. Griffith to Chief Letsie, Ha RaKhuite, 13 February 1880, no. 56A, ibid.

21. C. D. Griffith to Mabille, Morija, 11 March 1880, no. 107A, ibid.

22. C. D. Griffith to Mabille, 25 February 1880, no. 75A, ibid.

23. Letter of "Letsie Morena oa BaSutos, ka [written by] Tsekelo Moshoeshoe," to Ellenberger, 13 February 1880, Ellenberger Papers, LEC/PEMS Archives, translation mine, emphasis in original.

24. Ellenberger, Masitisi Mission Station, to C. D. Griffith, 19 February 1880, ibid.

25. C. D. Griffith to Letsie, 12 March 1880, no. 111A, S9/1/3/4, LNA.

26. C. D. Griffith to Letsie, 3 April 1880, no. 141, ibid.

27. C. D. Griffith to Letsie, 8 April 1880, no. 151, ibid.

28. C. D. Griffith to Letsie, 15 May 1880, no. 201, 17 May 1880, no. 204, 11 June 1880, no. 236, 11 June 1880 (again), no. 237, 15 June 1880, no. 240, ibid.

29. C. D. Griffith to Letsie, 19 June 1880, no. 246, ibid.

30. Burman, *Chiefdom Politics*, 138.

31. C. D. Griffith to SNA, 29 June 1880, S9/1/2/2, LNA.

32. Orpen to SNA, 13 September 1882, ibid.

33. Lagden, *The Basutos*, 2:511.

34. Mosebi Damane, interview with author, June 1989.

35. Charles Dube Molapo, interview with author, June 1989.

36. Patrick Lehloenya II, interview with author, June 1989, translation mine.

37. C. D. Griffith to SNA, 23 June 1880, S9/1/2/2, LNA.

38. Burman, *Chiefdom Politics*, 140–41.

39. Damane interview.

40. Ibid.

41. Lehloenya II interview; Charles D. Molapo interview.

42. Charles D. Molapo interview.

43. C. D. Griffith to SNA, 13 July 1880, S9/1/2/2, LNA.

44. Ibid.

45. C. D. Griffith to SNA, 8 March 1880, S9/1/4/1, LNA.

46. C. D. Griffith to Chief Masopha, 21 July 1880, S9/1/3/4, LNA.

47. C. D. Griffith to Chief Masopha, 22 July 1880, ibid.; and C. D. Griffith to SNA, 18 August 1880, 9/1/2/2, LNA. He reported that those taking part in the depredations were Masopha, Lerotholi, Leshoboro, Lesaoana, Lepoqo (the eldest son of Masopha), Mapeshoane, Bereng Letsie, Nkoebe Letsie, Alexander Letsie, Peete Lesaoana, Smith Posholi, and Jeremiah Jobo; some were reported to have already made restitutions.

48. Griffith to "Chiefs Lerotholi, Joel, Molapo & others who signed a petition to the Governor and High Commissioner," S9/1/3/4, LNA.

49. C. D. Griffith to SNA, 13 December 1880, S9/1/2/2, LNA.

50. A. C. Manyeli, interview with author, June 1989.

51. C. D. Griffith to SNA, 14 July 1880, S9/1/2/2, LNA.

52. Lagdon, *The Basutos*, 2:494.

53. Ibid., 2:494, 495, 496.

Chapter 6. Hidden Discourse in the Public Transcript

1. This and subsequent evidence from this meeting are found in: Minutes enclosed by the Governor's Agent in his letter to the Secretary for Native Affairs, no. 2/109, 14 July 1880, Cape Archives, N.A. 278, reprinted in Burman, *Justice*, 93–104. These minutes were written and submitted to the Colonial Office by Charles Maitin.

2. Burman, *Justice*, 104 n.13.

3. Ibid., 104 n.14.

4. C. D. Griffith to SNA, no. 2/109, 14 July 1880, Cape Archives, N.A. 278, reprinted ibid., 93.

5. Austen to Ellenberger, 5 July 1880, PFII, Ellenberger Papers, LEC/PEMS Archives.

6. C. D. Griffith to SNA, 22 July 1880, S9/1/2/2, LNA.

7. Austen to Ellenberger, 13 August 1880, PFII, Ellenberger Papers.

8. C. D. Griffith to Letsie, 31 July 1880, marked "confidential," S9/1/3/4, LNA.

9. Lagden, *The Basutos*, 2:468–69.

10. C. D. Griffith to Letsie, 31 July 1880, marked "confidential," S9/1/3/4, LNA.

11. C. D. Griffith to SNA, 4 August 1880, S9/1/2/2, LNA.

12. Ibid.

13. C. D. Griffith to Letsie, 4 August 1880, S9/1/3/4, LNA.

14. C. D. Griffith to Letsie, 11 August 1880, ibid.

15. Lagden, *The Basutos*, 2:514.

16. C. D. Griffith to Letsie, 15 August 1880, S9/1/3/4, LNA.

17. Ibid.

18. C. D. Griffith to Letsie, 17 August 1880, ibid.

19. C. D. Griffith to SNA, 18 August 1880, S9/1/2/2, ibid.

20. C. D. Griffith to Letsie at Ha Rakhuite, September 1880, S9/1/3/4, LNA.

21. C. D. Griffith to Letsie, 28 February 1881, ibid.

22. C. D. Griffith to SNA, 24 March 1881, S9/1/2/2, LNA. In a postscript Griffith noted that "the original letter is in the hand writing of Dr. Casalis of Morija."

23. Burman, *Chiefdom Politics*, 141, 221 nn.56, 57, citing correspondence of Griffith on 2 August 1880. Bereng Letsie confiscated property in the Thaba Bosiu District, and when the District Magistrate (Davies) "subsequently served Bereng with a summons, the chief tore it up, burnt it, and threatened to punish the bearer: and Davies was quite unable to punish Bereng."

24. C. D. Griffith to Letsie, 5 September 1880, S9/1/3/4, LNA. Outstanding, detailed coverage of people, troop movements, and other events of the war can be found in Tylden, *The Rise of the Basuto*, 137–86, who consulted with Charles J. Maitin.

25. Burman, *Chiefdom Politics*, 145.

26. A. Barkly to Sir Henry Barkly, 15 September 1880, quoted in Barkly, *Among Boers*, 182–86. Also quoted in Burman, *Chiefdom Politics*, 145–46, where the word "policies" is incorrectly written "polices."

27. Lagden, *The Basutos*, 2:521.

28. Ibid., 2:520.

29. Ibid., 2:521.

30. Ibid., 2:523; Burman, *Chiefdom Politics*, 150.

31. Lagden, *The Basutos*, 2:523.

32. Burman, *Chiefdom Politics*, 149–50; Tylden, *The Rise of the Basuto*, 164.

33. Burman, *Chiefdom Politics*, 152–53. See the letters of C. D. Griffith to the SNA, to troop commanders, to Letsie, and to Lerotholi, February–April 1881, S9/1/2/2, S9/1/3/4, LNA.

34. Originally printed in the local *Eastern Star* paper, reproduced in Tylden, *The Rise of the Basuto*, 173–78.

35. Orpen to SNA, 21 September 1881, 26 September 1881, S9/1/2/2, LNA.

36. Orpen to SNA, 30 September 1881, ibid.

37. Orpen to SNA, 19 November 1881, ibid.

38. Orpen to SNA from Thaba Bosiu, 19 January 1882, dispatch no. 2, ibid.

39. Burman, *Chiefdom Politics*, 157.

40. Ibid., 160.

41. Orpen, 15 February 1882, S9/1/3/5, LNA.

42. Ibid.

43. Orpen to SNA, telegram, 15 February 1882, S9/1/2/2, LNA. He expressed similar views in a letter two weeks later; see Orpen to SNA, 8 March 1882, ibid.

44. "Translation of letter by Letsie sent to High Commissioner," 5 March 1882, ibid. With the support of Orpen the High Commissioner sent the letter on to the SNA.

45. The High Commissioner consulted with the Cape government ministers, who advised him prior to his repeal of the law. See Lagden, *The Basuto,* 2: 533; Burman, *Chiefdom Politics,* 161.

46. Orpen to SNA, 13 September 1882, S9/1/2/2, LNA.

47. Lagden, *The Basuto,* 2:534–35. Burman concludes that Sauer was duplicitous in his dealings by encouraging both Gordon's overtures to Masopha and Lerotholi's expedition of troops to use coercion, although Sauer clearly did not trust Gordon and kept his moves and words under observation by the Inspector-General of the colonial forces. See Burman, *Chiefdom Politics,* 167–69.

48. Lagden, *The Basuto,* 2:535.

49. Burman, *Chiefdom Politics,* 139.

50. The choice of the name "Senate," pronounced as three syllables, presumably reflects the long-standing Western influence already pervasive at the time of her birth and the long-standing respect of the BaSotho for Roman-derived Western traditions of democratic governance.

51. Motsoene also contested the inheritance of his grandfather Molapo, further confusing the inheritance fight between Jonathan and Joel.

52. SeSotho law provided for the eldest son of the senior wife of a chief to succeed him; her status was determined by the payment of her bridewealth, *bohali,* by the chief's people. She was his "first" wife, and normally (but not necessarily) she was the first wife he married. If her eldest son were incapacitated or deemed unable to fulfill his duties, her next son would therefore be the legal heir, as she was the wife who had been explicitly chosen to produce the heir, as recognized at the time of her marriage in the source of the bridewealth.

53. Lagden, *The Basuto,* 2:539.

54. Ibid., 2:540–51.

55. Quoted in Burman, *Chiefdom Politics,* 176.

56. Ibid., 177.

57. Matt Blyth, Acting Governor's Agent, to Acting Resident Magistrate of Leribe, 3 October 1883, no. 477E, S9/1/3/6, LNA.

58. Blyth to Acting Resident Magistrate of Leribe, 3 November 1883, ibid.

59. Quoted in Burman, *Chiefdom Politics,* 179.

60. Blyth to President Brand, Orange Free State, 6 July 1883, no. 333E, and Blyth to Letsie, no. 316E, S9/1/3/6, LNA. I do not have any further information about these letters.

61. Blyth to Letsie, 27 June 1883, ibid.

62. Lagden, *The Basuto,* 2:555.
63. Ibid., 2:556.

Chapter 7. Lerotholi and "Masopha's War"

1. Lagden, *The Basuto,* 2:559.
2. Ibid., 2:561–62.
3. Burman, *Chiefdom Politics,* 228 n.8.
4. Ibid., 166.
5. Lagden, *The Basuto,* 2:566–67.
6. Ibid., 2:570–71.
7. Ibid., 2:571.
8. Ibid., 2:574–75.
9. Ibid., 2:576.
10. Ibid., 579.
11. Lagden to Lerotholi, 6 July 1897, S8/2/2/5, LNA.
12. Lagden to Lerotholi, 13 July 1897, S7/3/14, LNA.
13. Lerotholi to Lagden, 14 July 1897, ibid.
14. Lagden to Lerotholi, 18 July 1897, S8/2/2/5, LNA.
15. Lerotholi to Lagden, 21 July 1897, S7/3/14, LNA; the original SeSotho of the final phrase reads, "Ho qala Seaka mohla u reng re lira tsa tlaho ho fihla kajeno."
16. Leshoboro to Lagden, 22 July 1897, ibid.
17. Lerotholi to Lagden, 25 July 1897, ibid.
18. Lagden to Lerotholi, 25 July 1897, ibid.
19. Lerotholi to Lagden, 28 July 1897, ibid.
20. Attached to Lerotholi's letter to Lagden, 28 July 1897, ibid., date illegible.
21. Lagden to Lerotholi, 20 September 1897, S8/2/2/5, LNA.
22. Lerotholi to Lagden, 2 October 1897, S7/3/14, ibid.
23. Lerotholi to Lagden, 4 October 1897, ibid.
24. Masopha (as David Masupha Moshesh) to Lerotholi, 3 October 1897, ibid.
25. Lerotholi to Lagden, 6 October 1897, ibid.
26. Masopha to Lerotholi, 23 October 1897, ibid.
27. Lagden to Lerothodi, 30 October 1897, S8/2/2/5, LNA.
28. Lagden to Lerothodi, 17 November 1897, ibid.
29. M. Dieterlen, letter in *Journal des Missions Évangéliques,* 20 December 1898; Damane interview; Moeketsi Moseeka, interview with author, 6 February 1982.
30. Moseeka interview; Damane interview; Charles D. Molapo interview.
31. Lagden to Lerothodi, 26 November 1897, S8/2/2/5, LNA.

32. Lagden to Lerothodi, 29 November 1897, ibid.

33. Lagden to Lerotholi, 5 December 1897, S8/2/2/6, LNA.

34. Lagden to Lerotholi, 7 December 1897, ibid.

35. Lagden to Lerothodi, 9 December 1897, ibid.

36. Ibid.

37. Ibid.

38. Lagden to Lerotholi, 10 December 1897, ibid.

39. Lagden to Lerotholi, 17 December 1897, ibid.

40. Lagden to Lerotholi, 21 December 1897, ibid.

41. Lagden to Lerotholi, 24 December 1897, ibid.

42. Lagden to Lerotholi, 26 December 1897, ibid.

43. Lagden to Lerotholi, 7 January 1898, ibid. Emphasis in original.

44. Lagden to Lerotholi, 8 January 1898, ibid.

45. Lagden to Lerotholi, 9 January 1898, ibid.

46. Lagden to Lerotholi, 10 January 1898, ibid.

47. Lagden to Lerotholi, 10 January 1898 (second letter), ibid.

48. Lagden to Chief Maama, 12 January 1898, ibid.

49. Maama had engaged in brinkmanship against Lerotholi with armed forces twice in 1894. The first time Lerotholi had been fined by the Resident Commissioner for precipitously attacking Maama while negotiations were under way. At the end of 1894, when a similar situation arose, Lerotholi sought Lagden's support first, and both men had ridden to the scene of standoff between armed men. This time Maama was given two hours to surrender, and Lagden approved Lerotholi's use of military force if necessary. Maama had waited until the deadline expired before turning himself over for trial, during which Lerotholi's right to exercise authority over Maama's people was affirmed in court.

50. Lagden to Maama, 13 January 1898, S8/2/2/6, LNA.

51. Lagden to Lerotholi, 16 January 1898, ibid. Emphasis in original.

52. Lagden to Lerotholi, 22 January 1898, ibid.

53. Lagden to Lerotholi, 24 January 1898 (first letter), ibid.

54. Lagden to Lerotholi, 24 January 1898 (second letter), ibid.

55. Lagden, *The Basuto*, 2:596–97; *Journal des Missions Évangéliques* (February 1898): 91–95; "La Fin des Troubles," *Journal des Missions Évangéliques* (March 1898); and Great Britain, *Colonial Reports—Annual* No. 255, *Basutoland*, Cd. 9046–23, 7.

56. Lagden to Lerothodi, 4 February 1898, S8/2/2/6, LNA.

57. Lagden to Lerotholi, 9 August 1898, S7/3/14, LNA.

58. Mojela Letsie to the Resident Commissioner, 18 August 1898, ibid.

59. Mojela Letsie to Resident Commissioner, 22 August 1898, ibid.

60. Lagden, *The Basuto*, 2:594.

61. Lagden to Lerothodi, 4 February 1898, S8/2/2/6, LNA.

Chapter 8. Of Laws, Courts, and Chiefs

1. Lagden served as Resident Commissioner from 1893 until he was called in 1901 to serve under Milner in the Transvaal, where he served beyond the end of the war until his retirement in 1907. Supportive of Milner's broader goals during and after the war, Lagden nevertheless feared that all his work as a colonial officer in Basutoland, whose progress was measured in schools, hospitals, and Westernization in general, would come to naught if Lesotho came under the rule of a unified, white-ruled Union of South Africa, and he especially feared the destructive results of possible land alienation. His two-volume book, which was published in 1909 as the issue of the incorporation was pending in London, made the case for the protection of the BaSotho, law-abiding people who paid their taxes to support British colonial governance. See Lagden, *The Basuto*, 2:646, 626–49.

2. Great Britain, *Colonial Reports—Annual* No. 255, *Basutoland*, 28.

3. Lagden, August 1899, in Great Britain, *Colonial Reports—Annual* No. 288, *Basutoland*, 4.

4. Lagden, *The Basuto*, 2:597.

5. Lagden, August 1899, in Great Britain, *Colonial Reports—Annual* No. 288, *Basutoland*, 7, 17.

6. S. Barrett, ibid., 47.

7. Lagden to Lerotholi, 15 March 1898, S8/2/2/6, LNA.

8. See the correspondence between Lagden and various chiefs, including Lerotholi, Maama, Masopha, and Jonathan, in S8/1/1/6 and S7/3/14, LNA.

9. Lerotholi to Lagden, 31 March 1898, S7/3/14, LNA.

10. Lerotholi to Maama, 18 May 1898, ibid.

11. Lagden to Lerotholi, 30 June 1898, ibid.

12. Lerotholi to Lagden, 1 July 1898, and Lagden to "the chiefs of Leribe," 5 July 1898, ibid.

13. Lagden, August 1899, in Great Britain, *Colonial Reports—Annual* No. 288, *Basutoland*, 6.

14. Poulter, "The Place." On historical and postindependence aspects of laws and legal systems in Lesotho see Poulter, *Legal Dualism in Lesotho;* Maqutu, *Contemporary Constitutional History;* and Machobane, *Government and Change.*

15. See the correspondence between Lerothodi and Lagden and between Lerotholi and Acting Resident Commissioner Herbert C. Sloley for 1899–1902 in S7/3/14 and S8/2/2/6, LNA.

16. Lagden, *The Basuto*, 2:600–610.

17. Ibid., 2:605–6.

18. Ibid., 2:609.

19. Great Britain, *Colonial Reports—Annual* No. 313, *Basutoland*, 40.

20. L. Wroughton, Government Secretary, to Lerotholi, 14 October 1903, S8/2/2/7, LNA.

21. High Commissioner via Sloley to Lerotholi, 13 October 1903, ibid.

22. Selborne, High Commissioner's office, Johannesburg, to Lerothodi, 30 June 1905, ibid.

23. Sloley, Resident Commissioner, to Paramount Chief Letsie II, 16 June 1908, ibid.

24. Letsie II to Sloley, 12 May 1908, ibid.

25. Sloley to Letsie II, 10 October 1908, and Sloley to Alex Maama, 16 October 1908, ibid.

26. Wroughton, Acting Resident Commissioner, to Letsie II, 31 December 1908, ibid.

27. Sloley to Letsie II, 22 July 1909, ibid.

28. Sloley to Paramount Chief Griffith, 30 September 1914, S8/2/2/9, LNA.

29. See correspondence between Paramount Chief Griffith Lerotholi and Resident Commissioner R. T. Coryndon, November 1916 and May 1917, S7/4/10 and S8/2/2/9, LNA.

30. For this and other details of this episode in BaSotho history see Edgar, "Lesotho and the First World War"; and Mabille, *Mokhosi oa Fora.*

31. Griffith to Coryndon, 29 November 1916, S7/4/10, LNA.

32. Ibid.

33. Coryndon to Griffith, 21 February 1917, no. 166, Coryndon to Griffith, 28 February 1917, no. 170, S8/2/2/9, LNA.

34. Macgregor, Deputy Resident Commissioner, to Griffith, 12 May 1917, no. 218, ibid.

35. Macgregor, "To the Paramount Chief and Chiefs of the Basuto," 27 May 1917, ibid.

36. See the correspondence of Griffith and other chiefs in S7/4/12 and S8/2/2/9, LNA.

37. Macgregor to Griffith, 14, 16, and 19 July 1917, and Resident Commissioner Coryndon to Griffith, 4 August 1917, S8/2/2/9, LNA; Griffith, "Notice to Chiefs," 5 August 1917, S7/4/12, LNA.

38. Charles E. Boyes, Government Secretary, to Griffith, 11 December 1917, S7/4/12, LNA.

39. *Memorandum Prepared by the Parliamentary Committee.* Gen. Jan Smuts was Prime Minister of the Union of South Africa from 1919 to 1924 and again from 1939 to 1948. James Barry Hertzog was Prime Minister from 1924 to 1939.

40. Khama, *Statement.*

41. Lord Lugard, "South Africa and the Protectorates: A Complex Problem," and "South Africa and the Protectorates: Home Government's Past Neglect." The dramatic use of four headlines using half a page above each article indicated the interest in the issue in London at the time.

42. The legal and political issues involved in the "transfer" or "incorporation" question have been assessed in a number of government and scholarly

studies. See, for example, Union of South Africa, *Negotiations;* Doxey, *The High Commission Territories;* Spence, "British Policy"; Glass, *South African Policy;* Stevens, "The History"; Torrance, "Britain."

43. Whether out of deference or ignorance, when the *Leselinyana* ran Paramount Chief Griffith's obituary after his death in 1939 it stated incorrectly that Griffith had been heir and successor to his elder brother Paramount Chief Letsie II because the latter had had no children. Letsie II had more than one biological male child and one male child born to a legitimate wife and eligible to inherit but still a toddler at the time of his father's death.

44. Maama Letsie, 17 Hlakubele 1913, to the Government of Lesotho, H.C. no. 36/13, LNA.

45. Acting Resident Commissioner to Gladstone, High Commissioner, 1 February 1913, H.C. no. 16/13, LNA. The Resident Commissioner, Sir Herbert Slolely, was out of the country at the time, and it is not clear who was Acting Resident Commissioner, as the letter from the files is an unsigned copy kept by the sender; it may have been L. Wroughton, who had previously served as Acting Resident Commissioner.

46. Ibid.

47. Maama Letsie, 17 Hlakubele 1913, to the Government of Lesotho. On these events see also Machobane, *Government and Change,* 106–8.

48. Griffith to the Government of Lesotho, 29 March 1916, H.C. no. 34/16, LNA. I have quoted the government translation attached to the original because it accurately conveys the meaning and language of the SeSotho, but I have indicated more precisely several terms used in the letters.

49. Laydevant, *Bophelo.*

50. Ibid., 52.

51. The designation of a principal wife whose firstborn would become heir to a chief was known by everyone because of the collection of cattle for bridewealth from all areas that fell under his authority. In the case of the Paramount Chief, cattle to pay the bridewealth were gathered and sent from all districts of the country. Not only the chiefs but also everyone living within their jurisdictions were subject to the demand for a contribution, although in practice the numbers were limited and the responsibility lay with the chiefs, who could then demand compensation for any of their own cattle sent from the herds of their followers. For junior wives of a chief bridewealth was provided exclusively from the herds owned by his father (or paternal uncles), legitimating any children as belonging to the male line of descent but not indicating birthright as an heir. For further explanation of the role of bridewealth in the nineteenth and early twentieth centuries that governed the actions of Lerotholi and other chiefs in this era see Eldredge, *South African Kingdom,* 136–44.

52. Crais, "Conquest," 27–28; and Tylden, *The Rise of the Basuto,* 152–53, 158.

53. Laydevant, *Bophelo,* 33–36.

54. Ibid., 32–33.

55. I have not seen an explanation for this name, but the spelling of a word with a double letter in SeSotho indicates the sound is produced twice, so that the name Aa might have been pronounced as Ah-ah, which is used as a negative, "no," *tjee,* in SeSotho and may refer to Sebueng's previous refusal of her husband, Griffith. This is only speculation, however.

56. According to Laydevant she said, "Ha eba ke le thibelo tsokolohong ea hao, ke kopa hore Molimo a ntlose lefatseng lena" (*Bophelo,* 49).

57. Ibid., 50–51, 53.

58. Ibid., 68–70; Machobane, *Government and Change,* 139–49. Machobane points out that these events caused a vocal backlash against the Paramount Chief on the part of the *bahlalefi,* the educated elite who had formed the Basutoland Progressive Association and who were pressing for greater representation of commoners on the Basutoland National Council.

59. *Leselinyana la Lesotho,* 8 Mphalane 1926, 15 Mphalane 1926, 22 Mphalane 1926, 29 Mphalane 1926, 5 Pulungoana 1926, 12 Pulungoana 1926, 19 Pulunguana 1926, 26 Pulungoana 1926, 3 Tsitoe 1926. The assembled Principal chiefs did not take seriously the oblique references to the possibility that Griffith might not have been the biological father of Seeiso. They also dismissed other evidence as insignificant, such as 'MaSeeiso's own opinions, which reflected her preferences rather than points of law regarding her marriage, bridewealth, desertion, and return. They also evidently dismissed suggestions that because Bereng had thrown the first dirt at a funeral his seniority was recognized, since Seeiso indicated he had been told to wait for the priest to throw the first dirt, not expecting Bereng to do so before him. My conclusions more accurately reflect the sentiments of the chiefs at the hearing than do those of Machobane, who assumes the seniority of Bereng's mother based on a more limited reading of the evidence. Machobane, *Government and Change,* 188–95.

60. See Machobane, *Government and Change,* 195, for additional information on this meeting.

61. To avoid confusion here their surnames, indicating their fathers, are used, so that the child heir is referred to as Bereng Seeiso and his uncle as Bereng Griffith.

62. For further details see Machobane, *Government and Change,* 198–200.

63. *Financial and Economic Position.*

64. Lord Hailey, *The High Commission Territories,* 82.

65. Ibid., 88.

66. Machobane, *Government and Change,* 199.

Chapter 9. Of Paramente and Power

1. It was pointed out to me that Paramente screamed because it was customary for a person on the point of death to scream to the ancestors to announce

they were coming to the afterlife; this underscores the point that Paramente knew he was going to die when he saw the crowd of men approach him.

2. This testimony and all of the evidence that follows about the Paramente case is from the court record: Court Cases. CR 252/48–1/2/49, records of the High Court, LNA.

3. Whitworth, writing on behalf of Reverend Threlfall, to Nourse, 29 April 1824, in Theal, *Records of South Eastern Africa,* ix, 47.

4. Backhouse, *A Narrative,* 281.

5. Brownlee, *Reminiscences,* 238–40.

6. Casalis, *The Basutos,* 256–57.

7. Arnold A. Lili Molibeli, Tajane, 28 August 1960, to Marion How, Papers of Marion How, LEC/PEMS Archives.

8. See "Appendix A: List of murders believed to be Medicine murders," in Jones, *Medicine Murder,* 79–103, ref. no. 1.

9. Ibid., ref. no. 7.

10. Ibid., ref. no. 14.

11. Ramseyer, "La Circoncision."

12. Anonymous typescript, "Buka Ena e Matsohong a Batho Ba Baholo Feela," LEC/PEMS Archives.

13. Haliburton, "Edward Lion of Lesotho," 66, quoting the report of a colonial administrator.

14. The evidence for this case is discussed extensively by Murray and Sanders, *Medicine Murder,* 99–117, who also provide additional and valuable insights into the local politics and persons involved in both murders.

15. Rev. Albert Brutsch, interview with author, 30 July 1993.

16. Harragin, "The High Commission Territories," 5.

Chapter 10. Discourse and Subterfuge

1. Formally designated as the Regent Paramount Chief, 'Mantsebo was usually referred to in colonial documents as Paramount Chief, without reference to her name, and more rarely as Regent or as Paramount Chieftainess.

2. Circular no. 1 of 1946, Office of the Paramount Chief, Matsieng, Basutoland, 10 January 1946, emphasis added. Papers of Marion How, LEC/PEMS Archives.

3. Circular no. 28 of 1946, Office of the Paramount Chief, Matsieng, 31 July 1946.

4. Ibid., emphasis added.

5. Circular no. 42 of 1947, Office of the Paramount Chief, Matsieng, 4 November 1947.

6. Circular no. 8 of 1948, Office of the Paramount Chief, Matsieng, 9 April 1948. Signed by David Theko Makhaola, who served as Acting Paramount

Chief for a period of four months for 'Mantsebo; I have not been able to determine the reason for this.

7. Circular no. 46 of 1948, Office of the Paramount Chief, Matsieng, 18 December 1948.

8. Notice, Medicine Murders, A. D. Forsyth Thompson, Maseru, November 1948. Papers of Marion How, LEC/PEMS Archives.

9. Ibid., emphasis in original.

10. Ibid.

11. Machobane, *Government and Change*, 237–48.

12. Arden Clarke to his mother, 19 September 1944, quoted in Rooney, *Sir Charles Arden-Clarke*, 61.

13. Ibid.

14. Douglas-Home, *Evelyn Baring*, 198.

15. Typescript marked "Private. First Impressions of Basutoland. January 1947," Forsyth Thompson Collection, Killie Campbell Library.

16. Great Britain, *Annual Report on Basutoland for the Year 1947*.

17. This and the following references to his diary are from the diary of A. D. Forsyth Thompson, "South African Diary 1948," Forsyth Thompson Collection.

18. Douglas-Home, *Evelyn Baring*, 199.

19. Sir Evelyn Baring, High Commissioner, Pretoria, to Forsyth Thompson, 19 November 1949, Forsyth Thompson Collection.

20. In their exhaustive new study on medicine murder in colonial Lesotho in the 1940s and 1950s, Murray and Sanders provide extensive details on how Jones came to be invited to undertake his study. Murray, an anthropologist, and Sanders, a colonial official turned historian, have focused on the more exotic and sociological explanations for the problem. Besides providing the standard survey of historical events regarding colonial administrative changes that so many colonial officials and historians, and Jones, identified as the stimulus for a "crisis," they investigate numerous cases in depth, with attention to political motives, instigators and accomplices, plots, processes of entrapment, mutilation, and disposal of victims' bodies, and judicial processes in cases brought to trial. Their attention to my preliminary presentation of a portion of my work on the subject in a 1997 conference paper is flattering if misleading, and my central argument is misrepresented (Murray and Sanders, *Medicine Murder*, 288). Their voluminous coverage of the data is impressive, and many of their observations are important, but I strongly disagree with their line of argument that the medicine murder crisis arose *because* of a cultural propensity and traditional beliefs and practices.

21. Jones, *Medicine Murder*, 10–11.

22. Ibid., 12. In SeSotho orthography the term is spelled *liretlo* but pronounced as if spelled with a *d*.

23. Ibid., 18.

24. Marion How, handwritten notes on the Jones report, 24, Papers of Marion How, LEC/PEMS Archives.

25. "Secret. Analysis of Ritual Murders and Their Relation to Various Administrative Events," typescript manuscript, no author, 9. Private copy, see note 33.

26. How, notes on Jones report, 63.

27. Jones, *Medicine Murder*, 19.

28. Ibid., 20, 62.

29. Murray and Sanders provide compelling evidence that in some of the later crimes some participants were willing accomplices who as witnesses in trials deliberately changed their stories and told contradictory stories to undermine court cases against themselves.

30. Jones, *Medicine Murder*, 34–35, emphasis added.

31. Ibid., 66.

32. Ibid., 67.

33. They appear to have reached this conclusion because of the location of the documents in the Ashton papers in Cape Town as well as in the Jones collection at Cambridge University. The reports had recently been brought to light at the time I was conducting research in Lesotho in 1988 and 1989, and copies from both Cambridge and Cape Town came into my hands from two different sources, but in Lesotho access to them was carefully restricted at the time. Two other scholars suggested to me that they were unsure of the authorship of these reports, which they thought might be the work of Hugh Ashton.

34. Murray and Sanders also indicate the lack of a clearly designated author for these reports (*Medicine Murder*, 446 n.12).

35. Ashton, "Medicine, Magic, and Sorcery."

36. Ashton, *The Basuto*, 306–16.

37. "Secret. Analysis of Ritual Murders and Their Relation to Various Administrative Events," anonymous typescript, 7. See note 33.

38. "Secret. Mokhotlong District," anonymous typescript, 31.

39. Ibid., 32–33.

40. Ibid., 32.

41. Ibid., 33–34.

42. Ibid., 6–7.

43. Ibid., 1–5. Of these, Mahlomola had been convicted at the time of the report, and the cases of the others were pending.

44. "Secret. Analysis of Ritual Murders," 6.

45. As is evident from the records, from cases described by Mark Epprecht, and from cases described to me in an interview with C. D. Molapo in June 1989, some deaths were mistakenly attributed to medicine murder, and some clients were acquitted. But the evidence against Bereng, Gabashane, 'Mantsebo, and Matlere is damning. See, for example, from the Jones report Case 33 (HC 303/46), Case 42 (HC 335/47), Case 74 (HC 36/48), Case 46, Case 49 (HC

301/46), Case 86 (HC 36/49), and others. I disagree with Epprecht's conclusions about medicine murder in an otherwise strong work, "Women, Class and Politics."

46. "Secret. Analysis of Ritual Murders," 6.

47. Ibid.

48. Interview of Chief Makhaola in the *Friend,* an Orange Free State newspaper, quoted in "Basutoland Murders: Opinion of Basuto Chief," *Basutoland News,* 7 September 1948.

49. "Basuto" to Marion How, Mokhotlong, 27 May 1954, Papers of Marion How.

50. Ibid.

51. Damane, "Sotho Medicine."

52. A. C. Manyeli, interview with author, June 1989.

53. Jingoes, *A Chief Is a Chief,* 188, 201–2.

54. "Secret. Mokhotlong District," 33.

55. Unsigned letter with postscript, Forsyth Thompson to Lord Hailey, Resident Commissioner's office, Maseru, 15 January 1951, Forsyth Thompson Collection.

56. Douglas-Home, *Evelyn Baring,* 162–95.

57. Jones, *Medicine Murder,* 70–73.

58. Forsyth Thompson to Sir Evelyn Baring, 29 November 1950, Forsyth Thompson Collection, marked "Personal and Confidential."

59. Letter signed by G. J. Armstrong and initialed by A. D. Forsyth Thompson, 8 March 1950, Maseru, marked *"Confidential. Basutoland.,* Q.N.L. No. 1., S. 298 A. /DKD," 4, par. 15, Forsyth Thompson Collection.

60. Ibid., 8, par. 36.

61. Ibid., 8, par. 37.

62. Machobane, *Government and Change,* 247.

63. My biographical information on Constantine Bereng Seeiso comes from ibid., 266–74; and Lekoatsa, "Bophelo."

64. Machobane, *Government and Change,* 266–67, based on his interview of the sister, Mufumahali 'Mampoi (Makhaola) Seeiso, 30 December 1988.

65. Ibid., 271–75.

Chapter 11. Seeking Sovereignty and the Rule of Law

1. Machobane, *Government and Change,* 257–63.

2. Haliburton, *Historical Dictionary of Lesotho,* related entries on parties and leaders. See also Weisfelder, *Political Contention,* and Machobane, *Government and Change* for details on politics in Lesotho from the 1950s through independence in 1966 and beyond.

3. Weisfelder, *Political Contention,* 15–18. In the elections for District Councils (which provided the elected members of the Basutoland National Council)

held 20 January 1960 total votes cast were 35,302. Of these, the Basutoland Congress Party received 12,787 votes, and the Basutoland National Party won 7,002 votes, but the BNP did not win a majority, since Independents won 12,470, the Marema-Tlou Party won 2,182 votes, and the Basutoland Progressive Association won 231 votes. These statistics, from Great Britain's 1959 *Colonial Reports—Annual: Basutoland,* do not specify further about the delegates identified as "Independents" (110–11).

4. Mr. E. Rolland, 27 August 1879, in Great Britain, *Minutes of Evidence,* 85–86.

5. Said, *Culture and Imperialism,* xviii–xix.

6. Machobane, *Government and Change,* 220–48.

7. Khaketla, *Lesotho 1970,* 64–73.

8. Colonial dimensions of the politics of the late colonial period are reflected in Peter Sanders's recent autobiographical work, *The Last of the Queen's Men.* For controversies on the emergence and activities of parties and party leaders in the 1950s and 1960s see Machobane, *Government and Change,* 253–65, 282–306; Khaketla, *Lesotho 1970;* and Weisfelder, *Political Contention.*

9. Eldredge, *A South African Kingdom.*

10. Kimble, "'Clinging to the Chiefs.'"

BIBLIOGRAPHY

Archival Collections

BOLESWA Collection, National University of Lesotho
Killie Campbell Library, Durban, South Africa
  • Forsyth Thompson Collection
Lesotho Evangelical Church/Paris Evangelical Missionary Society (LEC/PEMS) Archives, Morija, Lesotho
  • D. F. Ellenberger Papers
  • Papers of Marion How
  • Miscellaneous documents
Lesotho National Archives (LNA)
  • Basutoland records, vols. 4–6
  • Correspondence files
  • Records of the High Court

Official and Government Publications

Cape of Good Hope. *Blue Book on Native Affairs.* Cape Town: Saul Solomon and Co. 1874 to 1883.
———. *Copies of Correspondence, Telegrams, etc. in re Morosi's Rebellion, Basutoland,* A. 49–79. Cape Town: Saul Solomon and Co., 1879.
———. *Report of the Select Committee on Hostilities in Basutoland.* A6–79. Cape Town: Saul Solomon and Co., 1879.
Financial and Economic Position of Basutoland: Report of the Commission Appointed by the Secretary of State for Dominion Affairs. London: January 1935. Cd. 4907. (Pim Report).
Great Britain. *Colonial Reports—Annual. Basutoland.* London: H.M.S.O., 1884–1939 and 1946–1964.
Jones, G. I. *Medicine Murder: A Report of the Recent Outbreak of Liretlo Murders in Basutoland.* London: H.M.S.O., 1951. Cmd. 8209.

Memorandum Prepared by the Parliamentary Committee for Studying the Position of the South African Protectorates. London: Headley Brothers, 1934.

Union of South Africa. *Negotiations Regarding the Transfer to the Union of South Africa of the Government of Basutoland, the Bechuanaland Protectorate and Swaziland 1910–1939.* Pretoria, 1952.

Books and Articles

Arac, Jonathan, ed. *After Foucault: Humanistic Knowledge, Postmodern Challenges.* New Brunswick, N.J.: Rutgers University Press, 1988.

Ashcroft, Bill, Gareth Griffiths, and Helen Tifin, eds. *The Post-Colonial Studies Reader.* London: Routledge, 1995.

Ashton, Hugh. *The Basuto: A Social Study of Traditional and Modern Lesotho.* London: Oxford University Press, 1952; 2nd ed. 1967.

———. "Medicine, Magic, and Sorcery among the Southern Sotho." University of Cape Town, Communications from the School of African Studies, n.s. no. 10, December 1943.

Atkins, Keletso E. *The Moon Is Dead! Give Us Our Money! The Cultural Origins of an African Work Ethic, Natal, South Africa, 1843–1900.* Portsmouth: Heinemann, 1993.

Atmore, Anthony. "The Moorosi Rebellion: Lesotho, 1879." In *Protest and Power in Black Africa*, ed. Robert I. Rotberg and Ali A. Mazrui, 3–35. New York: Oxford University Press, 1970.

Backhouse, James. *A Narrative of a Visit to the Mauritius and South Africa.* London: Hamilton, Adams and Co., 1844.

Barkly, Fanny A. *Among Boers and Basutos.* London: Remington, 1893.

Berman, Bruce, and John Lonsdale, eds. *Violence and Ethnicity.* Vol. 2 of *Unhappy Valley: Conflict in Kenya and Africa.* Athens: Ohio University Press, 1992.

Bernstein, H., and B. K. Campbell, eds. *Contradictions of Accumulation in Africa: Studies in Economy and State.* London: Sage, 1985.

Bhabha, Homi K. *The Location of Culture.* London: Routledge, 1994.

Boahen, A. Adu. *African Perspectives on Colonialism.* Baltimore, Md.: Johns Hopkins University Press, 1987.

Brownlee, Charles P. *Reminiscences of Kafir Life and History and Other Papers.* With an introduction and notes by Christopher Saunders. Pietermaritzburg: University of Natal Press; Durban: Killie Campbell Library, 1977; reprint of 2nd ed., 1916, orig. pub. 1896.

Burman, Sandra S. *Chiefdom Politics and Alien Law: Basutoland under Cape Rule, 1871–1884.* New York: Holmes and Meier, 1981.

———. *The Justice of the Queen's Government: The Cape's Administration of Basutoland, 1871–1884.* Cambridge: African Studies Center, 1976.

Cain, P. J., and A. G. Hopkins. *British Imperialism: Innovation and Expansion, 1688–1914.* London: Longman, 1993.

———. *British Imperialism: Crisis and Deconstruction, 1914-1990*. London: Longman, 1993.

Casalis, Eugene. *The Basutos; or, Twenty-three Years in South Africa*. London: James Nisbet and Co., 1861. Originally published as *Les Bassoutos ou Vingt-Trois Années d'Études et d'Observations au Sud de l'Afrique*. Paris: Société de Missions Évangéliques, 1859. 2nd ed. 1860; new ed. 1933; facsimile reprint, Morija, Lesotho: Morija Museum and Archives, Morija Printing Works, n.d.

Chabal, Patrick. *Power in Africa: An Essay in Political Interpretation*. New York: St. Martin's Press, 1994.

Clifford, James, and George E. Marcus, eds. *Writing Culture: The Poetics and Politics of Ethnography*. Berkeley: University of California Press, 1986.

Comaroff, Jean, and John Comaroff. *Of Revelation and Revolution: Christianity, Colonialism, and Consciousness in South Africa*. Vol. 1. Chicago: University of Chicago Press, 1991.

Comaroff, John L., and Jean Comaroff. *Of Revelation and Revolution: The Dialectics of Modernity on a South African Frontier*. Vol. 2. Chicago: University of Chicago Press, 1997.

Cooper, Frederick. "Conflict and Connection: Rethinking Colonial African History." *American Historical Review* 99, no. 5 (1994): 1516-45.

Crais, Clifton C. "Conquest, State Formation, and the Subaltern Imagination in Rural South Africa." In Crais, *The Culture of Power in Southern Africa*, 27-48.

———, ed. *The Culture of Power in Southern Africa: Essays on State Formation and the Political Imagination*. Portsmouth: Heinemann Press, 2003.

———. *White Supremacy and Black Resistance in Pre-Industrial South Africa: The Making of the Colonial Order in the Eastern Cape, 1770-1865*. Cambridge: Cambridge University Press, 1992.

Damane, Mosebi. "Sotho Medicine." *Lesotho Notes and Records* 10 (1973-74): 48-59.

Damane, Mosebi, and P. B. Sanders, eds. *Lithoko: Sotho Praise Poems*. Oxford: Clarendon Press, 1974.

Dieterlen, H. *La Médecine et les Médecins au Lessouto*. Paris: Société des Missions Évangéliques, 1930.

Douglas-Home, Charles. *Evelyn Baring: The Last Proconsul*. London: Collins, 1978.

Dove, Canon R. *Anglican Pioneers in Lesotho: Some Account of the Diocese of Lesotho, 1876-1930*. Maseru, 1975.

Doxey, G. V. *The High Commission Territories and the Republic of South Africa*. Oxford: Royal Institute of International Affairs, Oxford University Press, 1963.

Dreyfus, Hubert L., and Paul Rabinow. *Michel Foucault: Beyond Structuralism and Hermeneutics*. 2nd ed. Chicago: University of Chicago Press, 1983.

Dutton, E. A. *The Basuto of Basutoland*. London: Jonathan Cape, 1923.

Edgar, Robert. "Lesotho and the First World War: Recruiting, Resistance and the South African Native Labour Contingent." *Mohlomi: Journal of Southern African Historical Studies* 3–5 (1981): 94–107.

———. *Prophets with Honour: A Documentary History of Lekhotla la Bafo.* Johannesburg: Raven Press, 1988.

Eldredge, Elizabeth A. "Delagoa Bay and the Hinterland in the Early Nineteenth Century: Politics, Trade, Slaves, and Slave Raiding." In Eldredge and Morton, *Slavery in South Africa,* 17–165.

———. "Drought, Famine and Disease in Nineteenth-Century Lesotho." *African Economic History* 16 (1987): 61–93.

———. "Land, Politics, and Censorship: The Historiography of Nineteenth-Century Lesotho." *History in Africa* 15 (1988): 191–209.

———. Review of *African Workers and Colonial Racism: Mozambican Strategies and Struggles in Lourenço Marques, 1877–1962,* by Jeanne Marie Penvenne. *African Economic History* 24 (1996): 187–90.

———. Review of *Government and Change in Lesotho, 1800–1966: A Study of Political Institutions,* by L. B. B. J. Machobane. *Journal of Modern African Studies* 32, no. 2 (1994): 349–52.

———. Review of *Contesting Colonial Hegemony: State and Society in Africa and India,* by Dagmar Engels and Shula Marks, eds. *African Economic History* 24 (1996): 175–77.

———. "Slave-Raiding across the Cape Frontier." In Eldredge and Morton, *Slavery in South Africa,* 93–126.

———. "Sources of Conflict in Southern Africa c. 1800–1830: The 'Mfecane' Reconsidered." *Journal of African History* 33, no. 1 (1992): 1–35.

———. *A South African Kingdom: The Pursuit of Security in Nineteenth-Century Lesotho.* Cambridge: Cambridge University Press, 1993.

———. "Women in Production: The Economic Role of Women in Nineteenth-Century Lesotho." *Signs: Journal of Women in Culture and Society* 16, no. 4 (1991): 707–31.

Eldredge, Elizabeth A., and Fred Morton, eds. *Slavery in South Africa: Captive Labor on the Dutch Frontier.* Boulder, Colo.: Westview Press, 1994.

Ellenberger, D. Fred. *History of the Basuto Ancient and Modern,* trans. J. C. Macgregor. London: Caxton Publishing Co., 1912.

———. *Some Notes on the Origin and Causes of the Rebellion of the Baputhi Chief Morosi. February, 1879.* Aliwal North: Francis Hamilton, printer and publisher. First published anonymously in the *Northern Post,* 19 April 1879.

Engels, Dagmar, and Shula Marks. "Introduction: Hegemony in a Colonial Context." In Engels and Marks, *Contesting Colonial Hegemony,* 1–8.

———, eds. *Contesting Colonial Hegemony: State and Society in Africa and India.* London: British Academic Press, 1994.

Epprecht, Marc. "Women's 'Conservatism' and the Politics of Gender in Late Colonial Lesotho." *Journal of African History* 36 (1995): 29–56.

Feierman, Steven. *Peasant Intellectuals: Anthropology and History in Tanzania*. Madison: University of Wisconsin Press, 1990.

Foucault, Michel. *The Archaeology of Knowledge and the Discourse on Language*, trans. A. M. Sheridan Smith. New York: Pantheon, 1972. French ed. 1969.

——. *Discipline and Punish: The Birth of the Prison*, trans. Alan Sheridan. 1978; New York: Vintage Books, 1979. French ed. 1975.

——. *The History of Sexuality*, vol. 1, *An Introduction*, trans. Robert Hurley. 1978; New York: Vintage Books, 1990. French ed. 1976.

——. *Language, Counter-Memory, Practice: Selected Essays and an Interview*, ed. with an introduction by Donald F. Bouchard, trans. Donald F. Bouchard and Sherry Simon. Ithaca, N.Y.: Cornell University Press, 1977.

——. *Madness and Civilization: A History of Insanity in the Age of Reason*, trans. Richard Howard. 1965; New York: Vintage Books, 1988. French ed. 1961.

——. *Power/Knowledge: Selected Interviews and Other Writings, 1972–1977*, ed. Colin Gordon, trans. Colin Gordon et al. New York: Pantheon Books, 1980.

——. "The Subject and Power." In Dreyfus and Rabinow, *Michel Foucault*, 208–26.

——. "Two Lectures: Lecture One, 7 January 1976, and Lecture Two, 14 January 1976." In Foucault, *Power/Knowledge*, 78–108.

Gallagher, Catherine, and Stephen Greenblatt. *Practicing New Historicism*. Chicago: University of Chicago Press, 2000.

Germond, R. C. *Chronicles of Basutoland*. Morija, Lesotho: Morija Sesuto Book Depot, 1967.

Gill, Stephen J. *A Short History of Lesotho*, foreword by L. B. B. J. Machobane. Morija, Lesotho: Morija Museum and Archives, 1993.

Glass, Harold M. *South African Policy towards Basutoland*. Johannesburg: South African Institute of International Affairs, University of Witwatersrand, 1966.

Gramsci, Antonio. *Selections from the Prison Notebooks*. New York: International Publishers, 1991.

Guha, Ranajit, and Gayatri Chakravorty Spivak, eds. *Selected Subaltern Studies*. Oxford: Oxford University Press, 1988.

Hailey, Lord William Malcolm. *The High Commission Territories: Basutoland, the Bechuanaland Protectorate and Swaziland*. Pt. 5 of *Native Administration in the British African Territories*. London: Commonwealth Relations Office, 1953.

Haliburton, G. H. "Edward Lion of Lesotho." *Mohlomi: Journal of Southern African Historical Studies* 1 (1976): 64–70.

——. *Historical Dictionary of Lesotho*. Metuchen, N.J.: Scarecrow Press, 1977.

Harragin, Sir Walter. "The High Commission Territories." *Foundation*, April 1953, 5–6.

Hobsbawm, Eric, and Terence Ranger, eds. *The Invention of Tradition*. Cambridge: Cambridge University Press, 1983.

Hoy, David Couzens, ed. *Foucault: A Critical Reader.* Oxford: Basil Blackwell Ltd., 1986.

———. "Power, Repression, Progress: Foucault, Lukes, and the Frankfurt School." In Hoy, *Foucault*, 123–47.

Jingoes, Stimela Jason. *A Chief Is a Chief by the People: The Autobiography of Stimela Jason Jingoes*, recorded and comp. John and Cassandra Perry. London: Oxford University Press, 1975.

Keegan, Timothy. *Colonial South Africa and the Origins of the Racial Order.* Charlottesville: University Press of Virginia, 1996.

Khaketla, B. M. *Lesotho 1970: An African Coup under the Microscope.* Berkeley: University of California Press, 1972.

Khama, Tshekedi. *Statement to the British Parliament and People.* London: Anti-Slavery and Aborigines Protection Society, 1935.

Kimble, Judy. "'Clinging to the Chiefs': Some Contradictions of Colonial Rule in Basutoland, c. 1890–1930." In Bernstein and Campbell, *Contradictions of Accumulation in Africa*, 25–69.

Kimble, Judith M. *Migrant Labour and Colonial Rule in Basutoland, 1890–1930.* Grahamstown: Institute of Social and Economic Research, 1999.

Lagden, Sir Godfrey. *The Basutos: The Mountaineers and Their Country.* 2 vols. London: Hutchinson and Co., 1909; New York: Negro Universities Press/Greenwood Publishing Co., 1969.

Landau, Paul Stuart. *The Realm of the Word: Language, Gender, and Christianity in a Southern African Kingdom.* Portsmouth: Heinemann, 1995.

Landry, Donna, and Gerald Maclean, eds. *The Spivak Reader: Selected Works of Gayatri Chakravorty Spivak.* London: Routledge, 1996.

Lanham, Peter, and A. S. Mopeli-Paulus. *Blanket Boy: A Novel of South Africa.* New York: Thomas Y. Crowell Co., 1953.

———. *Blanket Boy's Moon.* London: Collins Fantana Books, 1956.

Larson, Pier M. "'Capacities and Modes of Thinking': Intellectual Engagements and Subaltern Hegemony in the Early History of Malagasy Christianity." *American Historical Review* 102, no. 4 (1997): 969–1002.

Laydevant, François, OMI. *Bophelo ba Morena Natanael Griffiths Lerotholi K.C.S.P., C.B.E., 1871–1939.* Mazenod, Lesotho: Mazenod Institute, 1953.

Lekoatsa, F. J. "Bophelo ba Morena e Moholo Constantinus Bereng S. Griffith." *Sesotho*, 9 August 1960, 3–8.

Lincoln, Bruce. *Discourse and the Construction of Society: Comparative Studies of Myth, Ritual, and Classification.* Oxford: Oxford University Press, 1989.

Lonsdale, John. "The Moral Economy of Mau Mau: Wealth, Poverty and Civic Virtue in Kikuyu Political Thought." In Berman and Lonsdale, *Unhappy Valley*, 315–504.

Lugard, Lord. "South Africa and the Protectorates: A Complex Problem: Pledge That Must Be Fulfilled: Bechuanaland's Case." *Manchester Guardian*, 27 May 1935.

———. "South Africa and the Protectorates: Home Government's Past Neglect: Date of Transfer: The Natives' Part in the Transaction." *Manchester Guardian*, 28 May 1935.

Lyotard, Jean-François. *The Postmodern Condition: A Report on Knowledge*, trans. Geoff Bennington and Brian Massumi. Minneapolis: University of Minnesota Press, 1984.

Mabille, H. E. *Mokhosi oa Fora*. Morija, Lesotho: Morija Sesuto Book Depot, 1948.

Machobane, L. B. B. J. *Government and Change in Lesotho, 1800–1966: A Study of Political Institutions*. London: Macmillan, 1990.

———. "The Political Dilemma of Chieftaincy in Colonial Lesotho with Reference to the Administration and Courts Reforms of 1938." National University of Lesotho Institute of Southern African Studies Occasional Paper No. 1, 1986, 12.

Mallon, Florencia E. "The Promise and Dilemma of Subaltern Studies: Perspectives from Latin American History." *American Historical Review* 99, no. 5 (1994): 1491–515.

Mangoaela, Z. D., comp. *Lithoko Tsa Marena a Basotho*. Morija, Lesotho: Morija Sesuto Book Depot, 1921; reprint, 1981.

Maqutu, W. C. M. *Contemporary Constitutional History of Lesotho*. Mazenod, Lesotho: Mazenod Institute, n.d.

Martin, Minnie. *Basutoland: Its Legends and Customs*. London: Nichols and Co., 1903; reprint, New York: Negro Universities Press, 1969.

McClendon, Thomas. "Coercion and Conversation: African Voices in the Making of Customary Law in Natal." In Crais, *The Culture of Power in Southern Africa*, 49–63.

Melao ea Lerotholi (e hlophisitsoeng). Rev. ed. Morija, Lesotho: Morija Sesuto Book Depot, 1959; 10th reprint, 1981.

Moffat, Robert. *Missionary Labours and Scenes in Southern Africa*. London: John Snow, 1842; reprinted with an introduction by Cecil Northcott, New York: Johnson Reprint Co., 1969.

Mohapeloa, J. M. "The Essential Masupha." *Lesotho Notes and Records* 5 (1965–66): 7–17.

Motlamelle, M. P. *Ngaka ea Mosotho*. Mazenod, 1937; 2nd ed., Morija, Lesotho: Morija Sesuto Book Depot, 1950; reprint, 1985.

Murray, Colin, and Peter Sanders. *Medicine Murder in Colonial Lesotho: The Anatomy of a Moral Crisis*. Edinburgh: Edinburgh University Press, 2005.

Orpen, Joseph M. *History of the Basutus of South Africa*. Cape Town: Saul Solomon and Co., 1857; reprint, Mazenod, Lesotho: Mazenod Book Centre, 1979.

———. *Principles of Native Government Illustrated and the Petitions of the Basuto Tribe Regarding Land, Law, Representation and Disarmament to the Cape Parliament Considered*. Cape Town: Saul Solomon and Co., 1880.

Penvenne, Jeanne Marie. *African Workers and Colonial Racism: Mozambican Strategies and Struggles in Lourenço Marques, 1877–1962*. Portsmouth: Heinemann, 1995.

Potholm, Christian P., and Richard Dale, eds. *Southern Africa in Perspective*. New York: Free Press; London: Collier Macmillan Publishers, 1972.

Poulter, Sebastian. *Legal Dualism in Lesotho: A Study of the Choice of Law Question in Family Matters*. Morija, Lesotho: Morija Sesuto Book Depot, 1981.

———. "The Place of the Laws of Lerotholi in the Legal System of Lesotho." *African Affairs* 71, no. 283 (1972): 144–62.

Prakash, Gyan. "Subaltern Studies as Postcolonial Criticism." *American Historical Review* 99, no. 5 (1994): 1475–90.

Ramseyer, Paul. "La Circoncision chez les Bassoutos." *Revue d'Ethnographie et des Traditions Populaires* (1926): 40–70.

Roberts, Andrew, ed. *The Colonial Moment in Africa*. Cambridge: Cambridge University Press, 1990.

Rooney, David. *Sir Charles Arden-Clarke*. London: Rex Collings, 1982.

Rosenau, Pauline Marie. *Post-Modernism and the Social Sciences: Insights, Inroads, and Intrusions*. Princeton, N.J.: Princeton University Press, 1992.

Said, Edward W. *Culture and Imperialism*. New York: Vintage Books, 1994.

———. *Representations of the Intellectual*. New York: Pantheon, 1994.

Sanders, Peter. *The Last of the Queen's Men: A Lesotho Experience*. Johannesburg: Witwatersrand University Press and Morija Museum and Archives, 2000.

———. *Moshoeshoe: Chief of the Sotho*. London: Heinemann, 1975.

Sarkar, Sumit. "Hegemony and Historical Practice." In Engels and Marks, *Contesting Colonial Hegemony*, 277–81.

Scott, James C. *Domination and the Arts of Resistance: Hidden Transcripts*. New Haven, Conn.: Yale University Press, 1990.

Setiloane, Gabriel M. *The Image of God among the Sotho-Tswana*. Rotterdam: A. A. Balkema, 1976.

Shillington, Kevin. *The Colonisation of the Southern Tswana, 1870–1900*. Braamfontein: Ravan Press, 1985.

Smith, Edwin W. *The Mabilles of Basutoland*. London: Hodder and Stoughton, 1939.

Spear, Thomas. "Neo-Traditionalism and the Limits of Invention in British Colonial Africa." *Journal of African History* 44 (2003): 3–27.

Spear, Thomas, and Isaria N. Kimambo, eds. *East African Expressions of Christianity*. Oxford: James Currey; Athens: Ohio University Press, 1999.

Spence, J. E. "British Policy towards the High Commission Territories." *Modern African Studies* 2, no. 2 (1964): 221–46.

Stevens, Richard P. "The History of the Anglo–South African Conflict over the Proposed Incorporation of the High Commission Territories." In Potholm and Dale, *Southern Africa in Perspective*, 97–109.

Taylor, Henry. *Doctor to Basuto, Boer & Briton 1877–1906: Memoirs of Dr. Henry Taylor*, ed. Peter Hadley. Cape Town: David Philip, 1972.

Terdiman, Richard. *Discourse / Counter-Discourse: The Theory and Practice of Symbolic Resistance in Nineteenth-Century France.* Ithaca, N.Y.: Cornell University Press, 1985.

Theal, George M., ed. *Basutoland Records.* Vols. 1–3. Cape Town: C. Struik, 1964; facsimile reprint of 1st ed., 1883.

———, ed. *Records of South Eastern Africa.* Vol. 9. Cape Town: C. Struik, 1964; facsimile reprint of 1st ed., 1903.

Thompson, Leonard. *Survival in Two Worlds: Moshoeshoe of Lesotho 1786–1870.* Oxford: Oxford University Press, 1975.

Torrance, David E. "Britain, South Africa, and the High Commission Territories: An Old Controversy Revisited." *Historical Journal* 41, no. 3 (1998): 751–72.

Tylden, G. *The Rise of the Basuto.* Cape Town: Juta and Co., 1950.

Vail, Leroy, and Landeg White. *Power and the Praise Poem: Southern African Voices in History.* Charlottesville: University Press of Virginia, 1991.

Weisfelder, Richard F. *Political Contention in Lesotho 1953–1965.* Morija, Lesotho: Morija Printing Works, Institute of Southern African Studies, 1999.

Widdicombe, John. *Fourteen Years in Basutoland: A Sketch of African Mission Life.* London: Church Printing Co., 1891.

Willet, Shelagh M., and David P. Ambrose. *Lesotho.* World Bibliographical Series, 3. Oxford: Clio Press, 1980.

Unpublished Works

"Buka Ena e Matsohong a Batho Ba Baholo Feela." Anonymous typescript. LEC.

Circular No. 1 of 1946, Office of the Paramount Chief, Matsieng, Basutoland, 10 January 1946. Papers of Marion How, LEC/PEMS Archives.

Circular No. 28 of 1946, Office of the Paramount Chief, Matsieng, 31 July 1946. Papers of Marion How, LEC/PEMS Archives.

Circular No. 42 of 1947, Office of the Paramount Chief, Matsieng, 4 November 1947. Papers of Marion How, LEC/PEMS Archives.

Eldredge, Elizabeth A. "Medicine Murder and Power: The Consolidation of Colonial Control in British Basutoland in the 1940s." Paper presented at the South African Historical Society, Sixteenth Biennial Conference, Pretoria, 6–9 July 1997.

———. "Colonial Eyes and Hegemonic Lenses: Sir Godfrey Lagden and the Denial of Reality in Basutoland, the View from 1909." Paper presented at the African Studies Association Annual Meeting, Houston, Texas, November 2001.

Epprecht, Marc. "Women, Class and Politics in Colonial Lesotho, 1930–1965." Ph.D. dissertation, Dalhousie University, Halifax, Nova Scotia, 1992.

Notice. Medicine Murders. A. D. Forsyth Thompson, Maseru, November 1948. Papers of Marion How, LEC/PEMS Archives.

"Secret. Mokhotlong District." Anonymous typescript, n.d.
"Secret. Analysis of Ritual Murders and Their Relation to Various Administrative Events." Anonymous typescript, n.d.

INDEX

Alfred, Prince, 97

Aliwal North, 50, 60, 106; Treaty of, 114–15

AmaMpondo. *See* Mpondo

AmaMpondomise. *See* Mpondomise

AmaNgwane (Ngwane people, chiefdom), 28, 177

AmaXhosa. *See* Xhosa

AmaZulu. *See* Zulu

Anglican Church in Lesotho, 36, 115, 153, 154, 223. *See also* Widdicombe, John

Anglo-Boer War. *See* South African War

anthropology, 3–4, 15–18, 200–201, 245 n.20. *See also* Ashton, Hugh; Comaroff, Jean and John; Jones, G. I.; Murray, Colin

Anti-Slavery and Aborigines Protection Society, 150

Apostolic Faith mission, 180–81

Arden Clarke, Charles (Resident Commissioner, 1942–46), 184–86, 188–89, 196, 197

Arrowsmith, E. P. (Resident Commissioner, 1952–56), 212

Ashton, Hugh, 194, 200–201, 208–9, 210, 246 n.33; *The Basuto*, 201; "Medicine, Magic, and Sorcery," 201. *See also* Jones, G. I.

Assistant Commissioners. *See under* colonial officials

Atkins, Keletso E., 20

Atmore, Anthony, 231 n.1

Austen, John (Resident District Magistrate, Cornet Spruit and Quthing districts), 43, 47–48, 50–54, 56–63, 66–68, 73, 93, 100, 107

authority: of chiefs, 41, 64, 120, 141–43, 187, 202–3; colonial in Lesotho, 40–41, 55, 108, 118–20, 131, 133–35, 210–12, 215–16; as component of power, 4–5, 13; indigenous discourse on, 95, 97, 124–27, 131–32, 205–8, 213; of men, 131–32; of Paramount Chief, 64, 66–67, 85, 121–28, 132–33, 140–43, 188, 202–3, 239 n.49; of police, 186

Ayliff, William (Secretary for Native Affairs, Cape Colony), 49–50, 59–60, 63–68

Backhouse, James, 177

bahlalefi (educated elite), 243 n.88

BaPedi, 47, 99

BaPhuthi (people and chiefdom in Lesotho), 32, 41–54, 55–70, 76, 99, 101, 141, 153. *See also* Mocheko L. Moorosi; Moorosi; Moorosi's Rebellion; Quthing

Baring, Evelyn (High Commissioner), 187–88, 190–91, 192, 193, 201, 209–10, 211